The Rise of the
Accounting Profession

The Rise of the Accounting Profession

From Technician to Professional
1896-1936

By John L. Carey
Former Administrative Vice President
American Institute of Certified Public Accountants

AMERICAN INSTITUTE OF CERTIFIED PUBLIC ACCOUNTANTS
666 FIFTH AVENUE   NEW YORK, N.Y. 10019

To
ELIZABETH ARLISS NICHOLSON,
whose contributions to the progress
of the accounting profession can never
be adequately acknowledged

NOTICE TO READERS

The author is solely responsible for the contents of this book. In publishing it the American Institute of Certified Public Accountants accepts no responsibility for the accuracy of factual statements or for the validity of interpretive comment.

Table of Contents

Preface to Volume I

W HEN THE Institute's executive committee asked me to write this book, we all conceived it as a history of the Institute—one of those institutional publications containing the dates, the names, and the principal achievements, viewed with pride.

As I dug into the records, however, it became increasingly clear that the rise of the accounting profession in the United States has been a significant and fascinating sociological phenomenon. To do it justice, it seemed necessary to expand the scope of the inquiry. This has resulted in a lengthier narrative than was originally expected. In order to make the book manageable, it has been divided into two volumes.

This first volume covers the period ended in 1936. The second volume, covering the period from 1937 to 1967, will be released as soon as production is completed.

It has been said that those who ignore history are bound to repeat it. With this in mind I have tried to relate the development of the profession to the changing environment, and to record the mistakes and the missed opportunities, as well as the victories and achievements.

There are striking parallels between problems confronting accountants many years ago and those facing them today. Lessons can be learned from the failures as well as the successes of the past.

It is inevitable that the book is written from the viewpoint of the Institute, in whose employ I have spent my entire working life. As a result, the contributions of other accounting organizations, including the state societies of certified public accountants, have received less than their due. In extenuation it can be claimed that the Institute has been an active participant, or at least a close observer, in every important development at the national level which has affected the professional practice of accounting.

The space available is limited, even in two volumes. Consequently I have been obliged to make arbitrary decisions about which events and which individuals to mention or describe. Apologies are offered to all who disagree with these decisions.

To make the book as readable as possible I have refrained from sprinkling its pages with distracting little numbers or asterisks referring to sources of information. The sources are listed in an appendix.

Like most authors, I have had a lot of help from other people. The following members of the Institute have given useful suggestions and advice, and some of them have reviewed portions of the manuscript:

FREDERICK B. ANDREWS	LINCOLN G. KELLY
HORACE G. BARDEN	RALPH E. KENT
ANDREW BARR	I. H. KREKSTEIN
WILLIAM M. BLACK	ARTHUR F. LAFRENTZ
CARMAN G. BLOUGH	SAMUEL D. LEIDESDORF
PERCIVAL F. BRUNDAGE	A. C. LITTLETON
M. C. CONICK	RALPH B. MAYO
THORNTON G. DOUGLAS	WILLIAM A. PATON
SCOTT H. DUNHAM	GEORGE E. PERRIN
STANLEY G. H. FITCH	JOHN W. QUEENAN
ARTHUR B. FOYE	HASSEL TIPPIT
THOMAS G. HIGGINS	J. S. SEIDMAN
ALVIN R. JENNINGS	EDWARD BYERS WILCOX

JAMES B. WILLING

Also I am indebted to the following members of the Institute's staff, who advised, researched, typed, edited, and finally produced the book: Elizabeth Arliss, Jo Darling, John Lawler, Joan Lucas, Katherine Michaelsen, Charles Noyes, Beatrice Sanders, and Stewart Schackne.

None of these advisers and assistants, however, has any responsibility for what finally appears in these pages. That burden must be borne by me alone.

JOHN L. CAREY

New York
January 15, 1969

The Rise of the Accounting Profession

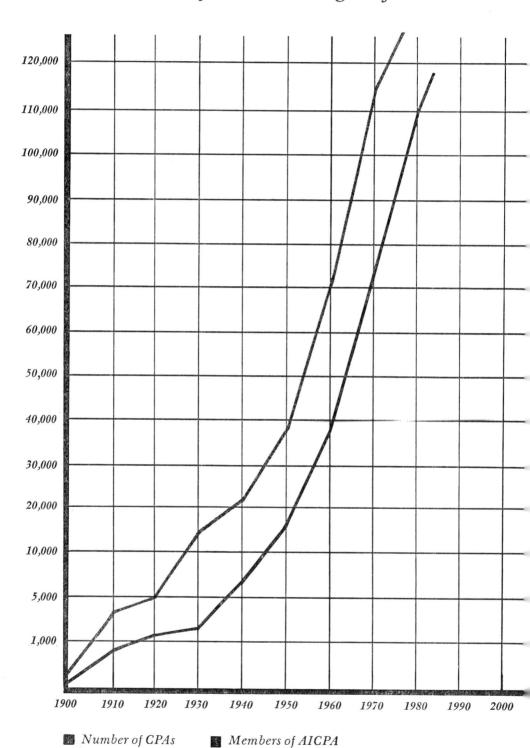

Number of CPAs   Members of AICPA

CHAPTER 1

Present, Past and Future

THE dramatic rise of the accounting profession in the United States has only recently come to public notice. Even now, a mere fragment of the public is aware of what has happened, or how great is the influence of this profession on society.

The Present

Dramatic is not too strong a word to describe the phenomenon. The accounting profession in the United States has come from nowhere, literally, in just over 80 years, to a position of crucial importance in the American economy. The certified public accountants can fairly claim to be the only true profession in the field of finance and management.

There are more than 100,000 certified public accountants in the United States today. (There were none until 1896.) The vast majority are college graduates—and an increasing number of them have advanced degrees. They have demonstrated competence by passing a rigorous two-and-a-half-day written examination, which has been uniform throughout the country since 1952. They are subject to stringent ethical restraints, based on codes enforced by disciplinary procedures. The ethical codes incorporate by reference an expanding body of technical standards. These standards are accepted by government agencies and are admissible as evidence in courts of law.

CPAs have developed a "common body of knowledge" which is taught today, in whole or in part, in more than 600 colleges and universities.

CPAs are licensed under state laws. They are highly organized in national and state associations, which are as effective as those of any of the professions, and more so than many. Despite the fact that membership is voluntary, these associations include about 80 per cent of all CPAs in the country.

The CPAs' sense of social responsibility has been amply demonstrated. They have invested millions of dollars in research directed toward improvement of financial reporting, and toward tightening their own technical procedures. Through their professional societies they co-operate with government at all levels, and with lawyers, bankers, financial analysts, corporate financial executives (many of whom are CPAs themselves), stock exchanges, and business and trade groups. Individually, CPAs serve in countless capacities in civic and community affairs. Some of them have occupied the positions of mayor, governor, Congressman, Senator, Commissioner of Internal Revenue, Director of the Budget, Comptroller General of the United States, Secretary of the Navy, Secretary of Commerce, members of federal regulatory commissions and Presidential advisory commissions, and holders of thousands of high-level government jobs—in times of war and times of peace.

A True Profession

The seven criteria which distinguish professions from other pursuits are: (1) a body of specialized knowledge; (2) a formal educational process; (3) standards governing admission; (4) a code of ethics; (5) a recognized status indicated by a license or special designation; (6) a public interest in the work that the practitioners perform; and (7) recognition by them of a social obligation.

According to these criteria certified public accountants can fairly claim to be the only true profession in the field of finance and management.

But what about the claim that they occupy a crucial position in our economy?

The capital markets depend on reliable financial information. It is largely the influence of the accounting profession that has made the financial reports of American corporations the most informative in the world—even though much room for improvement remains. It is the American Institute of Certified Public Accountants which has the leading role in setting standards for corporate reporting, which are backed by the Securities and Exchange Commission and the stock exchanges.

The vast dispersion of bank credit has been made possible in part, at least, by the availability to bankers of financial statements audited by CPAs.

The self-assessing income-tax system is buttressed by honest returns of millions of business and individual taxpayers prepared or reviewed by CPAs.

Internal controls—financial, cost, inventory, production, administrative controls—have been strengthened by CPAs in tens of thousands of businesses, large and small, with consequent improvement in efficiency and profitability.

The Rapid Rise

All this is little known to most of the public. Accordingly, too many young men and women are unaware of the career opportunities in this still young, still growing and extraordinarily vigorous profession. Why?

The very speed with which certified public accountants have advanced from a technician class to attain professional status has made it difficult for most people to keep up with the change. The impression that a CPA is only a superior bookkeeper still prevails in some quarters, despite the fact that it has been false for many decades.

What, then, brought about this rapid transformation from technician to professional?

The accounting profession today is the product of an industrial, free-enterprise economy, supported mainly by private capital, but subject to widespread government regulation. Economic and social change created the *need* for an accounting profession—but accountants themselves *created* the profession by constantly raising their standards of performance, by improving their own education and training, by enlarging the scope of their services, and by accepting heavier responsibilities.

All this has not been easy. Progress at times has seemed slow, and often it has been painful. CPAs, being human, have rarely embraced change with enthusiasm, or happily abandoned the security of the familiar. Many of their advances, indeed, have been the result of outside pressures. But to do them credit, the CPAs have had the intelligence to recognize the significance of those pressures—and to react to them before it was too late. Much of the progress must be credited to a succession of gifted, perceptive and courageous leaders who have foreseen the need for change and persuaded their colleagues to accept it—not always without internal conflict, and almost always only after protracted debate.

The Past

As every student of accounting knows, the earliest civilizations developed simple record-keeping methods. They had to. But the art evolved slowly over thousands of years, until trade and commerce reached a state of complexity which required something better. In the fifteenth century, double-entry book-keeping was invented. This invaluable technique was refined and elaborated throughout Europe for several hundred years. Still, however, the accountant was the servant of his employer.

Then, in England in the second half of the eighteenth century, came the Industrial Revolution. Large pools of capital were needed to finance the factories and machinery which could satisfy the yearning for higher standards of living. Partnerships, joint-stock companies, and finally the modern corporation, evolved to meet this need.

In the mid-nineteenth century English law created the independent auditor as a protection to stockholders against the incompetence or malfeasance of the managements to whom investors had entrusted their money. With the acceptance of responsibility to investors as well as to the employer, the accountant-auditor assumed the mantle of professionalism. He became a "public accountant," accepting a responsibility to the public as well as to the client who paid his fee.

Thus, while the *art* of accounting is ancient, the *profession* of accounting, in comparison with law and medicine, for example, is very young.

To secure public confidence, the public accountants had to

develop professional organizations, to formulate technical and ethical standards, to establish a system of training their successors, and to acquire symbolic evidence of competence and responsibility. For these purposes the Scottish and English institutes of chartered accountants were founded.

American Beginnings

In the late nineteenth century, some of these chartered accountants came to the United States, where British capital was being invested in the growing American industries. With the encouragement and participation of these visitors from overseas, a handful of native public accountants in 1887 formed the American Association of Public Accountants—the direct predecessor of the present American Institute of Certified Public Accountants.

No statutory requirement for independent audit of corporations existed in the United States, and without this leverage the progress of the profession in this country was slower than it had been in Great Britain. However, public identification was obtained by enactment of state laws providing for issuance of certified public accountant certificates to qualified candidates— beginning in New York in 1896 and extending throughout the nation over the next quarter of a century.

The bankers who financed the rapidly growing American industries encouraged independent audits. United States Steel, for example, published its first audited financial statements in 1903. They set a precedent.

The income-tax law of 1913 created a new demand for accounting services, and a new role for CPAs.

Cost accounting, as an aid to efficiency and profitability, was developed very early to an advanced stage by American accountants. This brought them into the ever-widening field of advisory services to management.

The advent of the first federal regulatory agencies—the Interstate Commerce Commission, the Federal Trade Commission, the Federal Reserve Board—further stimulated the demand for financial information, and thus the demand for the services of CPAs. Later, the intervention of the federal government in every phase of the economy—as regulator, lender, insurer, entrepreneur, and dispenser of welfare—added massive requirements for the kinds of information CPAs provide.

Problems Confronted

In the past 30 years especially, CPAs have been hard pressed to meet the demands which confronted them. They have suffered a chronic shortage of qualified personnel, despite the explosive growth of their numbers, and despite the fact that they are among the most highly paid of professions.

Yet they have been forced, at the same time, to improve their standards and techniques at what, in retrospect, seems breakneck speed.

These achievements would have been impossible without vigorous professional societies. The state societies of certified public accountants and the American Institute have played a major role in every area of professional concern—a greater role, it may well be, than that of the organizations of any other profession. The constant pressure of external forces required co-operative action.

But the success of the professional accounting societies is directly attributable to the deep involvement in their work by the ablest members of the profession, from the smallest to the largest firms, with complete disregard of personal convenience or expense.

Problems Ahead

Success, of course, is a comparative term. The record to date is good. Whether it is as good as it should be is a subjective judgment. That it must be improved in the years ahead is beyond question. Consequently, although a sound beginning has been made, the most important part of the accounting profession's history lies in the future. It will be even more exciting than the past, and its challenges will be worthy of the best minds the profession can attract.

Since the present is only a strange interlude between past and future, it is possible by projecting historical trends to perceive, at least dimly, the probable shape of things to come.

The Future

CPAs work in the field of information. Essentially, they assemble and convert data into information and interpret it. Information has been called the fastest-growing field in the world. References to the "information explosion" are common. Information systems of various kinds are in urgent demand. The computer vastly increases the capacity to provide information.

The familiar balance sheets and income statements with which CPAs are generally associated provide one very important kind of information which is essential to investors and credit grantors. As the numbers of investors increase beyond the present 24 million, and the volume of bank loans increases commensurately, it is already evident that more and better information of this kind will be demanded.

Indeed, the familiar forms of financial statements may undergo radical change. The accounting concepts and procedures on which such statements are based must be refined. Criteria must be established continually to determine what method of accounting would be most appropriate in given circumstances.

Projections of future results may be required. Distinctions may be made between the needs of investors, credit-grantors and other users, so that "all-purpose" financial statements will yield to special forms for special purposes.

Auditing long ago ceased to be a routine, detailed checking of books and vouchers. Auditors today push pencils far less than they push their brains, and, in the days ahead, auditing will become increasingly an analytical exercise. Appraisal of the effectiveness of internal control will become more important as additional data are stored in computers. Sampling methods will become more scientific as a result of experience, already successful, with statistical applications. The objective of financial auditing is no longer an item-by-item verification, but an assessment of the validity of information for the purposes of those who use it.

Auditing is extending to non-financial areas, such as compliance with regulations of government agencies. Audits of costs are likely to increase, as they already have done for purposes of defense procurement and Medicare. Some CPAs believe that independent audits of tax returns, with an appropriate form of opinion, may greatly reduce the scope of field examinations by Internal Revenue agents.

The advisory role of CPAs has limitless possibilities which have only begun to be realized. In the field of information systems, controls, cost reduction, financial planning, and many other areas where management needs information and advice, CPAs have potentially more to offer than any other identified profession.

Further out lie the possibilities of audits of management performance and "social accounting"—the development of techniques for evaluating cost-benefit relationships of social programs and non-profit activities of all kinds.

A Description of Accounting Practice

In 1966 the American Institute of Certified Public Accountants issued a "Description of the Professional Practice of Certified Public Accountants," a brief statement of what CPAs were doing and were likely to do in the foreseeable future. It is worth quoting here:

> Accounting is a discipline which provides financial and other information essential to the efficient conduct and evaluation of the activities of any organization.
>
> The information which accounting provides is essential for (1) effective planning, control and decision making by management, and (2) discharging the accountability of organizations to investors, creditors, government agencies, taxing authorities, association members, contributors to welfare institutions, and others.
>
> Accounting includes the development and analysis of data, the testing of their validity and relevance and the interpretation and communication of the resulting information to intended users. The data may be expressed in monetary or other quantitative terms, or in symbolic or verbal forms.
>
> Some of the data with which accounting is concerned are not precisely measurable, but necessarily involve assumptions, and estimates as to the present effect of future events and other uncertainties. Accordingly, accounting requires not only technical knowledge and skill, but even more importantly, disciplined judgment, perception and objectivity.
>
> Within this broad field of accounting, certified public accountants are the identified professional accountants. They provide leadership in accounting research and education. In the practice of public accounting CPAs bring competence of professional quality, independence, and a strong concern for the usefulness of the information and advice they provide, but they do not make management decisions.
>
> The professional quality of their services is based upon the requirements for the CPA certificate—education, experience and examination—and upon the ethical and technical standards established and enforced by their profession.
>
> CPAs have a distinctive role in examining financial statements submitted to investors, creditors and other interested parties, and in expressing independent opinions on the fairness of such statements.

This distinctive role has inevitably encouraged a demand for the opinions of CPAs on a wide variety of other representations, such as compliance with rules and regulations of government agencies, sales statistics under lease and royalty agreements, and adherence to covenants in indentures.

The examination of financial statements requires CPAs to review many aspects of an organization's activities and procedures. Consequently they can advise clients of needed improvements in internal control, and make constructive suggestions on financial, tax and other operating matters.

In addition to furnishing advice in conjunction with their independent examinations of financial statements, CPAs are engaged to provide objective advice and consultation on various management problems. Many of these involve information and control systems and techniques, such as budgeting, cost control, profit planning, internal reporting, automatic data processing, and quantitative analysis. CPAs also assist in the development and implementation of programs approved by management.

Among the major management problems depending on the accounting function is compliance with tax requirements. An important part of the practice of CPAs includes tax planning and advice, preparation of tax returns, and representation of clients before government agencies.

CPAs also participate in conferences with government agencies such as the Securities and Exchange Commission, and with other interested parties, such as bankers.

Like other professional men, CPAs are often consulted on business, civic and other problems on which their judgment, experience, and professional standards permit them to provide helpful advice and assistance.

The complexities of an industrial society encourage a high degree of specialization in all professions. The accounting profession is no exception. Its scope is so wide and varied that many individual CPAs choose to specialize in particular types of service.

Although their activities may be diverse, all CPAs have demonstrated basic competence of professional quality in the discipline of accounting. It is this which unites them as members of one profession, and provides a foundation for extension of their services into new areas.

This statement suggests the vast opportunities that lie ahead of the profession in coming years.

Perhaps most attractive are the opportunities for service to society in the broad sense. A profession skilled in the classification, analysis and interpretation of data could be helpful in determining the financial impact of tariff negotiations on American business. It could contribute to the measurement of productivity for purposes of collective bargaining. It could participate in efforts to devise statistics which would reveal trends in the economy as a whole. It could assist in analyzing the impact of the antitrust laws.

The opportunities available to the profession, in fact, are almost limitless.

The key word, however, is "opportunities." To exploit them the profession must improve itself in many ways. An examination of what has happened, and why, and how, may facilitate the determination of what yet needs to be done.

This is the purpose of the pages which follow.

CHAPTER 2

How It All Began

How did accounting begin?

The story has been told by many scholars. One who has told it very well is Professor A. C. Littleton of the University of Illinois.[1] This chapter is based largely on his book.

Ever since men have lived in organized social groups, they have kept track of their affairs by making marks on whatever surfaces were most convenient—stone, clay tablets, papyrus, paper, cards, punched cards, magnetic tapes.

For thousands of years, anyone involved in this record-keeping task must have been pretty much on his own. He had to invent his own accounting system or adapt it from someone close at hand who had done it before.

The Romans, for example, kept elaborate records, and no doubt their systems were standardized for such purposes as military payrolls and the accountability of provincial governors.

---

[1] A. C. Littleton, *Accounting Evolution to 1900*, American Institute Publishing Co., Inc., New York, 1933.

But they did not develop any system of commercial bookkeeping. Since numbers were expressed in terms of letters of the alphabet, they were severely handicapped by the lack of an easy means of computation.

The ingenious Italians of the Renaissance period—roughly from the fourteenth to the sixteenth century—are regarded as the fathers of modern accounting. They pursued trade and commerce vigorously, and felt the need for better ways of determining their profits. From the Arabs they learned the numerals which are used today, and the basics of arithmetic. Extensive record-keeping followed, as the use of capital and credit on a large impersonal scale developed. An evolutionary trend toward double-entry bookkeeping was developing.

Double-Entry Bookkeeping

Two years after Columbus discovered America an Italian monk wrote a book on arithmetic which included a text on double-entry bookkeeping. This is presumed to be the first published work on the subject. Every student of accounting knows the name of Fra Luca Pacioli and his work, *Summa de Arithmetica Geometria Proportioni et Proportionalita.*

Pacioli did not "invent" double-entry bookkeeping, but he formalized the practices and ideas which had been evolving in the years before, and presented his world with the essentials of bookkeeping as it is known today.

Double-entry bookkeeping for the first time enabled a business organization to keep a complete and co-ordinated record of all its transactions, showing both ownership equity and period results.

The printing press with movable type had been invented shortly before Pacioli's famous book appeared. Other men in other countries began to write about the subject, and various

versions of double-entry bookkeeping spread rapidly throughout Europe.

Financial Statements

Financial statements of one sort or another no doubt date
back to the time when the first master entrusted his slave or
servant with the management of goods or property.

Records of "charge and discharge" accounting—sometimes
called "agency accounting"—were developed in England following the Norman Conquest and the evolution of the feudal
system. This type of financial statement merely showed collec-
tions (as of rent or taxes) and disbursements, without reference
to proprietorship or indebtedness.

Statements of profit and loss, and statements of balances
leading to the modern balance sheet, emerged about 1600.
Later came the development of separate financial statements.

Littleton says, "It seems that the primary motive for separate
financial statements was to obtain information regarding capital: this was the center of the interest of partners, shareholders,
lenders, and the basis of the calculation of early property taxes.
Thus, balance-sheet data were stressed and refined in various
ways, while expense and income data were incidental—in fact,
the latter in the seventeenth century were presented merely
as a 'proof of estate'—to demonstrate by another route the correctness of the balance sheet."

As continuing business organizations replaced isolated ventures, such as a single voyage of a single vessel, it was necessary
to develop accounting records and reports reflecting a continuing investment of capital employed in various ways, and periodically summarizing the results of the activities. Proprietorship
accounting evolved. The nineteenth century saw bookkeeping
expanded into accounting. Emphasis shifted to the concept that

the owners' original contribution, plus or minus profits or loss, indicated net worth. Profit was considered an increase in net assets from any source. The concepts of cost and income had not yet been fully developed.

In the late nineteenth century the "entity theory" of accounting evolved, stressing the separateness of the business and the owners. Profit became the excess of proceeds recovered over outlays advanced during the business process—thus a reward for managerial skill.

The Corporation

The origin of the business corporation greatly accelerated accounting thought and practice. In the corporation the capital of many individuals could be pooled in aggregate amounts larger than individuals or small groups could furnish. The transferability of shares and the limited liability of shareholders made investment in corporations more attractive, but the fact that the capital was administered by delegated management for absentee owners required periodic reports on which investors could rely.

The fact that a corporation is presumed to continue its activities indefinitely, as contrasted with a single venture, led to careful distinctions between capital and income. The profits available for dividends without impairing capital became a central accounting issue.

The corporation evolved in England as a result of experience in joint ventures, through which individuals contributed capital in return for shares in the profits of trading voyages. As early as in the mid-seventeenth century the East India Company had developed the idea of a permanent invested capital. Distributions to the participants became a share of profits earned, rather than a division of gains from single ventures.

The corporation was legally established in England in 1845 by a statute which immediately began to stimulate the development of accounting standards, independent audits and the organization of an accounting profession.

Independent Audits

Preliminary legislation authorizing joint-stock companies had not prevented frauds and excessive speculation. The new law, which was amended frequently, set up rules designed to safeguard shareholders against improper actions by promoters and directors. Dividends were permitted only from profits of the business. Accounts were required to be kept, and to be audited by persons "other than directors." The directors were required to compile a "full and fair balance sheet," sign it and deliver it to the auditors, and to send a printed copy of the balance sheet, and the auditor's report on it, to the shareholders ten days before the general meeting.

The 1845 version of the law provided that "every auditor shall have at least one share in the undertaking, and he shall not hold any office in the company, nor be in any other manner interested in its concerns, except as a shareholder." But at the same time, the statute opened the way for the outside accounting expert as follows:

> It shall be lawful for the auditors to employ such accountants and other persons as they may think proper, at the expense of the company, and they shall either make a special report on the said accounts, or simply confirm the same; and such report or confirmation shall be read together with the report of the directors at the ordinary meeting.

The auditors, of course, could be amateurs. Anyone could call himself an accountant. There was no organized profession of accountants, nor were there any standards of qualification for accountants and auditors.

The purpose of the early audit was obviously to permit the shareholders to exercise some control over the management to whom they had delegated responsibilities. Since the audit was not designed to assist credit grantors, there was no emphasis on financial liquidity. Nor was there any concern with internal controls as an aid to managerial efficiency.

"The present resourcefulness in financial investigation," says Littleton, "and the independence of mind which is now expected of every public practitioner were not quickly achieved, nor was a really professional status easily established. Yet resourcefulness has grown and a professional standing has been achieved. The circumstances in which this development occurred are, therefore, a part of the background of modern accountancy, and as such deserve consideration."

The Industrial Revolution

The Industrial Revolution had catapulted England into an unrivaled prosperity. By the middle of the nineteenth century Great Britain led in production of coal, pig iron, and cotton textiles, and it had laid nearly 5,000 miles of railway lines. In addition, it was the financial center of the civilized world. In the 1870's bank deposits in London were three times those in New York. There was naturally a demand for accountants— much of it in the winding up of bankrupt companies which failed in the surging competition.

Men with some experience in bookkeeping or a liking for the subject became accountants. Some of them had gone into "public practice" as early as the mid-seventeenth century. Often they held regular jobs at the same time, or engaged in other businesses in addition to accounting.

As early as 1799 there were 11 practicing accountants in London. Less than 50 years later 210 accountants were listed—and the numbers in other principal cities had grown commensurately.

The English corporation laws made inevitable the development of an organized profession of accounting whose practitioners were identified as competent and independent.

Professional Organizations

In 1854 a small group of accountants organized the Society of Accountants in Edinburgh under a royal charter, which permitted the members to use the designation "chartered accountant." The Glasgow accountants and actuaries received a similar charter in 1855, and the accountants in Aberdeen in 1867. However, it was not until 1951 that these three groups combined under a new charter as the Institute of Chartered Accountants of Scotland.

The succession of Companies Acts greatly increased the demand for accounting services. Local societies of accountants were formed in London, Liverpool, Manchester, Sheffield and other cities. The Liverpool and London Institutes combined in 1870. Then groups of accountants from other parts of the country suggested to the London Institute that a national organization was needed to represent the profession. As a result, membership in the London Institute was made available to accountants in all parts of the United Kingdom, and the name was changed from the "Institute of Accountants in London" to "Institute of Accountants." Membership was confined to professional practicing accountants.

In 1872 a Society of Accountants in England was formed in competition with the Institute. Its requirements for membership were less stringent, and it grew more rapidly than the Institute, having 220 members in 1877 as compared with 154 in the Institute.

After unsuccessful efforts to get a bill through Parliament incorporating a national institute of accountants—in the course of which there were bitter arguments between the Society of Accountants and the Institute—application was made for a Royal Charter. "Among the great advantages of charters were the fact that the tradition surrounding them dated back to the fourteenth century, the prestige attaching to them and the characteristics of monopoly they conferred."[2]

The terms of the petition were approved by all the existing bodies of accountants, including the Society of Accountants and several provincial organizations.

The charter was approved by Queen Victoria, on May 11, 1880. The new Institute of Chartered Accountants in England and Wales brought together all the accountancy organizations in those parts of Great Britain. Five hundred eighty-seven members formed the nucleus of the new body, and 606 additional members were admitted on the basis of their experience.

Steps were immediately taken to establish standards of conduct and examinations for admission to the Institute. The members were entitled to use the designation "chartered accountant" and the initials "FCA" (Fellow Chartered Accountant, signifying a partner or proprietor in practice) and "ACA" (Associate Chartered Accountant, signifying a qualified member of an accountant's staff, or a member not in practice).

The motivation for professional organization was naturally, in large measure, to distinguish skilled accountants of integrity from self-styled accountants whose competence had not been demonstrated. Protection of the public was a major objective. But once organized the Institute necessarily embarked on the development of standards and self-improvement.

---

[2] *The History of the Institute of Chartered Accountants in England and Wales*, compiled by Sir Harold Howitt at the request of the Council of the Institute, William Heinemann, Ltd., London, 1965.

An independent periodical, *The Accountant,* had been established in 1874. It became the recognized voice of the chartered accountants, and has continued publication to this day. The earliest issues contain references to the responsibilities and procedures of auditors.

In the 1880's lectures were given before student societies, and were published in professional periodicals, which listed a number of specific steps to be taken by auditors—covering, for example, an examination of the bookkeeping system, articles of incorporation, board minutes; examination of the cash book and checking vouchers; examination of journals and ledgers; counting of securities and cash; aging of accounts receivable; examination of inventories; valuation of fixed assets and provision for depreciation; and examination of liabilities and capital stock.

The first certificates signed by auditors stated, according to the law, whether or not in the auditor's opinion the balance sheet was a "full and fair" balance sheet, properly drawn up so as to exhibit a "true and correct view of the state of the company's affairs as shown by the books of the company." As time went on, the statutory form of an auditor's certificate was modified and his responsibilities were gradually increased.

Export to America

These developments in the British Isles had great significance for the United States. Even before the colonies achieved independence there was, of course, extensive trade between American colonies and the mother country. British accountants visited the United States to check on investments and to wind up bankruptcies.

In the late nineteenth century, as the American industrial economy developed rapidly, large amounts of British capital were invested in the industries of the United States. Scottish and British chartered accountants, filled with professional pride in their recently organized societies, came to the United States to check on such investments. Some of them stayed. A number of present-day American accounting firms can trace back their origins to Scottish or English accountants who settled in the United States.

Native American accountants also began to hang out their shingles, in response to the same kind of economic needs as had developed earlier in Great Britain. A few American firms of native origin, still in existence, predate the twentieth century.

City directories indicated that in 1850 there were 14 accountants offering their services to the public in New York, four in Philadelphia, and one in Chicago. By 1886, these numbers had grown to 115 in New York, 87 in Philadelphia, and 31 in Chicago. Also by 1886 there were 41 in Boston, 20 in Baltimore, seven in Detroit, six in Pittsburgh, 11 in St. Louis, five in New Orleans, and 40 in San Francisco.

Groups of accountants and bookkeepers banded together in various small societies in the different cities. No one knows which of them was first. But the first society formed by and for accountants engaged in public practice, and the first which aspired to national scope, was the American Association of Public Accountants—the direct predecessor of the American Institute of Certified Public Accountants. The year was 1887— and a new era for accounting was beginning.

CHAPTER 3

Accounting Practice at the Turn of the Century

Profound economic and social changes were taking place in the United States. The country had emerged from the Civil War with a predominantly agricultural economy. The transcontinental railroads had been completed only a few years after the war. Vast western territories remained to be explored. Invasion of these areas by cattlemen, sheep herders, miners and farmers involved decades of Indian fighting. In fact, it was only a year before the Association's formation that the Apache chief, Geronimo, surrendered to the government.

The United States was a young country, and the accounting profession was a mere infant. But things were on the move. Iron mines, steel mills, and oil wells were added to meat-packing, textile manufacturing and breweries as major industries—along with railroading and shipping. By 1900 the country was one of the world's greater manufacturing centers, as well as a major center of extractive industry. Yet the value of farm products even then exceeded the value of industry's.

The industrial development, however, was marred by financial abuses. Over-capitalization and speculation in the securities markets caused panics in 1873 and 1893. Watered stocks of railroads became a national scandal. Monopolistic tendencies provoked concern. And exploitation of the working class brought on the labor unions and the first big, violent strikes.

Cries for reform were heard in the land, and they were not long in being answered.

At the time the American Association of Public Accountants was organized Congress passed the first Interstate Commerce Act—and, three years later, enacted the Sherman Antitrust Act. While it was years before these laws were adequately enforced—partly due to the reluctance of the Supreme Court to embrace the new theories—the beginnings of federal regulation of business were visible.

With the assassination of McKinley in the fall of 1901, Theodore Roosevelt became, at the age of 43, the youngest man ever to reach the highest office in the land. He was a liberal-conservative—a "progressive." He accepted the new industrial order, but recognized its excesses. He felt that government regulation was necessary. He knew it was impossible to turn back the economic clock, and though heralded as a "trustbuster," he recognized the inevitability of combinations in business. The only answer, in his view, was a corresponding increase in governmental power over big business.

The Sherman Antitrust Law was being evaded. The "trusts" were buying up companies to the point of monopoly of entire industries. Common stocks of the trusts were unloaded on the public by the bankers, competition was crushed, and prices then soared.

Roosevelt persuaded Congress to set up a new Department of Commerce and Labor to gather facts needed for enforcement of the antitrust laws. Railway regulation was broadened. The Interstate Commerce Commission's powers were extended from railways to steamship, express and sleeping-car companies. The Commission was also empowered to prescribe maximum rates and to set up a uniform system of accounting—the first use of accounting by the federal governent as an instrument of regulation.

In 1905 there was an investigation of the great insurance companies which also led to reform and regulation.

Big business was here to stay, but it was also here to be regulated.

Nature of Accounting Practice

What was the practice of accounting like in those early days, and what kind of people were they who practiced it? The records are incomplete, but they provide some clues.

Advertisements by accountants of the late nineteenth century reflect one type of accounting service in that time. A circular refers to "planning and remodeling books for business firms, preparation and adjustment of partnership accounts, and more especially the periodical auditing and verification of books and statements as a safeguard not only against fraud but against error."*

Another article stated, "The duty and service of the public accountant are by no means limited to the matter of searching out and reporting upon the possible shortages in the cash and securities of trusted employees. The proper departmenting of accounts, the planning of books and formulas, assisting and advising in the general organization and duties of office, so that proper safeguards and methods may be adopted to insure correctness with dispatch . . . are also parts of the duty and service of the specialist in this line."

Another firm of accountants offered to advise clients on "how

---

*NOTE: For much of the information which follows relating to the period 1886-1905, credit is due to Norman E. Webster's *The American Association of Public Accountants—Its First Twenty Years,* American Institute of Accountants, 1954.

single articles are to be priced in order to yield a required percentage of profit."

Still another accountant's circular pointed out "the advantage to any business of proper books of account correctly opened and thoroughly kept . . . and the advantage of regular and systematic auditing of accounts . . . the only existing safeguard against errors, and fraud."

The emphasis of smaller accounting firms was on accounting aids to management—bookkeeping systems, statement preparation, and audits to detect irregularities. In smaller businesses audited financial statements for third-party use were rarely necessary.

However, there was another, and more important, phase of practice not reflected in advertisements—the auditing of the large corporations, many of which by mergers became rapidly larger.

An Early Accounting Firm

For example, the clients of Barrow, Wade, Guthrie & Co., the first English firm established in New York, included the New York, Ontario and Western Railway Company, which James T. Anyon[1] said was the first railroad in the United States to employ public accountants to act as auditors and to certify to the correctness of its annual statements to its stockholders. Other important clients were British insurance companies with operations in the United States, and a textile concern in New York. The going wasn't easy at first. Mr. Anyon's book states candidly that at the end of the first six months of his tenure in 1886 the operations resulted in a "gross service credit" of $4,842.08, and a net profit, after charging his salary of $1,250.00 for the half year, of $2,133.50.

---

[1] James T. Anyon, *Recollections of the Early Days of American Accountancy 1883-1893*. James T. Anyon, New York, 1925.

The amount of business was so limited that Mr. Anyon could not afford to engage any assistant, except an office boy. He, therefore, did everything himself, except dusting, filling the ink stand, mailing letters and running errands, which were the duties of the boy.

The British Invasion

In the late 1880's more English and Scottish chartered accountants appeared in New York, representing prominent British accounting firms. They were sent to examine the financial condition and earning power of American industries which English syndicates had purchased, and whose securities were floated on the English market.

The presence of these British colleagues provided the American accountants, according to Mr. Anyon, with a greater insight into the nature and responsibility of professional accounting work. Bankers and financial men also began to understand better the nature and value of accounting and auditing.

Some of these British firms established permanent offices in the United States. After Barrow, Wade the first to do so was Price Waterhouse & Co., already firmly established in London, which in 1890 and 1891 sent two agents, Jones and Caesar, to reside in this country. For a while they practiced as individuals, then as Jones, Caesar & Co., but to all intents and purposes they were Price Waterhouse in America, and eventually the entire American practice was absorbed under the latter name.

American industrial concerns were beginning to incorporate under the laws of the various states, and their securities were offered to the American investing public. Bankers usually employed accounting firms to make examinations and reports on the financial condition and earnings. Consolidation of industrial enterprises, to the extent permitted by the antitrust laws, also became popular, and accountants were employed to examine the earnings of the companies which were to be combined, but most of the important auditing work at first went to the British firms.

A typical certificate of the early days is the following, covering the accounts of St. Louis Breweries Ltd., signed in London by Price Waterhouse & Co.:

> We have examined the above accounts with the books and vouchers of the company, and find the same to be correct. We approve and certify that the above balance sheet correctly sets forth the position of the company.

In 1899, Jones died, and in 1900 Caesar retired. London offered the senior partnership of the American firm, which soon reverted to the name of Price Waterhouse & Co., to Arthur Lowes Dickinson. Dickinson was a superior man. He held a master's degree from Cambridge University, and was both a chartered accountant and a Fellow of the Institute of Actuaries. In addition, he had an attractive personality and extraordinary leadership capacity. He had a strong interest in elevating the status of the accounting profession, and played a prominent part in strengthening the professional organizations in the United States.

In 1902 Price Waterhouse & Co. was elected, by shareholders of the United States Steel Company at their first annual meeting, as auditors of the company, which the firm continues to be to this day. The auditor's certificate issued in 1903 read as follows:

> We have examined the books of the U.S. Steel Corporation and its Subsidiary Companies for the year ending December 31, 1902, and certify that the Balance Sheet at that date and the Relative Income Account are correctly prepared therefrom.
>
> We have satisfied ourselves that during the year only actual additions and extensions have been charged to Property Account; that ample provision has been made for Depreciation and Extinguishment, and that the item of "Deferred Charges" represents expenditures

reasonably and properly carried forward to operations of subsequent years.

We are satisfied that the valuations of the inventories of stocks on hand as certified by the responsible officials have been carefully and accurately made at approximate cost; also that the cost of material and labor on contracts in progress has been carefully ascertained, and that the profit taken on these contracts is fair and reasonable.

Full provision has been made for bad and doubtful accounts receivable and for all ascertainable liabilities.

We have verified the cash and securities by actual inspection or by certificates from the Depositories, and are of opinion that the Stocks and Bonds are fully worth the value at which they are stated in the Balance Sheet.

And we certify that in our opinion the Balance Sheet is properly drawn up so as to show the true financial position of the Corporation and its Subsidiary Companies, and that the Relative Income Account is a fair and correct statement of the net earnings for the fiscal year ending at that date.

When U.S. Steel was organized in 1901 through consolidation with a number of other enterprises, the lawyers and bankers wished to present to the stockholders the accounts of the parent company alone. Dickinson insisted that consolidated accounts were necessary, and supporting statements and schedules were provided. To a large extent, United States Steel established a standard for financial reporting during the early years of the century. The disclosure of significant facts and figures, in which Dickinson played an influential role, contributed to a realization on the part of the business world of the importance of accounting and auditing.

In 1905 the life insurance business was put under the spotlight of a public examination, as a result of widespread publicity about the internal difficulties of some of the larger companies. A Joint Legislative Committee of the State of New York was appointed for the investigation. Legal counsel was Charles Evans Hughes. The newly elected chairman of the Equitable Life Assurance Society engaged Price Waterhouse & Co. and Haskins & Sells to make a thorough examination of the past transactions of this large insurance company in order to ascertain its condition at the time he assumed office. The New York Life Insurance Company also engaged the two firms for similar purpose. The reports were signed by Price Waterhouse & Co. as chartered accountants, and Haskins & Sells as certified public accountants.

Early American Firms

Haskins & Sells, one of the oldest native American accounting firms, was founded in 1895 by Charles Waldo Haskins and Elijah Watt Sells.

Haskins, after some years in private accounting work, had begun the public practice of accounting in New York City in 1886. Sells' previous experience had been in accounting work for railroads in the Midwest. His last post in 1893 was as secretary and auditor of the Colorado Midland Railway.

The two founding partners met in 1893, having been designated as experts to assist a Congressional commission investigating the operating methods of the Executive Department in Washington and to recommend improvements and economies.

Mr. Haskins was the first president of the New York Board of Examiners of Public Accountants, and also the first president of the New York State Society of Certified Public Accountants. He took a leading part in the founding of the School of Commerce Accounts and Finance of New York University, becoming its first dean.

Mr. Sells was also active in professional affairs. He was one of the organizers of the first International Congress of Accountants, and for two years he served as president of the American Association of Public Accountants.

Robert H. Montgomery's book, *Fifty Years of Accountancy*[2]

---

[2] Ronald Press Company, New York, 1939.

throws much light on the nature of accounting practice in the formative days of the profession. Montgomery was a native-born American, and the firm of which he became a member, Lybrand, Ross Bros. & Montgomery, founded in 1898, had no British origin. But Montgomery readily conceded that he benefited much from his association with Dickinson and the other Englishmen and Scots who were among the pioneers.

Montgomery, who became an outstanding leader of the profession, was employed at the age of 16 as an office boy by John Heins, a public accountant of Philadelphia, then president of the American Association of Public Accountants, which had been organized only two years before.

Montgomery said, "As office boy, I would have gained an insight into all the secrets of the national organization if there had been any secrets. The activities were few. Often I sent a telegram that there would be no quorum, hence no meeting."

Montgomery became a junior accountant with the Heins firm, spending much of his time checking postings from one book to another.

In the early days, prior to the turn of the century, many financial statements of both large and small businesses had the symbols "E.O.E." in the lower left-hand corner. It meant "Errors and Omissions Excepted." So many of these statements were erroneous, wrote Montgomery, that it gave rise to one of the favorite jokes of his contemporaries, "The real meaning is Errors and Omissions Expected."

Montgomery also said that his firm in the early days frequently verified all of the transactions in the books, wrote "audited and found correct," and did not make a single constructive suggestion. He felt it wrong to accept fees for routine checking of footings and postings, without finding errors sufficient to pay for the accountant's time.

When an audit was started the accountants were handed what were known as all the books of account: ledgers, journals, cash, purchase and sales books, with canceled checks and paid bills. When the accountants verified the entries and vouched all the payments, they were pretty much through with the job.

Later the Heins firm began to analyze the trial balance, and look at shipment books, cash-sales records and other evidences of transactions which might not have found their way into the books with which the auditors were furnished. Often they were refused access to subsidiary records, but they kept insisting, because they found many defalcations they were not supposed to find, which would not have been discovered by checking the formal books of account.

The accountants were not supposed to know much about inventories, but they tried to learn what they could. Montgomery said that the first time he asked to see the insurance policy covering the stock in process and on hand, "I might as well have thrown a bomb." But his rule was that if there was any reluctance to show him what he wanted to see, he would keep on asking—"or else." In some cases auditors were not permitted to read the minutes of boards of directors. The mere fact that permission was denied was a cause for suspicion.

One of the reasons for detailed checking was that the instructions often included bringing the books into exact balance. Frequently the books of businesses had been out of balance for months or even years, and the discovery of the errors was a terrific task. One junior accountant would call off an amount from a ledger to another junior who compared it with an item in a book of original entry. One hollered the amount, and the other ticked it off. The function was known as "holler and tick."

It gradually became apparent that when the books were in balance the integrity of the records could be determined by comprehensive tests as well as by verifying all items.

Out-of-Town Work

Accountants traveled a good deal in those days, since their firms had not established branch offices in many different parts of the country. Some of the conditions in which they worked were primitive. James T. Anyon told of a visit to a place called Mills Camp in Alabama in the 1890's. His train was hours late, and he arrived at midnight in a desolate part of the country where there was no railway station, but where he was allowed to dismount from the train. A night watchman met him and allowed him to sleep, in the rain, around a roaring fire among a group of convicts who were working at the camp. When morning came he was allowed to go to the house of the manager, where he was given coffee, and found other civilized amenities.

Robert Montgomery described a job in Vicksburg, Mississippi, where there was no hotel. He and his companion camped out in the mill. They drank and bathed in the muddy waters of the Mississippi. On another engagement, Adam Ross and Montgomery spent six weeks in a town in the mountains of North Carolina. They occupied a double bed and used one washbowl. In the morning the water was frozen. To finish the job on time, they worked nights and Sundays and all night on the final day. The cooking was so bad that they lived on boiled eggs—six or eight a day!

Montgomery's tireless service in the professional organizations will be mentioned frequently in this book. He wrote, "My personal opinion is that it is far easier to rise in one's trade or profession by attendance at meetings and by friendly intercourse with those in the same line as ourselves than in any other way."

Professional Pioneers

Many other firms which later became prominent were founded in the late nineteenth and early twentieth centuries.

It was, of course, an advantage to these early accounting firms to be on the scene when the American economy was in the first stages of its great industrial growth. They formed important connections with influential bankers, lawyers and industrialists which in many cases led to rapid expansion of the practices of these firms.

But it must be remembered that many other firms which came on the scene about the same time did not prosper, and have long since been forgotten. Those that survived were able to deliver the goods. Their partners were not wealthy men at first. They worked hard, held to high standards, gave their clients valuable service, and through sound internal policies developed strong organizations of their own.

In spite of the head start enjoyed by these firms, many other firms which were founded much later have also achieved great success through application of the same formula.

In those pioneering days from 1886 to 1906, some of the American accountants were jealous of their British colleagues, who seemed to be favored by the bankers, and thus obtained many of the most lucrative engagements. In retrospect, however, the accounting profession clearly gained much from the presence of the English and Scottish chartered accountants.

They brought with them a background of discipline, professional training, standards, and professional pride, derived from the simple fact that in their home countries the profession had already been organized for 20 years or more, and had attained status and recognition. This in turn was due to the industrial development in Great Britain, and the acquisition of investment capital in that country which preceded similar developments in America by roughly half a century.

The chartered accountants were self-confident, since they knew their jobs; they were articulate, and were generally well educated. They were hard workers and astute businessmen. For the most part they were dedicated to high standards, and earnestly desired to enhance the status of their profession in their adopted country.

The same things can be said of the native American accountants who followed their example and had the vision to see the opportunities in the young profession. It is not surprising that some of these pioneer firms developed into the large national organizations of today.

The partners of the larger firms became comparatively well-to-do. They had time also to give to the affairs of the infant professional organizations.

The contributions of these men are too numerous to be described individually. In the aggregate they were invaluable. If they had chosen to devote their attention exclusively to the development of their own practices, without concern for the accounting profession as a whole, that profession would not enjoy the status which it has today.

CHAPTER 4

The First "National" Association

W HILE the organization of a national professional accounting society was inevitable, it might have been delayed for many years if it had not been for a visit to New York by an Englishman in 1883.

In that year Edwin Guthrie, of the firm of Thomas, Wade, Guthrie & Co., Chartered Accountants of London and Manchester, England, was receiver in bankruptcy of a financial concern in England. He found it necessary to come to the United States to ascertain the value and status of certain property and assets which the bankrupt concern owned in this country. He intended to employ an accounting firm here to assist him, but could not find one.

Being a perspicacious gentleman, Mr. Guthrie saw an opportunity to establish an accounting practice in New York, which as far as he then knew would be the first of its kind in the country. He met an actuary named John Wylie Barrow, and with him organized in 1883 the firm of Barrow, Wade, Guthrie & Co., Public Accountants, New York, the English partners supplying the necessary working capital.

In 1886 Barrow died. Mr. Guthrie then brought to this country James T. Anyon, a senior assistant and a chartered accountant of England, who became the partner in charge of the firm in New York.

Mr. Anyon, a stranger in a strange land, looked about for American colleagues in his chosen profession. He found a firm called Veysey & Veysey, with a staff of two or three assistants, a James Yalden & Co., and several individual practitioners. In Philadelphia John Heins appeared to be the leading accountant in public practice, and in Boston Rodney McLaughlin was similarly situated.

Since Mr. Guthrie had remained in New York to provide for the conduct of the firm's practice there, Mr. Anyon arranged for him to meet the accountants with whom Anyon had become acquainted.

Six or seven individuals attended the meeting, including Mr. Heins of Philadelphia.

Mr. Guthrie expressed his pleasure at meeting the American accountants, but indicated regret that the profession here had not attained much public recognition. He said that in England, on the contrary, the profession was on a high plane, being recognized as one of the leading professions. He suggested that a body similar to the Institute of Chartered Accountants in England and Wales should be started in the United States.

Since the English Institute had been in existence for only six years, Mr. Guthrie's allusions to the high standing of his profession may have involved some poetic license, excusable on the grounds of national pride.

Nonetheless, his suggestion was received with enthusiasm. It was moved and seconded that the accountants present at the meeting should form themselves into an association for the advancement and protection of the interests of the accounting profession, and that the qualification for membership should be ability and fitness to practice accounting in a public capacity.

At first, it was proposed to select as a name, "The Chartered

Accountants' Institute." However, Mr. Guthrie strongly advised the use of some other name than "chartered accountants." He pointed out that this would be likely to conflict with the use of the same title in the United States by English and Scottish accountants who might visit the United States on professional business for clients in Great Britain. This loomed as a serious objection at that time, since the most important and responsible engagements entrusted to accountants in those days were given to visiting British accountants.

Accordingly, it was resolved to organize a society entitled the American Association of Public Accountants. A committee was appointed, a second general meeting was held, the Association was incorporated, a constitution was adopted, and a Council and officers were elected. The certificate of incorporation was filed on September 20, 1887.

The first president was James Yalden, the vice president was John Heins, the secretary was James T. Anyon, and the treasurer was W. H. Veysey. At this time there were 31 members— 24 fellows and seven associates. Fellows were persons who had practiced as public accountants continuously for three years prior to their admission to membership.

Most of the members and associates merely had desk space, with no assistants, and some had offices in their homes. A few had firms with regular offices, names on the door, and several staff assistants.

The formation of the Association did not immediately change things very much.

The new society had to struggle for survival. It was the first American organization intended to represent the public practitioners of accounting. But whereas the English Institute had started with more than 1,000 members, there were few public accountants in the United States from which to draw membership. The Association was also the first organization to aspire to national coverage, but the bulk of its members were in New York, and transportation being what it was, the Association had little to offer those in other parts of this vast nation.

Legal Base Lacking

There was nothing in the United States similar to the required statutory audit of corporations in England, which had greatly stimulated the development of the accounting profession there. Nor did the United States provide a Royal Charter, which automatically had given status to the chartered accountants of Scotland and England. The Institute in England had actually introduced a system of examinations as early as July 1882. It was not until 1897 that any professional accounting examinations were required in the United States—and those only in the State of New York.

There was no recognized title for qualified public accountants here. There was no native accounting literature to speak of, nor any system of education and training for young accountants.

The first two years of the tiny American Association were occupied with internal affairs. Where matters stood in 1889 is reflected in the address of President James Yalden:

> The profession of accountancy having hitherto been but little known in the United States, and the recognized want of a well-organized body of professional and public accountants, whose ability, character, and strict business conduct could be relied upon, being called for by the leading commercial and financial representatives of the country, led to the formation of our Association—the lines being taken mainly from the older countries, notably England, in the formation and the ruling and conduct of our Order.
>
> It is much to be regretted that our Association is not stronger in number. At the present time we have but 25 fellows, and seven associates, which I am sure you will agree is not enough to give the Association that standing and recognition we all desire, and it is of paramount importance to the profession that some means should be adopted to increase our membership.

But things moved slowly. By 1892 the membership had increased only to 35. The Association had no employees. Everything was done by volunteers. The officers were required to spend a good deal of time and energy on mere administrative details—the arrangement of meetings of trustees and members, the writing of minutes, the sending out of notices and invitations to membership, discussion of amendments to bylaws, debates over proposed activities, and efforts to obtain publicity and recognition.

Nor did the Association have the field entirely to itself. There were various organizations of bookkeepers and accountants in New York, among the most vigorous of which was the Institute of Accounts. Its members were mostly accountants in private employment, but included a number of public accountants, among whom were even some of the leading members of the Association.

Societies of public accountants had also been organized in a number of the states. From time to time the Association was faced with the competition of other national organizations, though they were short-lived. The most influential of these was the Federation of Societies of Public Accountants in the United States of America (the state societies).

At times the leaders of the Association must have been tempted to throw in the sponge. By January 1894, its membership had grown to 48 fellows and 17 associates. But in January 1896, the membership had dropped again to 27 fellows and five associates.

Adventure in Education

Over a period of several years in the early 1890's, the Association invested an enormous amount of its scarce resources, and the time and energy of its members, in efforts to establish a school or college of accounting where young men could be trained for the profession.

The certificate of incorporation of the American Association included as one of its objectives "establishing a high standard of professional attainments through general education and knowledge and otherwise."

In 1892 the Association began an effort to establish a college of accounts with degree-conferring powers, under the jurisdiction of the Regents of the University of the State of New York and the immediate guidance of the Association. The project was supported by a number of business and financial leaders. *The New York Times* commented editorially on the proposal. A delegation from the Association attended a hearing before the Regents on June 8, 1892. But the petition for a charter for a college of accounts was not approved by the Regents. This august body resolved that it was not prepared to endorse the entire proposal of the petition, but was ready to open examinations for such persons as desired to become public accountants.

The Association returned to the attack with better preparation. In December 1892 it presented another petition to the Regents for a charter to establish a professional school to be known as the New York School of Accounts. The petition stated that $5,000 had been subscribed as a guarantee of support for the school; that suitable accommodations had been leased; and that all necessary furniture, books and supplies would be provided within a reasonable time. The petition was supported by a resolution of guarantee, an outline of a proposed curriculum in detail, and a paper elaborating the reasons for the establishment of such a school, the proposed method of financing it, the qualifications of the proposed board of trustees and other details.

This time the effort was successful. The Regents granted a temporary charter for two years. A dean and faculty were appointed, members of the Association were designated to lecture, and letters and prospectuses were sent to several thousand prospective students.

Alas, this herculean effort was doomed to failure.

At a meeting of the faculty of the school in June 1894, the following resolution was passed:

> Resolved, That in the opinion of the faculty it is unadvisable to continue the School of Accounts, and they recommend that the Trustees take such action as they may decide upon to surrender the charter to the Board of Regents or otherwise. Carried.

In September 1894, at a meeting of the trustees of the school, Richard F. Stevens, president of the Association, reported:

> Our members gave freely of their time and experience, and everything that the Association could do with the limited means at its command was done. A year has passed since its inception, and what has been accomplished? A class of seven pupils have gone through the year's course, that is all, not a businessman has come forward to aid us in any way, the whole burden has fallen upon the shoulders of a few members, now disheartened and disillusioned, the Board of Regents of the University has stood silent and aloof, not a word has been said about commissioning or licensing our members, and communications addressed to them on the subject of legalizing the profession by legislative enactment have remained unanswered. The members, under this state of affairs, naturally have ceased to take an interest in the school, the professors have resigned or been slack in their attendance, the scholars supine, and further continuance of the school, in its present status, seems idle.

The school was abandoned. However, several proprietary schools of accounting were started a few years later, quite likely as a result of the Association's pioneering effort. The growing interest in accounting education also led the universities to establish courses in the subject.

The Wharton School of Commerce and Finance had been established at the University of Pennsylvania in 1881, and the introduction of accounting instruction there encouraged the growth of public accounting in Philadelphia. The School of Commerce, Accounts and Finance of New York University was established in 1900, on the initiative of the New York State Society of Certified Public Accountants. In 1902 the Association established an annual scholarship of $100 at the New York

University School, which was gratefully acknowledged by the University authorities.

In 1906, the Pace Institute of Accountancy was founded, which survives today as Pace College, now a degree-granting institution.

The unsuccessful efforts of the American Association in the field of education at least started some ripples by pointing up the need, and the need was finally filled in better ways than those originally attempted. The question of "licensing our members" had also arisen in connection with this adventure in education—and that was to be the subject of successful action.

The First CPA Law

The idea of legislative recognition of the public accounting profession had fascinated members of the Association from the beginning. Tentative approaches to the Board of Regents had not received encouraging responses. But in 1894 a serious attempt was made to have a bill enacted by the New York State Legislature.

Several draft bills were prepared by different individuals—and argued over. A Mr. Gottsberger wrote his own bill and put it in the hands of a senator, apparently without submitting it for approval of the Association. The Institute of Accounts, most of whose members were privately employed, but some of whom were also public accountants, also drafted a bill and had it introduced in the Assembly.

Failure because of conflicting bills was feared. A "Committee of Fourteen" was formed, and a meeting of all interested public accountants was held in New York to discuss the situation. The committee included representatives of the American Association, the Institute of Accounts, and public accountants belonging to neither organization. The bills already introduced were read at this meeting.

The Gottsberger bill was restrictive. It prohibited practice as a public accountant in New York without a license, and provided the means by which such licenses could be obtained.

The other bill (by the Institute of Accounts) was permissive. It provided for the issuance of a certificate to practice as a "certified public accountant," but did not restrict the practice of public accounting to persons who obtained this title.

There ensued a long debate in which various opinions were expressed as to the merits of the two bills. Apparently, the Regents had expressed a preference for the permissive bill. The minutes of the meeting state, "Richard M. Chapman thought that of the two bills . . . the one endorsed by the Regents was the most desirable to act upon. . . ."

Meetings were held in Albany with the secretary of the Board of Regents, and with a committee of the Assembly. Finally the Association endorsed and approved, with some amendments, the permissive bill providing solely for the issuance of the CPA certificate.

The bill was defeated in the Senate.

Nothing daunted, the accountants renewed the effort in 1896. The Committee of Fourteen rallied all interested accountants in support of identical permissive bills in the Senate and Assembly. Representatives of the Association appeared at the legislative hearings. The bill became law on April 17, 1896. It provided for issuance of a certificate conferring the title "certified public accountant" upon qualified persons, and prohibited use of that title by others. It provided for examination of applicants but included no education or experience requirement. "Waiver certificates" could be issued without examination to public accountants already in practice.

The passage of this law marked the beginning of an *accredited* profession of accounting in the United States.

The question has often arisen as to why the title "certified public accountant" was selected.

It was no doubt a temptation to adopt the term already established in Great Britain—"chartered accountant." But it was pointed out in the discussions of this subject, as Mr. Guthrie had done ten years before, that this would conflict with the rights established by the Scottish societies, and later by the English, under Royal Charters. Moreover, the pioneers in the United States, with native pride, probably did not want to be accused of copying the British. In addition, the term "public accountant" was already fairly well established in the United States, and the simple addition of the prefix "certified" seemed to meet with general approval. It is also possible that the American Association of Public Accountants favored preservation of the last two words in its own title.

By the end of 1905, New York had issued 332 CPA certificates, of which 155 were issued by examination, the remainder by waiver.

The passage of the CPA law in New York was swiftly followed by similar legislation in other states, notably Pennsylvania (1899), Maryland (1900), California (1901), Illinois (1903), Washington (1903), New Jersey (1904), Florida (1905), and Michigan (1905).

The Struggle for Identification

The members of the American Association of Public Accountants had a compulsive desire for recognition. This was natural and understandable. They knew that they had skills which were useful to the community. They knew that their colleagues in Great Britain had already achieved professional status and a considerable degree of prestige. The Association members were impatient for wider opportunities for service in the United States, and for the public respect which they felt was due them as experts in a field which deserved, even if it had not yet attained, the title of "profession."

Yet in the view of most of the public they were indistinguishable from bookkeepers. In 1902, a publication known as *Business World* published a letter in which the writer said plaintively, "The term accountant to the public signifies bookkeeper." This feeling persisted for a long time. Robert H. Montgomery was fond of saying, humorously, "The public thinks a public accountant is a bookkeeper out of a job—who drinks."

It is not surprising, then, that much of the energy and financial resources of the new Association was directed to publicizing the profession. A committee on advertising was formed in 1888. Thousands of dollars were spent on advertising in the following years.

Booklets were printed and widely distributed containing the bylaws, objectives and membership of the Association. Paid advertising in contemporary business and financial newspapers and magazines described the services of accountants, the profession's objectives and the nature of its organization. Membership-promotion materials were distributed by the thousands.

Individual accountants, including members of the Association, also advertised their services through circulars distributed by mail and advertisements in periodicals. In England, the Institute of Chartered Accountants had begun as early as 1881 to stamp out advertising and "touting" for business, though it was over 20 years before the practice entirely died out. On occasion *The Accountant* (London) made critical remarks about "touting" by American accountants.

In 1893, at a meeting of the American Association, W. Sanders Davies offered a resolution "that the indiscriminate soliciting of business by the issue of touting circulars is unprofessional and unworthy of the profession of public accountants, and it is further resolved that a copy of the foregoing resolution be transmitted by the secretary to each member of the Association."

This action was characteristic of Mr. Davies. He had come to New York from England in 1891, and established a local firm—still flourishing as Davies and Davies—in which his son and grandson became partners. Sanders Davies was a man of uncompromising integrity, devoted to the highest standards of conduct. He was genial, humorous and fearless. Over a span of more than 40 years he was a tireless worker in the national organizations, a member of the governing bodies, twice serving as president.

However, his resolution of 1893 was laid on the table.

But in 1894 the Association adopted the following resolution:

> That all members of the Association be prohibited from advertising in any shape or manner their vocations and calling; and setting forth the nature or special features of their business, but that the insertion of a card in any regular authorized journals or papers indicating their profession and giving address, etc., is permissible.

There is no indication that this admonition was ever enforced, or that it succeeded in eliminating undesirable advertising, although it doubtless had a restraining effect on many of the members.

Although one of the objectives of the American Association of Public Accountants was to compel "the observance of strict rules of conduct as a condition of membership," no such rules were formulated in the first twenty years.

For one thing, the membership was so small that formal complaints against members by other members might have generated personal hostilities which would have torn the organization apart.

Nevertheless, the records indicate that the trustees of the Association were conscious of the importance of professional conduct, and actually did take disciplinary action in at least a few instances. Some applications for admission were refused on ethical grounds. One complaint or question which had official attention apparently caused the voluntary separation of a member.

Lack of Technical Standards

Very little was done in the first 20 years to develop standards of accounting and auditing. The first technical meeting held by the Association occurred in 1892. The subject was uniformity in practice. The main speaker proposed that at each meeting one or more members present a paper designed as a model for universal adoption on some phase of practice, which, after being discussed, would be laid over until the next meeting when it would be rejected or adopted: "As soon as sufficient matter be thus accumulated, it should be published in book form, with proper table of contents, index, etc., and placed on the shelves of every fellow member as the code of the Association."

This was an ambitious plan which showed awareness of the need for codification of standards of practice. It was too ambitious, however, to come to fruition.

The next record of a technical discussion was in March 1893. The preparation of balance sheets was the subject. In June 1893 papers were read on trading and profit-and-loss accounts.

Then there was a gap. No doubt the members were giving all their attention to the school fostered by the Association, and thereafter to the effort to secure enactment of the New York CPA law.

In June of 1893 a resolution was adopted to the effect that members be requested to present papers connected with the profession of accountancy at the regular meetings of the Association. In the following three years, 13 technical papers were presented, which were published in one or another of three contemporary financial magazines: *The Financial Record, Business,* and *The Banking Law Journal.*

Apparently, however, these technical meetings also died a natural death.

In 1901 the president of the Association called attention to the need for instructive literature related to the accounting profession in the United States.

There were British books on accounting, but most of those published in the United States were on bookkeeping. Little had been written primarily for the use of public accountants.

In 1902 there was a discussion by the trustees of the Association on the desirability of establishing a library. Thirteen books were acquired, mainly by gifts.

With regard to periodical literature, *The Accountant* (London) was apparently widely read in the United States. Technical articles on some aspects of accounting were also occasionally published in various business and financial magazines in the United States.

The 1904 Congress

The outstanding event of the first 20 years was the first International Congress of Accountants held in St. Louis, simultaneously with the Louisiana Purchase Exposition, in 1904.

The initiative for the Congress came from George Wilkinson of Chicago, who as president of the Illinois Society of Public Accountants had organized in 1902 the Federation of Societies of Public Accountants in the United States of America. He became the secretary of the Federation, and was a moving spirit in organizing the 1904 Congress.

Accountants in many of the states had organized local societies, though most of them were small. The American Association in 1904 had only a little over 250 members, with a heavy concentration in New York. Nearly one-third of its members had come from abroad, mostly from England and Scotland, and many of these were chartered accountants.

England was generally unpopular in America at the turn of the century. James T. Anyon, in writing of his early experiences, said that he had the disadvantage "of being an Englishman, for the people generally, at that time, did not take very kindly to men of this nationality. . . . There was somewhat of a national feeling of prejudice against Englishmen, arising I think in the old colonial days, which was still apparent. It was a fact nevertheless in spite of this feeling that if any real and important accounting work had to be done, it would in the majority of cases be given to the foreign-trained accountant in preference to the native one."

No doubt because of this preference, the native American accountants, particularly outside of New York, had some latent feelings of hostility toward the "foreigners," which may have carried over in some measure to the Association.

In any event, the Association was not doing much for the members outside New York, and this probably stimulated the organization of the Federation.

Meanwhile, the New York State Society of Certified Public Accountants had been organized in 1897, following enactment of the CPA law a year earlier. Many members of the Association naturally obtained CPA certificates, and some of them joined the New York State Society. But the Association had other members who were public accountants in states where CPA laws had not yet been enacted. Yet the bulk of its membership was in New York, and there is evidence that some of its leaders feared that the New York State Society would be competitive. They suggested, unsuccessfully, that the Association remain as the representative society of all public accountants.

A comparison of memberships showed that some CPAs belonged both to the American Association and to the New York State Society, some CPAs belonged only to the Association and not to the State Society, some CPAs belonged to the State Society but not to the Association, and the Association contained some accountants who were not CPAs!

Further to complicate the scene, the New York State Society chose not to join the Federation.

In these chaotic circumstances the International Congress in St. Louis provided a rallying point. The energetic George Wilkinson brought together all three organizations in a common cause. It was the first truly national meeting of professional accountants in the United States. The international flavor added glamour. Representatives from England, Canada and Holland attended.

It was a large meeting for those times. There may have been somewhat more than 150 persons present.

Arthur Lowes Dickinson was chairman of the committee on arrangements, George O. May was chairman of the local committee, and Joseph E. Sterrett was permanent chairman of the Congress. Other participants who later occupied prominent positions in the professional organizations were: William M. Lybrand; Robert H. Montgomery; John B. Niven; Ernest Reckitt; Elijah Watt Sells; and Walter R. Staub. Some of them had been active in the Federation, others in the Association.

Joseph E. Sterrett first came to national prominence as chairman of this Congress. He had joined the staff of a pioneer accounting practitioner in Philadelphia, John W. Francis, in 1891, and became Francis' partner in 1893.

Sterrett was instrumental in the organization of the Pennsylvania Association of Public Accountants in 1897, which following passage of the CPA law in that state changed its name to the Pennsylvania Institute of Certified Public Accountants. Sterrett became president of the state association, a member of the State Board of Examiners, and chairman of the committee on education. In this capacity he initiated the Evening School of Accounts and Finance, which later was merged with the Wharton School of Commerce of the University of Pennsylvania.

Francis died, and Sterrett continued the practice in his own name. In 1902 he had become interested in the Federation of Societies of Public Accountants, of which Arthur Lowes Dickinson, the head of Price Waterhouse & Co., was president in 1904. The friendship of these two men resulted in amalgamation of Sterrett's practice with Price Waterhouse & Co., Sterrett becoming a partner of the firm in 1907. He later moved to New York.

Sterrett's capacity as a negotiator, together with his competence and his personal sincerity, idealism and persuasiveness, made him one of the great leaders of the profession in his time.

The program of the 1904 Congress was largely devoted to technical papers, followed by discussion. Both papers and discussion were subsequently published in the official record, which must have been one of the most important professional accounting publications thus far produced in the United States.

In all respects, the Congress was a grand affair, and it undoubtedly contributed in many ways to acceleration of the progress of the profession in the following years.

Notably, the Congress laid a foundation for merger of the Federation with the Association a year later. All members of state societies associated with the Federation were admitted to the Association. Other national groups disappeared from the scene. A truly national organization of professional accountants was emerging.

In 1905 also, arrangements were made to take over a magazine launched by the Illinois Society, under the title *The Auditor*. The name was changed to *The Journal of Accountancy*, the first issue of which appeared in November 1905. It has been published ever since, under the editorial control of the American Association and its successor organizations.

In spite of disappointments and discouragements the Association had stuck to its guns. The little band of leaders who did most of the work kept on trying, and in the second decade their efforts began to be rewarded. They knew what it took to create a profession and they developed momentum in the right direction.

By 1906, the end of the first 20 years, the survivors could look back with satisfaction on their efforts. Their Association had become a going concern. It had 341 members and associates, from 25 states and two foreign countries. To be sure, the majority—200 of the members—resided in New York. But the foundations of a nationwide profession were being laid.

CHAPTER 5

The Impact of the Federal Government

V ASTLY strengthened by the merger with the Federation after the 1904 Congress the American Association of Public Accountants entered the second stage of its development with confidence and enthusiasm.

The first annual meeting of the Association following the merger, held in New York, October 17, 1905, was an occasion of self-congratulation and great expectations. The president, John R. Loomis, said at the banquet:

> This occasion celebrates the culmination of what is perhaps the most important movement ever inaugurated in the interest of the profession of public accountancy in this country—the fusion of the several state societies constituting the Federation of Societies of Public Accountants with the American Association of Public Accountants. The American Association of Public Accountants stands at this time as the grand national body, representing practically all pub-

lic accountants throughout the United States. Its object is the elevation of the profession, and the spreading of a knowledge and recognition of the utility and necessity for the public accountant in the industrial and financial development of our country. It is an organization that every society can stand by and that every individual member can work for. The hopes and plans of the past are now measurably realized, and upon a basis of absolute harmony and good feeling. We surely have abundant cause for rejoicing—the promise for the future is most encouraging.

There was reason for optimism. The United States economy was developing rapidly, and the nation was becoming a world power. The trend toward widespread investment in corporate securities, the extension of bank credit, the increasing intervention of the federal government in the economy, and the probability of an income tax, all forecast increasing need for reliable financial information.

Panic and Regulation

This need was highlighted by the panic of 1907, described by an editorial in *The Journal of Accountancy* for November of that year, as "one of the craziest, most spectacular panics ever recorded in the annals of finance." Within three days the banks in New York lost over $12 million in cash. Long lines of frightened depositors besieged the doors of two trust companies. One trust company suspended payment and several small banks closed their doors. There had been a sudden collapse of the credit system in New York. Investigations of the insurance industry and other companies had led to general criticism of corporate managements.

The *Journal* editorial pointed out that the financial statements of banks, railroads and insurance companies had not been made public, and that they had no independent certification in which the people could place confidence: "Publicity is a safe and conservative remedy for most corporate abuses. The certified public accountant is the authorized agent of publicity. Let popular discussion of this subject proceed until the people shall demand that the affairs of every public-service corporation, of every bank and of every insurance company shall be regularly examined by certified public accountants who are independent of the directors, if not also of the stockholders."

The panic of 1907 discredited big business in the eyes of the public, and created a political environment favorable to further regulation. President Theodore Roosevelt sought legislation, which Congress refused to enact until the Administration of President Wilson seven years later, in the form of the Clayton Antitrust Act. This measure strengthened the Sherman Act by prohibiting certain specified trade practices, and set up the Federal Trade Commission as an administrative agency clothed with police power to enforce the law.

Due to Roosevelt's inexhaustible energy, the federal government had grown rapidly in prestige and power in the preceding years. In 1908 Roosevelt controlled the Republican Convention, which nominated his favorite candidate, William Howard Taft.

During Taft's term in 1910 legislation was adopted further strengthening the Interstate Commerce Commission. More prosecutions for violation of the Sherman Act were instituted. Of special significance to the accounting profession was the Sixteenth Amendment of the federal Constitution, promoted by Taft, though not adopted until after his term, which permitted a federal tax on incomes.

Taft was succeeded in 1912 by Woodrow Wilson, who also was a liberal and a progressive. He believed in lower tariffs, conservation of natural resources, and regulation of banking and the big corporations.

In 1909 a corporation excise tax, based on income, had been enacted, but in 1913 this was replaced by a graduated federal tax on incomes, as a result of the Sixteenth Amendment, which had nullified an earlier Supreme Court decision that an income tax was unconstitutional.

An outstanding achievement of Wilson's first year was the

Federal Reserve Act of 1913, which reconstructed the national banking and currency system. The Federal Reserve Board was created to control the discount rate and superintend the 11 newly created federal reserve banks, which in turn were empowered to issue bank notes against commercial paper and other liquid assets. The Board and the banks needed reliable financial statements from the issuers of commercial paper. This need led to promulgation of the first authoritative guide for the conduct of independent audits.

All these developments were to add to the responsibilities and opportunities of the young accounting profession, which was small, little known to the public, virtually without political influence, and in truth not yet fully organized.

In 1905 there were still no authoritative rules or guidelines on accounting or auditing procedure, no comprehensive code of ethics or effective disciplinary machinery, no officially recognized system of education and training.

Only ten states had enacted CPA laws, and even in those states a large proportion of the certified public accountants had received their certificates by waiver of examination. There was as yet no nationwide system of examination and qualification for admission to the profession. Applicants were admitted to the Association on the basis of experience in public accounting.

At the annual meeting in 1906, the newly elected president, Elijah Watt Sells, in his inaugural address stressed three subjects: (1) a continuing elevation of the standards of professional ethics; (2) an increasing insistence upon the highest possible excellence of professional work; and (3) the encouragement and aid which many American educational institutions were giving in the development of accountancy education.

Incidentally, Mr. Sells, a native American, said: "In two of these fields of professional advancement, we have much to learn from Great Britain. As loyal Americans and as accurate observers, we are convinced that America is far ahead of Great Britain in the character of our professional accounting work. In the field of accountancy ethics and accountancy education, we are still, however, behind our English brothers."

Pressure for Financial Disclosure

As early as 1905 President Theodore Roosevelt had proposed legislation requiring full publicity of the accounts of corporations doing interstate business—specifically railway corporations. Some years later the Interstate Commerce Commission took charge of railroad accounting.

Disclosures resulting from investigation of the insurance industry in New York (to which reference has been made in an earlier chapter) stimulated demand for more thorough inspection of the affairs of insurance companies. In 1906 the president of the Equitable Life Assurance Society announced, "It will be the policy of the new administration of the Society to insist on an independent audit of its accounts as to its fiscal condition once each year, the results of which will be published."

Later in that year representatives of the American Association of Public Accountants met with the executive committee of the National Association of State Insurance Commissions. The accountants argued the necessity of remodeling forms of financial statements on the basis of sound accounting principles, and also the desirability of periodical independent audits by public accountants. Forms of statements theretofore in use were said to be inadequate, and largely responsible for the failure of the regulatory authorities to gain knowledge of the conditions revealed by the recent investigation.

An Association committee was also appointed, jointly with the New York State Society, to support legislation at Albany requiring audit of the accounts of life-insurance companies by public accountants, and improving the forms of annual statements. Arthur Lowes Dickinson was chairman of the committee. However, the accountants' efforts came to naught.

A bill providing for compulsory audit by certified public accountants of all corporations doing business in Pennsylvania was introduced in the state legislature but failed to pass.

In commenting on these developments *The Journal of Accountancy* again urged complete reports by private corporations of their financial condition to corporate stockholders. The editorial pointed out that many large corporations voluntarily presented audited statements—the United States Steel Corporation being conspicuous among the number.

In 1906 another Association committee conferred with the Chairman of the Interstate Commerce Commission to advocate employment of public accountants in connection with the preparation of statements for the use of railroads under the new law recently passed. The committee was courteously received, but that was all.

Government Accounting

In 1906 an Association committee of five was appointed to co-operate with the Committee on Department Methods of the United States Government (generally known as the "Keep Commission"), to assist that committee in framing recommendations for improving the business methods of the departments of the government. This seems to be the first occasion on which the organized profession had officially acted in an advisory role to a federal government agency.

The Association's committee had several meetings with Charles H. Keep, Assistant Secretary of the Treasury, and his associates on the investigating commission. The public accountants were briefed by the chairmen of "assistant committees" who were investigating specific aspects of departmental procedures, including accounting and auditing. Mr. Keep formally expressed appreciation of the Association's willingness to co-operate in the work of his committee.

In 1909 the Keep Commission proposed changes in procedures of government departments, which were actually put into effect. The changes included matters of internal organization, departmental relations, modes of purchasing and contracting, and many others. One of the most important suggestions was introduction of a comprehensive system of double-entry accounting in the Treasury Department. *The Journal of Accountancy* said, "The plan was approved by a select committee of public accountants appointed by the American Association of Public Accountants and was ordered put into operation."

Trust-Busting

In 1908, President Roosevelt was in an aggressive trust-busting mood. The results of the insurance investigations, violations of the law against rebates by railroads, and a fine levied against the Standard Oil Company in an antitrust case had created the impression that all managers of large business corporations were violating the law.

Mr. Sells, as president of the Association, addressed the New Jersey Society of Certified Public Accountants in defense of the free-enterprise system. He contended that private business was efficiently managed, that managers were generally honest, and that the notion that public officials could manage business better than private citizens was a fundamental dogma of socialism.

In comment a *Journal* editorial said, "There is a world of difference between government control and government management of corporations." While against management of railroads by government officials, the editor seemed inclined to believe that private management should be subject to considerable regulation. He said that the Interstate Commerce Act of 1887 created a commission "which had a long tail but no sting." It rendered opinions but couldn't enforce them.

"It is folly for Congress or for state legislatures to prescribe the rates that railroads shall charge ... or limit the amounts of their capitalization. Nevertheless, our railroad managers have the power ... to divert net income into the treasuries of barnacle companies at the expense of small stockholders, and to humbug the small investor by the concealment of facts or by the juggling of accounts. Such being the case, it will be impossible to convince the American public that the railroads should go unregulated."

This was a fairly liberal stance for a spokesman of a conservative profession which was dependent on the business community for its clientele. Yet it was not the only example of outspokenness on the part of the profession's leaders. The increasing involvement of accountants in public affairs, despite the failures of some specific missions, was gradually increasing public awareness that the profession existed.

Differences With Government

The results of government activity were not always benign from the profession's point of view. For example, the uniform system of accounts for railroads prescribed by the Interstate Commerce Commission resulted in 1913 in the discontinuation by one railroad of an annual independent audit by CPAs, on the ground that government supervision was an adequate substitute.

The Journal of Accountancy deplored this step. Conceding that "it is probably well within the mark to say that without the operations of the Commission railway accounting today would be far behind its present condition," the editorial nevertheless pointed out that on several occasions the Commission itself had indicated its hearty approval of audits by CPAs, and that at least seven of the great railway systems and many smaller roads as well were being regularly audited by independent accountants.

Again, the government showed a disposition to limit fees paid to accountants or other experts involved in improving government operations. In 1914 a proposed amendment to an efficiency bill in Congress would have provided that rates of compensation be specifically stated in the legislation providing for employment of such experts—unless government officials already authorized to fix such compensation should do so.

Robert H. Montgomery, as president of the American Association, submitted a memorandum on this bill. He pointed out that the employment of experts had increased greatly in recent years. He said that service could not continue if it should become the practice for a client to insist upon the right to deal directly with the organization of the "expert," including not only the individual members of the staff, but office employees such as stenographers, typists, proofreaders, telephone operators, and so forth.

He said, "The suggestion is made, however, that public accountants whose services are required by departments of the federal government shall delegate to the government the payment of their assistants, thus in effect imposing upon the latter the very doubtful policy of accounting to their employers for the difference between their normal salaries and the amount received from the government."

Montgomery pointed out that the fees of an accounting firm covered far more expense than the salaries of the staff engaged on a given audit or other service. "There must be considerable margin for unemployed time, sickness and vacation, as well as a proper proportion of the expense of maintaining the entire organization."

Apparently the distasteful amendment was never enacted.

The Comptroller of the Currency, too, made himself unpopular with the accountants when he announced that national bank examiners would be instructed to make two reports of each examination, one for the information of the Comptroller, the other for directors of the bank concerned. In explanation, the Comptroller said, "It is believed that the receipt by the boards of directors of national banks of these reports from the Comptroller's office twice a year will relieve many banks of a considerable expense to which they are now subject for periodical examinations by outside public accountants."

The *Journal's* editor took a dim view of this proposal, reminding his readers that a recent embezzlement in a national bank had led to the directors being held negligent, with a decree against them for $282,000. "This is one of the sort of economies that Mr. Williams' plan may frequently effect—if bankers can be induced to believe in it."

The Federal Trade Commission

Of overriding importance to the profession, however, were the Federal Reserve Act of 1913 and the Clayton Antitrust Act of 1914, which established the Federal Reserve Board and the Federal Trade Commission, respectively. The interest of these two bodies in financial reporting and auditing led to establishment of official standards, in the absence of which independent audits by public accountants might have been widely discredited.

Unsatisfactory audits and inadequate financial reports were not uncommon. Without authoritative guidelines, without control over the qualifications of its own members, and without disciplinary authority there was little the Association could do about the quality of independent auditing, except by exhortation. Yet its complex organizational structure prevented it from establishing the standards and controls which were necessary.

The Federal Reserve Act provided for the issuance of federal bank notes based upon rediscount of commercial paper offered by member banks. On November 10, 1914, the new Federal Reserve Board issued a circular outlining the discount policy. It would accept single- or double-name commercial paper for rediscount with the Federal Reserve banks. Member banks were warned, however, to be sure that single-name paper was of a self-liquidating nature, not issued for purposes excluded by the act, such as investment of a permanent or speculative nature. The circular added, "For the time being, certified accountants' statements will not be required. This matter is reserved for regulation at a later date." However, the essential information required in a balance sheet and profit-and-loss account to be in the credit file was briefly described in the circular.

An article on this subject appeared in the November 1914 *Journal* by Frederick G. Colley of Arthur Young & Company (which had been founded only eight years earlier by Arthur Young, a barrister from Scotland). Mr. Colley said, "The credit of the nation is therefore to be protected and provided for, as regards certainty of liquidation and the intrinsic value of commercial paper against which Federal Reserve notes (currency) are issued, by the filing of a sworn statement of the borrower which is to be examined by the bank."

Shortly thereafter the new vice-chairman of the Federal Trade Commission, Edwin N. Hurley, finding that his regulatory duties required intelligible and reliable financial data, indicated an intention to establish uniform accounting systems for all the principal businesses of the country. In 1915 Mr. Hurley made a speech advocating a standard system of bookkeeping and cost accounting. He recognized that no one form could be applied to all classes of business, and that special forms must be devised for each industry. He said that the Federal Trade Commission might help manufacturers and merchants by putting at their service the accountants, bookkeepers, and cost experts employed by the Commission.

The American Association of Public Accountants could not overlook these developments. Its committee on federal legislation, consisting of Robert H. Montgomery, chairman, Harvey S. Chase and George O. May, had a number of discussions in 1915 and 1916 with both the Federal Trade Commission and the Federal Reserve Board, regarding the former's proposal to prepare uniform systems of accounting, and the possibility that the Board might recommend and give preference to commercial paper accompanied by balance sheets certified by professional accountants. These discussions led to one of the most important events in the profession's history, the details of which will be described in due course.

The Corporation Excise Tax

The so-called Corporation Excise Tax Law of 1909 was an effort to evade a Supreme Court decision holding that an income-tax law enacted in 1894 was unconstitutional. While referred to as an excise tax, the 1909 tax was based on net income. However, net income was to be ascertained virtually on a cash-accounting basis—gross receipts less expenses plus "losses actually sustained." Furthermore, returns were to be filed on a calendar-year basis, as of December 31.

While the bill was before Congress 12 accounting firms jointly signed a letter to Attorney General George W. Wickersham, with copies to every member of Congress, pointing out the impracticability of these provisions.

The letter stated that many corporations were on fiscal years other than the calendar year, making it impossible for such companies to file a true return of profits as of December 31.

The accountants then referred to the provision that the tax was to be charged upon the "entire net income," which was to be "ascertained by deducting from the gross amount of the income . . . from all sources, (1) expenses actually paid, (2) losses actually sustained, (3) interest actually paid—within the year." The words "actually paid" conveyed the meaning of actual disbursements. The proper deduction should be, said the accountants, expenses actually incurred, losses actually ascertained, and interest actually accrued. A reasonable allowance for depreciation of property was also advocated. The fact that the difference between cash receipts and cash payments did not represent the profits of a manufacturing concern was explained. The accountants' letter closed with the statement that the law as framed was absolutely impossible of application.

In his reply, the Attorney General plainly showed that he did not comprehend the issues: "It may be inconvenient, but it is certainly not impossible, for any corporation which keeps just and true books of account to make up a return such as that required by the proposed law (that is, as of December 31), particularly as the return requires statements of actual receipts and payments and not as you recommend in your communication, of expenses 'incurred,' interest 'accrued,' and losses 'ascertained.' "

The Attorney General went on to say that the bill was purposely framed to deal with receipts and disbursements, and the words "actually paid" were employed advisedly. He concluded, "My personal acquaintance with you and a number of the other signers of the letter leads me to believe that you have underestimated your capacity."

The accounting firms responded by endeavoring to explain the impracticability of a tax on the excess of receipts over disbursements. They referred to the English income-tax law "which has stood the test of over half a century. . . . The accounts of corporations prepared in the regular course of business for their respective fiscal years are and always have been accepted as the basis for taxation, subject to minor provisions. . . ."

The accountants also pointed out that the accounts of railroads in the form prescribed by the Interstate Commerce Commission were not kept on a basis of receipts and disbursements, but on the basis of earnings, whether collected in cash or not, and of expenses, whether paid or not.

Illustrations were given of the difficulty of complying with the law on the part of a large manufacturing concern. In conclusion the accountants offered to appear before the Attorney General and discuss this matter with him.

The response was a brush-off. The Attorney General rejected the argument briefly, and concluded, "However, it is now too late to attempt to recast the corporation-tax amendment bill on the basis of such a proposition."

The executive committee of the American Association of Public Accountants thereupon wrote to all members of the Association, enclosing copies of the correspondence with the Attorney General, and urged members to convey their own views to their senators and representatives.

Despite these efforts, the law was enacted without change in the objectionable provisions. The battle had not been in vain, however. The administration of the tax was under the jurisdiction of the Secretary of the Treasury. In discussing the regulations issued by the Secretary, *The Journal of Accountancy* for December 1909 said, "It is understood that the Secretary of the Treasury has availed himself of the advice of accountants in formulating these rules, and evidence that this advice has been given and acted upon will be found in the various definitions...."

The regulations actually removed most of the difficulties which would have been encountered if the strict letter of the law had been followed. The Secretary had said that the law should be construed liberally for the purpose of producing revenues, and that the real intent was to collect a tax of one per cent on the net income, less $5,000, of the individual corporation liable to the tax.

The regulations stated that it was immaterial whether any item of gross income was evidenced by cash receipts or in such other manner as to entitle it to proper entry in the books of the corporation in the period; and also that it was immaterial whether deductions were evidenced by actual disbursements or in such other way as to be properly acknowledged by the corporate officers, and so entered on the books as to constitute a liability against the assets of the corporation.

In effect, these regulations said, in the words of the *Journal,* "Any corporation keeping its books in accordance with accepted ideas can determine for itself the income subject to tax.... The regulations provide specifically that no particular system of bookkeeping or accounting will be required by the Department, provided that the books are so kept that the return may be readily verified by an examination thereof, whenever such an examination is deemed necessary."

The requirement that returns be filed on a calendar-year basis, however, was not changed. The Association continued to press for an amendment to the law to enable corporations to report for their own fiscal years. Representatives of the Association had spent time in Washington arguing this point, and had secured a promise from the Treasury Department not to oppose the amendment. The support of business organizations had also been secured.

As a result, on December 5, 1912, Representative Harrison of New York introduced in the House of Representatives a bill to permit any corporation to change the date of filing its annual return under the Corporation Excise Tax Law from the close of the calendar year to the close of its own fiscal year.

On January 10, 1913, the Ways and Means Committee conducted a hearing on this bill, which was strongly supported by the Association. Robert H. Montgomery testified on its behalf. The Treasury Department and the Attorney General both had approved the legislation. The Commissioner of the Internal Revenue Department, speaking for the Treasury, appeared before the committee and recommended enactment of the amendment.

However, this effort was discontinued in the light of the almost certain enactment of a general income-tax law, following adoption of the Sixteenth Amendment of the Constitution. The accountants had made their point, nevertheless, and the new tax law of 1913 provided for fiscal-year filings.

The 1913 Income-Tax Law

The great debate on the proposed Constitutional amendment had been joined seriously in 1910. It was bitterly opposed, but in an environment of reform and social legislation a graduated tax on incomes had irresistible appeal to the mass of the voters. And the example of the income-tax law of Great Britain, a half-century old, exercised a powerful influence.

Meanwhile, the Corporation Tax Law of 1909, though short lived, had had an important impact on accounting, and had revealed problems to be dealt with in future tax legislation.

For example, an editorial in the *Journal* for February 1911 stated that the Commissioner of Internal Revenue had reported returns from the corporation tax during the first fiscal year of its operation. Total returns were nearly $27 million, and the net income of reporting corporations was slightly over $3 billion. The editor said: "It is doubtful that the figures in this report will ever be referred to by any man who wishes to get even approximate knowledge of the amount of business being done by corporations in the United States. Ever since the law was passed, it has been an open secret in business circles that corporation managers of all kinds have taken a keen interest in practical accounting, and have eagerly cast about for methods guaranteed to render profits temporarily intangible and invisible."

It was also said, as a well-known fact, that many concerns had given up the corporate form and were then doing business as either partnerships or associations in order to evade the tax.

Still another *Journal* editorial, in March 1912, dealt with depreciation in connection with the federal corporation tax. Depreciation, it said, was a charge which company officials had been rather prone to regard as flexible and adjustable to meet fluctuations from year to year in the profits from operations. A good year had frequently been made to bear a heavy depreciation charge, and in a bad year no provision, or an inadequate one, had been made. The acceptance of depreciation by corporation officials represented, "it is only fair to say, a development of comparatively recent years, due in no small degree to the persistent efforts of the public accountant."

Reference was also made to a ruling of the Treasury Department which, in effect, stated that depreciation to be admitted as a deduction in calculating taxable income must be recorded "unequivocally on the books as such." Said the *Journal*, "The cases which the rule was intended to reach were those in which a company's officials had claimed deductions for depreciation in making their return for taxable income and at the same time had reported to the stockholders that there was no depreciation. . . . Accountants will undoubtedly be in hearty accord with the endeavor to make corporations face the facts fairly and squarely."

The experience with issues of this kind was useful in administration of the 1913 income-tax law.

The bill providing for a general income tax was introduced in Congress early in 1913.

Robert H. Montgomery, as president of the American Association, testified at a hearing before the Ways and Means Committee on January 31, 1913.

He urged that every concession be made to the taxpayers so long as it did not interfere with the purpose of the tax law: "It will be apparent to anyone that the law which is most easily understood and most easily applied will bring the most satisfactory results to the government."

Montgomery stated that the 1909 corporation excise tax had been found to be unworkable, and that the Treasury Department's regulations had been at wide variance with the letter of the law. This divergence was necessary, he said, because otherwise the law could not have been applied. He advocated authorization to the Treasury Department to formulate regulations, so that the law itself need not go into details as to how net income was to be determined. He pointed out, for example, that mining companies and trading companies had different problems to meet, and if the Treasury Department were empowered to issue instructions, modified to meet varying conditions, there would not be so much dissatisfaction with the administration of the law as had existed under the 1909 Act.

He recommended that the new tax be based on the average result of the last three years' operations immediately preceding the taxing date—for which there was precedent in British income-tax practice—which would make the tax more equitable for corporations which had substantial profits in one year and less profits, or even losses, in another.

Finally, he offered the assistance of the American Association of Public Accountants in the preparation of efficient legislation.

The 1913 law did provide that tax returns could accord with natural fiscal years. However, the 1909 law had influenced so many corporations to close their books on a calendar-year basis that much damage had been done. The accountants, as a result, were forced to concentrate most of their work in the first three months of the year. Montgomery wrote later, "It was a blow from which we have not fully recovered. . . . This congestion has made the practice of public accounting far more hazardous than it should be. It is difficult and expensive to carry a competent staff throughout the year."

As president of the Association, Montgomery worked with Cordell Hull, then a member of the Ways and Means Committee of the House of Representatives, in framing the proposed law. Many years later Montgomery praised the fairness of Mr. Hull, and his courtesy in listening to the accountants' views: "The rates were microscopically small compared to those of today, but that did not influence him to insert any unfair or discriminatory provision."

The Association's committee on federal legislation also participated actively in framing the new income-tax bill, so that it would define income on proper accounting lines, making provisions, for example, for obsolescence and depreciation.

The committee reported that the work of the Association in Washington had brought recognition of the importance of the profession's advice. "The committee thinks the work done will be of service, when an opportune time comes, for pushing further the recognition by Congress of the accounting profession."

The law was enacted in the fall of 1913. The rate for corporations was one per cent. For individuals it started with one per cent and reached only 6 per cent on incomes over $500,000. The individual exemption was $4,000. However, the accountants realized that, while the rates were low, there was a strong probability that they would soon be increased. Accordingly, the accounting profession took an active interest in the law and its administration. Most lawyers felt that the income tax was a job for the accountants. Later, as will be noted, the opinion of the Bar on this point changed!

A *Journal* editorial in December 1913 said, "The income-tax law is bound to result in the engagement of accountants by many corporations and individuals who have not in the past availed themselves of such services. And even though such engagements may in the first instance be limited to purely income-tax questions, they will undoubtedly lead in many cases to a realization by the clients of the wider usefulness of the work of accountants and so to more extensive instructions." No more accurate prediction can be imagined. The deep involvement of the accounting profession in tax matters, from the very inception of income taxation, has greatly accelerated the profession's development.

The Leaders Look to the Future

The foresight, enthusiasm and energy of the profession's leaders in the period between 1905 and 1916 compel admiration. They were comparatively young men, busily engaged in building their own practices and in meeting the increasing demands of clients in a rapidly expanding economy. Yet they devoted incredible amounts of time—until 1911 without any full-time staff assistance—to the affairs of the American Association and the problems of the profession as a whole.

No less remarkable was their keen insight into political and social trends, and the effect these trends would have on the future of public accounting. For example, the president of the Association, Edward L. Suffern, partner of a local New York firm, made a speech at the annual banquet in 1911, which must have been extraordinary for that time.

He referred to decisions of the United States Supreme Court in dissolutions of large corporations—Standard Oil, the Dupont Powder Company, and the American Tobacco Company, among others. He said the results of these decisions had been approved by the "commercial conscience" of a large part of the American people. The meaning, he said, was that the government and the law were superior to any corporation, however large.

"I believe," he said, "that there has come a feeling of relief and assurance that the people are coming again into their own, and that the overlordship of the people had been re-established. . . . There are being evolved new standards of political morality, new conceptions of the relations of men in their several aspects—of employers to employees, of the duties of the state toward their children, toward their dependents, toward their delinquents, toward their unfortunates; new judgments concerning the obligations of corporations, and particularly of public-service corporations, to the public which they undertake to serve; and all these things together in my mind mean this, that there is to come about a readjustment in our industrial life; and in order that that readjustment shall be right, and in order that the proper relation shall be maintained, I believe that there will be a demand for our services in new spheres and in new ways, and in new degrees such as we have never seen before."

This seems a remarkably prescient observation for the year 1911. It is also evidence of the intellectual capacity and objectivity which characterized the leaders of this still-small and little-recognized organization of professional accountants.

At the annual meeting in 1912, in an address on "Federal Control of Corporations," the indefatigable Robert Montgomery also showed prophetic ability. After discussing the corporation excise tax, the antitrust laws, and other trends toward federal control, he said:

> Foolish laws, and more foolish laws, relating to taxation and regulation will not diminish the income of the professional accountant; on the contrary, the more involved and unscientific the law the more our profession will benefit financially. Before the Corporation Tax Law was passed, representative accountants suggested alterations which would have saved the government an immense amount of trouble and the corporations millions of dollars of useless expense. A few practitioners of narrow vision criticized such action on the ground that the suggestions, if adopted, would eliminate an immense amount of accountancy work. Fortunately accountants of that type

form a very small minority. The vast advance in accountancy in recent years has been along constructive lines. . . .

I am convinced that the question—"federal control or no federal control?"—has been decided affirmatively, and that the matter of the form which that control shall take is the serious problem before us. We know that a world-wide economic force has not been and cannot be arrested. The people are not afraid of big business. They want it, but they know that it must be controlled. . . . Without a knowledge of profits, there can be no regulation, no control. . . . No plan is feasible which does not require publicity of a sort which can be depended upon. Profits must be reported to every stockholder, and under modern conditions this means to the public generally. Therefore, every plan of federal control must provide for the certification of profits and balance sheets by independent accountants . . . who will be supported by public opinion when fearless in the performance of their duty, and made amenable to constitutional laws if recreant to their trust.

An editorial in the May 1914 *Journal* reflected similar thinking. The editor regretted the campaign of "trust-busting" which had spread over the country during the past few years. He said that when legislators were imbued with the idea that every combination of capital or enterprise was a menace to the public weal, the welfare of the country was seriously imperiled. However, it was recognized that there must be some control of the activities of the railroads and other corporations, and a strict supervision of the issuance of securities—"the mad financing of former years must be avoided in the future." A temperate and middle-road approach between indiscriminate attacks on big business and reasonable regulation was advocated.

These observations accurately forecast the shape of things to come.

CHAPTER 6

Emerging Professional Standards

Prior to the Congress of 1904 meetings of accountants devoted to technical matters had been few and far between; technical literature was sparse; and prior to the launching of *The Journal of Accountancy* in 1905 there was no effective medium of communication among American accountants on technical questions.

Following the merger of the Federation with the Association, however, technical discussions took on a new vitality. Annual meetings of the Association were held in different parts of the country, and the most talented members of the profession presented papers which were often the subject of lively debate and were later published in the *Journal*.

At the annual meeting of 1908 Joseph E. Sterrett of Pennsylvania was elected president of the Association. He was never a controversial figure. Everyone liked and respected him. He reconciled differences, and worked hard behind the scenes to get things done. He was interested in the fundamentals—technical standards, ethics, education—which he knew were the essential foundations of professional status.

The very meeting at which Sterrett became president reflected a growing awareness of the need for more technical knowledge.

A. Lowes Dickinson presented a paper on accounting practice and procedure, which included the following subtopics: annual examination and certification of accounts (in this portion he cited the English Companies Act and English practice); relations with the banker; form of accounts; investigation for purpose of certifying the profits and determining the purchase price for a business; receivers and assignees in bankruptcy and plans of reorganization; cost accounting and systems; consulting accountants; office organization; forms of report. This paper in itself was a textbook in capsule.

At the same meeting William M. Lybrand presented a paper on the accounting of industrial enterprises, which included the following subtopics: pools; trusts; holding companies; advantages of combination; evils of monopoly; accounts of a corporation; balance sheet of holding company; consolidated balance sheet; inventories; capital surplus; subsidiary company balance sheet; charges to fixed-asset accounts; deferred charges to operations; liabilities; sinking fund; reserve accounts; depreciation; income of holding company; consolidated profit-and-loss account; monthly balance sheet; stock accounts; cost accounts. Here was another small textbook.

Another session was devoted to a paper on railway accounting presented by Henry C. Adams, who was in charge of statistics and accounts for the Interstate Commerce Commission. This topic was of unusual interest because of the uniform system of accounts for railways recently promulgated by the ICC, which had great impact on accounting thought in the years ahead.

The fruits of this 1908 meeting were a valuable addition to the technical literature.

An uneasiness about the absence of authoritative standards began to manifest itself, partly, perhaps, because of the differences in opinion and practice revealed by these discussions.

An article on earnings and income by Seymour Walton in the April 1909 *Journal* stated:

> One of the unfortunate things about the profession of accountancy is the absence of any supreme tribunal which can pass on questions about which there is an honest difference of opinion, and can render a decision which will be binding upon individual practitioners. Our brethren of the law have their Supreme Court to whose dictates they must conform, however unwillingly, or be thrown out of court. In the absence of any corresponding arbiter in our profession it is left to each individual to be a law unto himself, and the result is a mass of conflicting opinions on many subjects, each one of which receives its value principally from the reputation of the person holding it, or the more or less convincing way in which he can express it.

This was an early and thoughtful recognition of the need for authoritative statements on accounting principles and procedure on which the profession as a whole could rely.

Accounting Terminology

Attention began to be paid also to accounting terminology. A special committee on terminology presented a report in 1909, including suggested definitions of scores of words and phrases used in accounting. The report was discussed at the annual meeting. In 1911 the committee presented additional definitions of 23 accounts used in financial statements, with suggestions regarding the nature of items to be included in each account. Two years later this industrious committee added definitions of 713 words and phrases to the 187 items reported previously. This report occupied 51 pages of the Association's *Yearbook*.

In 1915 the committee reported that it had carefully reviewed definitions of words previously presented, and submitted an initial list of words which the committee felt were worthy of official approval and ratification. After discussion, the report was adopted, and the definitions presented were accepted as a basis for the standardization of accounting terminology.

Thereafter, unfortunately, there was a hiatus of many years in the work undertaken in this area.

Responsibilities of Auditors

The responsibilities of auditors were also a subject of growing concern.

Remarks by the president of the Institute of Chartered Accountants in England and Wales regarding an auditor's duties were the subject of editorial comment in *The Journal of Accountancy* for November 1910:

> For example, he believes that the auditor is not "concerned in the volume of business a company does, whether it is overtrading, whether its working capital is insufficient, whether it is carrying on operations on too extensive a scale in countries where credit is bad and economic conditions are unfavorable"—nor should an auditor act or appear to act as a valuer. However, if assets appear to him to have been overvalued, he should say so.
>
> In the United States it is generally recognized that the duties of an auditor depend very much upon circumstances. An auditor may certify merely to the correctness of the account-keeping, if that is all the directors of the company desire. Frequently, however, audits are made on behalf, not of directors, but of banks or intending investors or dissatisfied stockholders, and in such cases it will not be generally admitted in this country that an accountant has done his full duty if he has discovered merely that the accounts and financial statements are technically correct. The accountant's work under such circumstances combines that of the investigator and of the auditor.

The annual meeting of 1912 was somewhat disturbed by a paper written by Alexander Smith of the banking firm of Peabody, Houghteling & Company, Chicago, entitled "The Abuse of the Audit in Selling Securities."

In the paper Mr. Smith asserted that the accountants' clients were both the stockholders or owners of a business, and the investing public and their agent, the banker. He went on to make specific complaints.

First, he referred to the "deadly average":

> The accountant's certificate may show, with absolute truth, that the average annual net earnings of a business represent a certain sum, which may appear to the investor to be ample for the protection of his interest and principal of his investment, and yet, an exact analysis of the component units of the average may reveal a condition highly alarming to the safety of the security involved. Earnings decreasing materially every year may still show a satisfactory average. . . .
>
> Another form of abuse . . . is concealed in the phrase, "Net earnings before charging interest."
>
> Less common, but equally misleading, is the covering up of depreciation charge in the statement of net earnings, generally by ignoring it altogether, but also by quoting the earnings as before charging interest and depreciation, and passing the matter off in this inconspicuous way.
>
> Another phrase that frequently covers a multitude of sins is to be found in the expression "Quick Cash Assets, or Working Capital." This is often the dumping ground for all sorts of questionable assets—unmarketable securities, prepaid insurance, loans to subsidiary companies, bills receivable from officers and stockholders . . . even horses and wagons, by some strange and subtle reasoning, are sometimes included in this item of working capital.

Mr. Smith also criticized inventory valuations, pointing to a case in which a large manufacturing corporation was audited by two prominent firms of public accountants—one valued manufactured products on hand at selling price, less certain reserves for expenses incidental to delivery; the other firm valued the manufactured product at cost.

Again, Mr. Smith said, some auditors maintained that bond discount and organization expenses were part of the cost of plant and properties acquired by the proceeds of the bonds, while another firm asserted with equal authority that bond discount was a charge against future operations.

Finally, Mr. Smith recommended that the American Association appoint a committee to investigate and report on the feasibility of adopting exact and uniform principles of accounting.

Arthur Lowes Dickinson led the discussion: "I think the evils to which he calls attention are real evils; they exist—there is no question about that. . . . There is no use blinding our eyes to the fact that certificates are given by accountants that should not be given. . . . I think the remedy is to provide better training and better experience for everybody. . . ."

However, with respect to Mr. Smith's suggestion that efforts be made to secure more uniformity, Mr. Dickinson said, "All of us know perfectly well there is no book for accountants . . . you have to take every case on its own merits and deal with it as you see it. If you should put down all the rules in the world you would have cases to which the rules would not apply. You have to use your experience . . . and that is the reason why we are here as professional accountants—because we have to gain experience, judgment, and tact in dealing with accounts, and taking the best of the many different ways of determining matters. . . . You cannot lay down definite principles, but you can lay down broad principles that will cover most cases. When you come to interpret the principles, you will have to take the case in point and do the best that you can with it upon a conservative basis."

This may be taken as an expression of the best thought of the profession at the time, and it prevailed generally for nearly 20 years. But as the issuance of securities became more and more widespread, and the numbers of individual and institutional stockholders increased, pressure for more definitive accounting principles mounted in strength.

Attempting to defend the profession against criticism *The Journal of Accountancy* charged that the fault lay largely with those responsible for the selection of the auditor:

> For one reason or another firms and individuals of known character and reputation are passed over, and stationery companies or other organizations are selected to prepare statements on which

financial arrangements of considerable magnitude are entered into. Much remains to be done by the profession in the way of educating the public to the point where it will distinguish between members of a profession regulated by law and bound by certain standards, ethics, and tradition, and those not influenced by any of these considerations.

Responsibility and Legal Liability

Again, in the May 1912 *Journal,* an editorial discussed the authority and responsibility of the auditor, stating that it was important that appointments of auditors should be made in a manner best calculated to insure maximum efficiency:

> It is well to have clearly in mind that the function of the auditor is primarily to safeguard the interests of the creditor and stockholder. . . . Unfortunately some accountants, and we fear their number is distressingly large, do not take their work with a sufficient degree of seriousness, and give audit certificates that deserve less confidence than they inspire. . . .
>
> Accountants may as well face the truth that is so luridly illustrated by conspicuous instances of clean certificates given to accounts grossly erroneous, and that have been the means to the entailing of heavy losses to creditors and stockholders. . . . Hitherto our state societies have shown a reluctance to deal with cases of professional misconduct. . . . There remain at least two other measures that would do much to strengthen an auditor's certificate and give it a more definite value.

The first measure recommended was the election of auditors by the stockholders at their annual meeting—a practice established by law in England. In the United States, it was said, the appointment of auditors was usually left to the board of directors though, in some instances, notably the U.S. Steel Corporation, the stockholders elected auditors.

The editorial continued, "The early adjudication of the auditor's legal liability is another matter, the determination of which will almost certainly do much to enhance the value of an auditor's certificate."

Previously, the *Journal* had suggested that it would be to the benefit of the accounting profession if the extent of the auditor's legal liability were to receive the adjudication of a court of law: "There has never been in this country any definite ruling; and until the decision of the courts has been given there will be a continuance of the present uncertainty." The editor went on to point out that there were two principal sources of civil suits against accountants: first, loss sustained by a client resulting from embezzlement of funds which might have been detected or prevented by an auditor; and second, "and perhaps the more important class of cases," those in which losses had been suffered by investors who had purchased securities relying to some extent on an auditor's certificate. The editor continued:

It would therefore seem to follow, if an auditor has failed to exercise reasonable care ... that he should be held in some measure at least, responsible for losses sustained by investors. . . . One of the strongest inducements to this exercise of conservatism in certification ... would be the possibility of fixing upon the auditor legal liability for statements made. The great majority of American accountants today regard the moral liability for their work as equally imperative with any legal liability, but it must be admitted that there are members of the profession—happily their numbers are small—who require to have some sort of legal obligation in order to stimulate their sense of honor and their respect for integrity. . . .

So far as we are aware the question of legal liability has never been brought before the courts of this country. In England there have been many cases. . . . In the early days of accountancy in America this matter was one which was not of paramount importance, but today the auditor is called upon to testify to the condition of accounts of all the great corporations, the great railroads, the great industries, and to a large extent to examine and verify the accounts of all incorporated business. . . . The auditor stands in a fiduciary capacity to both the owner and the manager—to stockholders and directors. . . . In order to protect the public against inefficiency ... and in order to protect the profession against the inclusion of undesirable members we strongly advocate the theory that if the laws today do not fix legal liability upon the auditor they should be so amended as to bring about that condition of affairs.

This urgent declaration, and the strong medicine it recommended, could hardly have been published without the approval of Association officials. In fact, the editorial appeared to echo an address by Joseph E. Sterrett before the American Economic Association in 1908, in which he said that the effect of a clearly defined civil liability would give confidence to the business public in the accountant's certificate as nothing else would do.

The leaders of the profession were clearly worried about the poor quality of auditing performed by too many public accountants.

Qualified Certificates

The subject of qualified certificates also came in for attention. Apparently many clients thought that a mere inspection of the books was enough to justify an accountant in certifying that things were as they should be. Some auditors tried to satisfy the client and at the same time protect themselves by reservations in their certificates.

"Looking at the matter from the highest ethical viewpoint," said a *Journal* editorial, "It must be admitted that the proper course for the accountant to pursue would be to refuse to conduct an audit unless opportunity were given for verifying inventories and accounts receivable and all other things having a bearing on the accounts.

"But here the difficulty arises that many clients would be estranged thereby, and unfortunately some accountants are not yet in a position to ignore the financial consideration. . . . The average accountant is not sufficiently independent to be able to dictate in this respect." The conclusion was that qualified certificates were inevitable, but that qualifications should be clearly stated.

"It may be perfectly correct, for example, to say that the accounts reflect the true condition of affairs as shown by the books, but it should never be forgotten that there is a considerable portion of the public which will not remember that there are things other than the books. A plain statement that conditions are correctly shown followed by some such ... formula as 'E. and O.E.'. . . is another instance of the technically correct assertion which may grossly deceive the public. . . ."

Disclosures

Disclosures in financial statements were often inadequate by present standards. For example, tangible and intangible assets were often lumped together. It frequently required persistent urging on the part of accountants to induce disclosure of substantial payments for goodwill, patents or other elements of intangible value.

The Journal of Accountancy made a survey in 1916 to determine how many corporations were making such disclosures, and presented a list—an "honor roll"—of about 100 companies which were following this practice. One of them, American Tobacco Company, had been doing so since 1897, and three others had instituted the practice prior to 1900. Others, however, had only begun as late as 1915.

Quite often financial publications criticized members of the accounting profession for signing misleading statements in deference to clients' wishes. Spokesmen stoutly defended the profession, and invited complainers to submit the facts to the American Association for disposition. Anonymous and destructive criticism, it was said, would help no one.

Everyone knew, however, that a good deal of auditing and

reporting on the part of public accountants was in fact indefensible.

The leadership was coming to the conclusion that something had to be done to improve the situation.

Professional Ethics

As the profession grew more visible, and the importance of independent audits began to be understood by government agencies, bankers and others concerned, the leaders of the Association also became more and more concerned with the subject of ethics. They knew that rules of conduct and means of enforcing them were necessary for two reasons: first, to improve the quality of auditing and financial reporting; and second, to induce behavior on the part of practitioners which would attract public respect and confidence.

The Association, however, was not in a strong enough position to move decisively in the direction of rule-making and enforcement. First of all, there were no restrictions on the practice of accounting, and all sorts of individuals and organizations outside the membership of the Association were offering accounting and auditing services—in competition with the members. But even within the membership itself there were strong differences of opinion on the extent to which discipline should be imposed. Furthermore, since a large segment of the Association were members by virtue of membership in constituent state societies, it would have been difficult, if not impossible, to expel or suspend such members without prior or concurrent action by the state societies to which they belonged.

States' rights were jealously guarded. Association policies were under the ultimate control of delegates from the state societies. Accountants were highly individualistic. For all these reasons, progress in the area of ethics—as in the field of technical standards—was inevitably slow.

This was one of the compelling reasons for reorganization of the Association in 1916, as will be explained later.

In 1906 the constitution and bylaws of the Association contained only two provisions related to ethics and discipline. There was no separate code of ethics.

Article VII of the bylaws provided for expulsion or suspension of a member if (1) he violated any of the bylaws, (2) he was convicted of a felony or misdemeanor or declared by a competent court to have committed any fraud, or (3) he "is held by the Board of Trustees on the complaint of any person aggrieved ... to have been guilty of any act or default discreditable to a public accountant."

In the same article, under the heading, "Miscellaneous," appeared the following two rules:

> 1. No member shall allow any person not being either a member of the Association or in partnership with himself as a public accountant to practice in his name as a public accountant.
>
> 2. No member shall directly or indirectly pay to any attorney, broker or agent any portion of his professional charges, nor accept any portion of the fees of any attorney, broker or agent who may be concerned in any professional work in which such member is engaged.

This was a reflection of the influence of the English Institute. Its charter of 1880 laid down certain "fundamental rules," with which the Association's provisions cited above were virtually identical.

Evidence of some activity in the area of ethics appears in the report of the committee on professional ethics as early as 1907. Four cases had been considered. One raised a question as to the relationships of an incorporated audit company. Another related to the right of a client to dictate or alter an auditor's report—the committee took the stand that this should never be permitted. The remaining two cases dealt with advertising and solicitation of an unprofessional and undignified character. No disciplinary action was reported, however. The role of the committee appears to have been advisory.

At the 1907 annual meeting a good deal of the program was

devoted to the subject of professional ethics. In an historic address, Joseph E. Sterrett began by saying, "This is probably the first time that the attention of a representative body of American accountants has been directed to the consideration of professional ethics."

He discussed the public accountant's relation to his client, to the general public and to his fellow accountants. His speech makes good reading today. It laid the groundwork for many of the rules of professional conduct to be formally adopted years later.

Amendments to the bylaws were adopted in 1907 to introduce an article headed "Professional Ethics." To the two rules already in the bylaws were added the following:

> 3. No member shall engage in any business or occupation conjointly with that of a public accountant, which in the opinion of the Board of Trustees is incompatible or inconsistent therewith.
>
> 4. No member shall certify to exhibits, statements, schedules, or other form of accountancy work, the preparation of which was not carried on entirely under the supervision of himself, a member of his firm, one of his staff, a member of this Association or of similar Association of good standing in foreign countries.
>
> 5. No member shall in his business advertisements use any initials as an affix to his name that is not either authorized by statutory enactment of this country or by the well-known associations established for a similar purpose in the British Empire, nor shall he affiliate or substantially recognize any society that is designated or in any way sets itself out to be a so-called certified public accountant society, without the state in which such society is organized having the requisite statutory enactment in full force and effect.

An additional proposal to prohibit contingent fees was not adopted.

A new article was also introduced in the bylaws providing that the board of trustees, sitting as a Trial Board, would adjudicate complaints or charges against members under the cited provisions of the bylaws.

In the years prior to 1916 frequent unhappiness was expressed—in committee reports, speeches, articles and editorials

—about the activities of "audit companies," about advertising and solicitation, and about competitive bidding.

Audit Companies

It was reported, for example, that a prominent Chicago financier, recently embarrassed, controlled an audit company as well as other corporations. The president of the audit company was vice president of one of the banks which the financier controlled. A *Journal* editorial said that there was no objection to the incorporation of accounting companies as such:

> The main and, indeed, the only reason which in our judgment justifies such incorporation, is the desire of members to transmit their interest in the goodwill of their concerns to their heirs. But while admitting the propriety of incorporating audit companies in which the directors are practicing accountants, and where professional secrecy and responsibility are preserved, the severest condemnation should be visited upon audit or accounting companies whose directors are not practicing accountants, who are relied upon to furnish business to the concern because of their various connections, and who usually expect a return in confidential information in addition to their dividends.

Advertising by audit companies, on a scale similar to that of banks and insurance companies, was also an object of complaint.

Bidding

Competitive bidding for audit engagements was frequently deplored. Consideration was given to the possibility of standardizing fees. Spokesmen maintained that accountancy was not a commodity. When *The New York Times* published an advertisement seeking proposals for a complete audit of the various departments of the city of Savannah, Georgia, and for the installation of a system of municipal accounting, the *Journal* said, "There are some things that cannot properly, or profitably, be placed upon the competitive basis."

Comparing accounting with legal and medical services, the editor continued, "To ask a competitive bid from a professional man is asking him to admit that his services are worth less than the fee ordinarily commanded by his profession."

Independence

An isolated incident in 1915 foreshadowed the intense debates to occur many years later on the subject of independence —a subject which had attracted little attention previously. A question arose whether it was proper for a firm of public accountants to certify statements of a corporation in which a member of the firm was acting as internal auditor. A *Journal* editorial was equivocal; it partly justified the relationship by comparing it with situations where accounting firms, which had installed systems of accounts for large corporations, had designated one of their members to act as controller or supervisory accountant until the system was in successful operation, while the firms continued as independent auditors.

Advertising

In the area of ethics, by far the most widespread and continuing concern was focused on undignified and unprofessional advertising and soliciting. The first move toward a rule on this subject was indicated in the report of the committee on professional ethics for 1911.

The report said, in part:

> After all, it is not the easiest thing in the world to say where the line shall be drawn. The insertion of a card in a financial or trade publication is probably generally considered to be not unprofessional. An announcement by mail or by advertisement of the opening of a new office, or of any change in firm relations is, of course, perfectly proper. The legitimate use of business or social connections cannot be condemned.
>
> Promiscuous solicitation of work, either by circularizing or by canvassers, is the one form of publicity which seems most open to question. Perhaps the best way to stop it would be to show the futility of it in the long run, if accountants concede that such is the fact, as we believe they do. It certainly does not lead the public to esteem our calling more highly. It tends to encourage unprofessional competitive bidding, which is bad for the accountant and the client alike.

The editor of the *Journal* hammered at this problem. He declared that the leading firms of accountants in the United States did not indulge in advertising which would tend to lower the dignity of the profession: they did not "tout for business." However, it was said to be good form for a new firm of accountants to publish a card announcing its presence, or for a firm opening an office in a new city to insert a card in the local newspapers.

It was conceded that it was still possible for a "cheap and pretentious practitioner" to obtain business in "some American communities" through undignified advertisements and circular letters.

On another occasion the editor said:

> We have several advertisements clipped from newspapers or magazines, in which various well-known accounting firms and audit companies solicit business in language that suggests, although it does not directly assert, their superior ability. Even if accountancy be viewed merely as a trade or a business, these advertisers are surely making a mistake. . . . In our opinion no business that is worth while can be got in that way.
>
> The business public of the United States certainly needs education

as to the meaning and importance of the work of the public accountant, and nobody is disposed to find fault with advertising literature that is both dignified and enlightening. That is the only kind of advertising that will increase the receipts of accountancy if it is a business, and it will probably not hurt the status of accountancy as a profession.

In 1914, it was reported that the subject most discussed at meetings of state societies was professional ethics, with particular reference to advertising: ".... many members of the Association feel that the national organization itself should do more than it has done in advertising accountancy. ..."

In the same year the committee on professional ethics deplored circular letters sent by members of the Association addressed to clients of other members. The committee was unanimous in the opinion that this method of obtaining clients was unethical. However, since the practice was common, it did not seem possible to challenge any one firm for indulging in it.

A Broad View

In March 1914 the *Journal* carried an article on "The Ethics of Accountancy" by J. Porter Joplin, partner of a local Chicago firm, who was to become president of the American Association within a few months. This was the most comprehensive treatment of the subject since the Sterrett speech of seven years before.

Mr. Joplin's article forecast some of the rules to be adopted years later. He dealt with advertising, encroachment on the practice of other professional accountants, the desirability of a successor accountant communicating with the retiring accountant, the importance of the confidential relationship with clients, the necessity of independence even though it involved the loss of a client, the responsibility to the public to make the wording of the accountant's certificate and any qualifications perfectly clear.

On this latter point the following quotation is significant:

> It is possible at times that the directors of incorporated companies may be desirous of showing the revenue of their company to be not quite so good as the actual facts would indicate, the purpose being to cause the shares of the company to be slightly reduced in price, so as to enable them to purchase to advantage; or it is possible that the profits may be so overestimated as to give those with inside information advantage over the general public. . . . That is the time when the accountant or auditor must stand firm for the principle to which he is obligated, and it is necessary that he should word his certificate in language so plain that there can be no mistaking the wording or the intent which it is desired to convey. A secret reserve may be a good thing for a company to have, but the intention in creating such reserve may not always be of the best.

Mr. Joplin went on to discuss the undesirability of contingent fees, and the undesirability of a uniform scale of fees. Competitive bidding came in for its share of disapproval. He advocated publicity through the professional societies, rather than through individual circularization or advertisement. The responsibility of the accountant to train his staff adequately was mentioned. Mr. Joplin also expressed disapproval of the practice of accounting by corporations, since the profession involved personal service—particularly audit companies in which directors and advisory boards were not professional accountants.

Differences of Opinion

As mentioned earlier, however, there was by no means universal agreement, even among the leaders, as to what should be done about ethical problems. The August 1914 *Journal* carried three articles on the question, "Should Accountants Advertise?" by John Alexander Cooper of Chicago, Edward E.

Gore of Chicago, and E. G. Shorrock of Seattle—all partners of prominent local firms and all active in Association affairs. There were differences in viewpoint among the authors. All regretted the advertisement of personal services in an undignified manner, but all felt it necessary to permit advertising in good taste, especially by newcomers to the profession.

One author said:

> It would be more dignified—more professional if you please—to refrain from it, but we should not stickle for dignity nor assume a professional pose while we are bidding against each other for engagements, like a parcel of hucksters at the close of market on a Saturday night, nor while we are ruthlessly grabbing the business of brother practitioners whose certificates "don't go" with the financial monarchs. . . . One must concede that advertising has nothing about it of which to be ashamed. As it is practiced by the majority, accountancy is more a business than a profession, and should be regulated by business rather than by professional ethics. When accountancy is established as a learned profession and is recognized as such by the public, it will be time enough to be horrified by advertising indulged in by its practitioners.

The editor, in commenting on these papers, said:

> One has only to look over the files of the papers of 15 or 20 years ago to find that nearly every accounting firm of those days conducted a more or less continuous and self-laudatory campaign of advertising. . . . The accountants throughout the country have spent an enormous amount of money in advertising and have as a rule reaped a very meager harvest therefrom. In the East the practice is now on the wane; in the Middle West it is not increasing; in the Far West it is still general. . . .
>
> In all probability the accountants of 20 years hence who look back over their files of the *Journal* for the year 1914 will be absolutely astonished to read a headline containing such a question as "Should Accountants Advertise?" It will appear as ridiculous to that coming generation of accountants as it would to the rest of us nowadays to have physicians or lawyers ask a similar question as to their codes of professional ethics.

The editor was prophetic. Twenty years from 1914 advertising had been absolutely forbidden by the professional societies, and virtually eliminated among all certified public accountants.

Yet dissents continued. John F. Forbes of California, who had established his own practice in 1906, but merged it with that of Haskins & Sells in 1912, delivered an address on professional ethics at the annual meeting of the Association at Seattle. Mr. Forbes opposed written rules of conduct.

He pointed out the difficulties of young men starting in public accounting practice. While deploring competitive bidding, he suggested that clients might properly require to know the amount of the fee in advance. He defended the right of the young accountant to work at whatever fee he thought his services would command, whether lower than the general standard or not.

All in all, much talk and little action sums up the record on professional ethics during this stage of the profession's development.

Spokesmen for the Association had to content themselves with saying that the precepts recommended by Joseph E. Sterrett in his 1907 address on ethics represented the standard of conduct voluntarily followed by members of the Association. But these precepts could not be enforced.

Time for a Change

Ten years after the 1905 merger of the Federation and the Association the leaders of the profession were well aware of the weak spots in its armor.

The lack of both technical and ethical standards which could be used in judging the performance of members was a severe handicap in the quest for public respect. Yet the Association could do little about it.

One obstacle was the reluctance, even among the policy-

makers, to be fenced in. The human aversion to rules and restrictions was a drag on progress.

But the other disability which the Association suffered was
its own loose structure, devoid of central authority. About this
something could be done, and many of the leaders were quietly
deciding that it was time for a change.

CHAPTER 7

Education and CPA Standards

T HE lack of adequate technical and ethical standards was not the only serious weakness in the structure of the aspiring accounting profession prior to 1917.

The standards for admission to the profession—for accreditation as a competent public accountant—were all over the lot. While accounting practice followed business activities across state lines, and while bankers and government agencies were beginning to urge uniformity in auditing and accounting, the requirements for recognition as a professional accountant were in the hands of the states which had enacted CPA laws. From state to state these requirements, including the level of examinations, ranged from very good to very poor.

Membership in the American Association, following the 1905 merger with the Federation, was attained mainly through membership in an affiliated state society. Where there were no CPA laws as yet, the state societies consisted of public accountants who had passed no examination at all, and whose education and experience had not been effectively evaluated by any common measurement device.

This untidiness was especially galling to the Association's leaders in the light of the shining examples across the Atlantic —the Scottish and English chartered accountants—whose societies and institutes had by 1905 established elaborate systems of training and examinations for those who sought the chartered accountant title.

These rigorous requirements were largely responsible for the prestige of the British accountants, which overshadowed that of the Americans—even in the United States.

If the Association had been able to secure authority comparable to that conveyed by the English Institute's Royal Charter, it is quite likely that the apprenticeship system established by the English chartered accountants would have been imitated in the United States. In that event the teaching of accounting in colleges and universities might have been delayed for many years—until the apprenticeship system proved unworkable, as it certainly would have in this country, and indeed may ultimately prove to be in England.

But the old Association was in no position to set itself up as a "qualifying body." Not only had it no legal authority to do so, but it had a hard enough time to attract members when the only requirement for admission was a few years of undefined experience in public accounting. In the circumstances the best way to create a supply of qualified recruits was through some formal educational process.

Efforts to Improve Accounting Education

It will be recalled that one of the first major efforts of the Association was an abortive attempt to establish a school of accounting. This failed, but it demonstrated the need, and several proprietary schools, as well as a few recognized universities, set about filling the vacuum.

The Association's interest in accounting education continued through the years.

At the 1907 annual meeting, Joseph French Johnson, Dean of the New York University School of Commerce, Accounts and Finance (and, incidentally, editor of *The Journal of Accountancy*) read a paper on accountancy education.

He said that ten years before only one university had recognized accountancy in its catalogue—the Wharton School of Finance at the University of Pennsylvania. However, in the past ten years a dozen or more institutions had followed the Wharton School's example: New York University in 1900, and then the Universities of Wisconsin, Illinois, California, Chicago, Michigan, Vermont, and Kansas, the Cincinnati School of Commerce and Accounts, and Harvard University. In addition, Dartmouth College had founded its graduate business school, The Amos Tuck School.

Dean Johnson predicted that in the next ten to 15 years CPAs would be receiving training not only in the use of figures, but in subjects that covered the whole field of the science of business. "I do not believe," he said, "the profession will receive the recognition from the public which is its due until we recognize the fact that a very broad and liberal education, a thorough education, is necessary to its professional practice." Five university professors commented on Dean Johnson's paper. All of them supported the idea of broader and better training of accountants at the universities.

From 1908 to 1916 the Association's committee on education—for most of the time under the chairmanship of Waldron H. Rand, head of his own firm in Boston—submitted a series of impressive reports. It kept close track of additions to the list of institutions which taught accounting, just what courses were being taught, what the Association's members thought should be taught, and related matters.

For example, in 1908 the committee reported the creation

of the Harvard Graduate School of Business Administration, and stated that several well-known members of the Association were among the lecturers. It also reported that several institutions had been added to the list of those providing instruction in accounting: Northwestern University, and the Universities of Minnesota and Colorado. In Boston an evening School of Commerce, Accounts and Finance had been established in connection with the YMCA. In St. Louis a new College of Law and Finance included accountancy in the curriculum.

In 1911 the committee reported results of a survey of all state universities and other institutions which had over 100 instructors or 1,000 students. The objective was to find out the exact status of higher education in commercial subjects, and particularly accounting. An elaborate questionnaire had been developed and sent to 100 institutions. Forty-three replies were received, from which it was learned that The Amos Tuck School, the Harvard Business School and 16 other institutions were giving courses in accounting and commerce.

In 1913 the committee reported results of a survey of Association members' opinions as to the subjects which should be included in the education of a certified public accountant. Commercial law, auditing, theory of accounts and economics attracted the largest number of votes. Finance, banking, organization management, penmanship and commercial arithmetic came next. (In contrast with attitudes of later days, English was not mentioned among all the other subjects suggested!)

The committee also presented an analysis of the requirements for the CPA certificate in those states which had passed CPA laws up to July 1913. The analysis showed wide variation in education and experience requirements, as well as variation in the subject matter of the examinations.

In 1916 the committee for the first time submitted a report on the experience requirement. A questionnaire had been sent to the state boards of accountancy, most of which indicated that they did not equate bookkeeping with practical accounting experience, that education in accounting was not deemed to be the equivalent of actual public practice, and that experience gained as a junior staff assistant with a reputable firm of public accountants was acceptable.

The 1916 report also described "laboratory" methods adopted in some of the colleges and universities which gave accounting courses.

A notable example was the accountancy laboratory installed at Columbia University, under the direction of the ubiquitous Robert H. Montgomery. The laboratory consisted of accounting records and some complete sets of books of business enterprises which had been discontinued by dissolution or bankruptcy. In addition there were a few "model" sets of books and collateral records, such as minute books, stock certificate books, and transfer books.

The laboratory also included a file of annual reports and statistical data from leading companies, together with organization charts, descriptions of systems in use, and similar material. Also the laboratory was expected to maintain an exhibit of office appliances, bookkeeping machines, and so on. All this was designed to give the student contact with the real world of accounting, as well as with the theory of the subject.

At New York University, John R. Wildman, both a teacher and a partner of Haskins & Sells, proposed a plan under which the student would be called upon to do accounting work under the supervision of a CPA, mainly in the audit of various charitable organizations, which it was said as a rule could not afford to pay for such service. In this proposal was the seed of the "internship programs" later attempted in conjunction with the formal educational process.

The Association's hardworking committee on education performed a useful service. By repeated questionnaires and correspondence, it continually reminded the university community of the profession's keen interest in accounting education. This undoubtedly encouraged the introduction of the subject in more and more institutions.

Furthermore, the committee's surveys identified significant interrelationships—between CPA requirements and education, for example, and between education and experience. These re-

lationships involved thorny problems which remained un-
solved for many years to come, but they were made sufficiently
visible to permit a start toward solutions.

Professional Literature

In those days there was not much technical literature with
which teachers and students could work.

One of the most valuable contributions by the Association
was its sponsorship of *The Journal of Accountancy*. It was the
principal medium—virtually the only medium for many years
—for the interchange of information, ideas and opinions among
both schools and practitioners throughout the nation.

From the time of the Association takeover in 1905 the *Journal* had the benefit of intelligent and imaginative editorial
guidance. The first editors were Dean Johnson, of NYU, and
Dr. Edward Sherwood Meade, Director of the Evening School
of Accounts and Finance, University of Pennsylvania. In 1912
A. P. Richardson, the new secretary of the Association, assumed also the post of editor. However, Dean Johnson continued as consulting editor until 1915.

The leaders of the Association were also the mainstays of
the *Journal*. Volume 1, No. 1, published in November 1905,
contained excellent articles by Messrs. Sterrett, Dickinson and
Montgomery.

Although the editors complained periodically, as editors are
wont to do, about the lack of enough manuscripts of high
quality, the content of the *Journal* in its first decade was surprisingly good, considering its limited circulation and its financial difficulties.

It was first published by the Accountancy Publishing Company which was controlled by the Association. Stock in this
company was sold to members of the Association.

By 1909 the circulation of the *Journal* was almost 2,000, but in 1910 it had sunk to 1,625, including only 219 members of the Association—much to the disappointment of the leaders. The magazine was having trouble in making ends meet. However, by 1914 circulation had risen to nearly 5,000, and almost half of the Association members had become subscribers.

An arrangement was then made with The Ronald Press Company, which contracted to publish the *Journal*, with editorial control remaining in the Association.

In 1916 the magazine had become a going concern. This was its most prosperous year to date. For the past three years it had been on a paying basis. Circulation was maintained at about 5,000, and advertising volume had grown. Profits were divided between The Ronald Press Company and the Association, which received some $2,900 as its share, of which $1,160 was devoted to payment of debts of the Accountancy Publishing Company. This practically wiped out the obligation to the creditors of that organization.

Aside from the *Journal*, however, there was an embarrassing paucity of American accountancy literature.

The most important book available was the American edition of *Auditing: A Practical Manual for Auditors*, by Lawrence R. Dicksee, professor of accounting at the University of Birmingham, England. The American version was edited by the amazing Robert H. Montgomery.

Dicksee's *Auditing*, first published in 1892, was a standard work on the subject in England. But so large a part of it was occupied with analysis of English court decisions and discussion of English practice that it was not applicable to the United States. Mr. Montgomery's adaptation contained only those portions adapted to American needs. Later American editions evolved into "Montgomery's *Auditing*."

The *Journal* for February and April 1908 carried articles on accounting literature by Leo Greendlinger, instructor in accounting at New York University. He said, "We not only do not possess a body of accountancy literature that could be called American, but if we inquire in some of our libraries or book stores for accounting books we generally receive the answer, 'You mean bookkeeping books.' "

The articles listed the available accounting literature for study or reference. In all they described some 130 books, including many dealing with special industry accounts, a number of books on cost accounting, and a number on auditing, prominent among which was Montgomery's American edition of Dicksee's *Auditing*. However, even some of the books included in this list were of English origin.

The extension of accounting courses in colleges and universities and the emergence of a number of distinguished accounting professors were soon to result in a number of textbooks and other publications, some of which became classics. In 1908 and 1909, for example, several outstanding books on accounting were published which served as a basis for instruction at the universities, and to a considerable extent as authority for practitioners for many years to come. They were Charles Ezra Sprague's *The Philosophy of Accounts*, William Morse Cole's *Accounts—Their Construction and Interpretation,* and Henry Rand Hatfield's *Modern Accounting*.

In the first 30 years of its existence, however, the American accounting profession had little native technical literature with which to work.

The CPA Movement

As a sponsor of the first CPA law, the Association was naturally dedicated to the enactment of similar legislation throughout the nation. Through merger with the Federation in 1905 the Association became in effect a federation of state societies. Inevitably it was the Association's official policy to encourage and assist state societies in bringing about enactment of sound CPA legislation. To this end, its committee on state legislation drafted a model CPA law.

The numbers of states enacting CPA laws increased rapidly. Almost every year one or more states were added to the list. By 1914 there were 33 "CPA states," and it was predicted that by 1916 there would be 40.

But gradually there were signs of disenchantment on the part of the Association's leadership with the diversity of requirements in the various laws, with questionable administration in some cases, with wide fluctuations in the level of the examinations among the states, and with the difficulty of establishing reciprocity among the states. Thoughts turned again to the desirability of obtaining recognition of the profession by the federal government.

The Association tried to prevent enactment of undesirable CPA laws, but occasionally failed. Sometimes it was not informed early enough. Sometimes, no doubt, its advice was ignored. Sometimes state societies were simply not strong enough politically to prevent enactment of objectionable provisions.

A case was cited in which CPA certificates originally issued without examination—"waiver certificates"—were made available to anyone who had any bookkeeping experience. In another instance an amendment to an existing law, subsequent to issuance of waiver certificates at the time of enactment, permitted issuance of CPA certificates without examination on affidavit that candidates had been in public practice for five years. Efforts to lower standards were not uncommon, and political influence on legislatures and on state board appointments was a cause of constant concern.

Even sound laws were not always well administered. Some state boards were too lax, others too tough. There were cases in which circumstances strongly suggested that state board members who were practicing accounting deliberately limited the number of CPA certificates issued—in order to minimize competition with themselves!

In 1908 a banker, James G. Cannon, addressed the American Association's annual meeting on "The Relation of the Banker to the Public Accountant." Described as a sincere friend of the profession and a bank president of influence, Mr. Cannon criticized the results of the requirements for the CPA certificate. He stated that of 617 candidates who tried the CPA examination in New York over a ten-year period, 409 were rejected. Possible reasons, he suggested, were a monopolistic intention on the part of the examiners or those who influenced them, "catch questions" in the practical accounting part of the examination, and inadequacy in the education or training of the candidates.

In 1913, the New York State Education Department reported: "There were 134 candidates who took the CPA examination, six of whom have passed in all topics." Two reasons were suggested for the failures: lack of education and training on the part of the applicants, and the character of the examinations themselves.

On the first count the New York State Regents stiffened the requirements for admission to the CPA examination, by providing that a candidate must have had five years' experience in the practice of accountancy, at least two of which must have been in the employ of a certified public accountant in active practice, in no less grade than that of a junior accountant.

The *Journal* applauded this change as one that would eliminate a large proportion of the unqualified applicants who were likely to fail the examination. However, the editorial did suggest that candidates who had done advanced work at schools of the highest type, "such as the Graduate School of Business Administration at Harvard—to take an illustration at a safe distance," might get credit for two years against the experience requirement.

On other occasions spokesmen for the profession deplored the elementary nature of the examinations for the CPA certificate in some states. It was said that the examinations were often too simple to serve as a standard for admission to a profession. A pleasing contrast was noted in the questions set by the Pennsylvania Board of Examiners of Public Accountants. Passing this examination, it was said, would require more than "cramming in three subjects and guessing in a fourth."

Reciprocity among the states was another goal toward which

the Association struggled with varying success. It was not until 1913, 17 years after enactment of the New York CPA law, that an amendment was enacted permitting issuance of New York CPA certificates to CPAs of other states. Yet, as the *Journal* said, "A large percentage of the practicing accountants [in New York] had been CPAs of other states, and while there was no reciprocity clause in the New York law it was impossible for those accountants to obtain the New York degree unless they elected to take the examination—an alternative not seriously to be considered by men who had already fulfilled the requirements of other boards."

The Association's committee on state legislation in 1916 recommended that the Association endorse the principle of reciprocity among states, without regard to place of residence. "The practice of accounting is so largely of an interstate nature," said the committee, "that we believe this matter should receive the careful consideration of an action on the part of the Association."

However, the variations in preliminary requirements and in the level of examinations enormously increased the difficulty of achieving reciprocity on a broad scale. States with higher standards were naturally reluctant to issue certificates to CPAs of other states whose standards were notoriously lower.

A hopeful sign appeared in 1916. The state boards of examiners in Missouri and Kansas collaborated in the preparation of a single CPA examination to be used in both states. Said the *Journal*, "The harmonious way in which this cooperative method has been brought about should encourage other states, particularly those which are near neighbors, to put into practice a principle which tends toward that uniformity of standard which is the aim of every friend of CPA legislation."

This incident may have started the thinking which soon led to the beginnings of a uniform written examination, ultimately adopted by all state boards of accountancy.

In addition to screening candidates, state boards had to concern themselves with unauthorized use of the initials "CPA."

In New York in 1913 a magistrate decided a case against

certain public accountants who were using the letters "CPA" after their names without having complied with the provisions of the CPA law. It was held that the use of the letters "CPA" was permissible only to persons who had complied with the law; that a person could not use the letters "CPA" in New York simply because he was a CPA of another state; and that although a firm name was used by public accountants, and one of its members was a certified public accountant, the letters "CPA" could be used only with his individual name.

At the time this evidently was an important precedent. "For many years," the *Journal* noted, "it has been a moot point whether or not the title authorized by the act could be restricted to those persons holding the degree under authority of the state in which they practice."

Even before such basic questions as this had been settled, even before some states had enacted CPA laws, even before the public had begun to learn the difference between a CPA and a public accountant, there was talk of restricting the practice of accounting to certified public accountants.

The regulation of the practice of law and medicine was cited as precedent. Naturally the idea had strong appeal. It was utterly impracticable at this stage of the profession's development, but it was bound to be tried out before long—and to become a source of internal conflict.

As the historic year of 1916 approached, the CPA movement, from a national viewpoint, looked extremely untidy. The prospect of uniformity of standards seemed hopeless. Time, energy and money were being expended by state societies, and to a lesser extent by the Association, on legislative and administrative problems which seemed almost insoluble. It appeared that little progress was being made in meeting the urgent needs for better education and training, higher standards of competence, and strengthened public confidence in CPAs.

More and more frequently mention was made of the possibility of federal CPA legislation.

And so decisions were made and steps were taken which in a few years resulted in splitting the profession in half. It took

15 years to put it together again. The experience was painful, but instructive.

In any event it settled some things, and in the end provided a foundation for the growth and development of the profession on a scale beyond the wildest dreams of those who were about to try a new approach to its problems.

CHAPTER 8

A Radical New Approach

THE benefits of the merger of the Federation with the Association in 1905 had been obvious and substantial. One larger group clearly could be more effective than two smaller organizations. But even more important, the new Association acquired a broader geographical base and a closer relation with the state societies than before.

The merger brought into the councils of the Association local leaders of the profession from the Midwest, Far West and South, whose point of view was less conservative—less insular, it might even be said—than that of the New Yorkers who had been most active in the Association from the beginning, many of whom were Scottish or English chartered accountants.

These men contributed a dedication to high professional standards, technical competence, and a sense of professional pride which few native American accountants had had the background and experience to acquire. At the same time, some of these men from Great Britain exhibited a typical conservatism, and a disposition to exercise authority somewhat arbitrarily, which did not coincide with characteristic American attitudes. The influx of leadership from the West and South, therefore, was a very good thing.

However, the price paid for these advantages was an extremely awkward organizational structure.

The merger required reconciliation of two quite distinct organizational philosophies. From the beginning, membership in the Association had been obtained by direct personal application, subject to requirements applied universally, regardless of place of residence. Theoretically, at least, this made it possible to exercise centralized disciplinary control.

On the other hand, the Federation, as its name implied, was an organization of local groups. Any individual who belonged to one of the federated local groups was automatically a member of the Federation. The local groups set their own admission standards. The Federation could not discipline such a member except through his local group.

An additional complication was the fact that CPA laws had been enacted in only a few states at the time of the merger. Both the Association and the Federation, therefore, were mixtures of certified and non-certified public accountants.

In 1906 the enlarged Association included 15 constituent state societies, of which eight were societies of certified public accountants, while seven, lacking CPA laws, were still societies of public accountants. All the members of these societies came into the Association. In addition, all the former members of the Association, whether members of a state society or not, and whether CPAs or not, continued as members of the merged organization.

The constitution and bylaws of the new organization, as amended at the 1906 annual meeting, contained in essence the following requirements for admission:

1. Fellows consisted of accountants who had been in continuous practice *on their own account* for at least three years prior to application for admission; or accountants who held CPA certificates and who had been in continuous practice on their own account *or in the office of a public accountant* for three years prior to application; or members of state or district societies of public accountants

admitted to membership in the Association, *provided that such members could individually qualify as fellows according to the above requirement.* (Emphasis supplied.)

2. Associates were those who were employed by members of the Association or other practicing public accountants; or persons engaged in practice on their own account for less than three years prior to application.

No examination was required; and CPAs had only a slight advantage over non-CPAs in seeking admission to the Association as fellows.

Furthermore, the fellows were distinguished as "fellows at large" and "society fellows," the first class being those who were fellows of the Association before the merger, plus those who might thereafter be admitted by direct application; and the second group being those fellows admitted by virtue of their membership in state or district societies admitted to the Association.

Direct application to the Association was not acceptable if the individual was eligible for membership in a state or district society affiliated with the Association. In other words, such individuals had to come in through the affiliated local group, but in states where no such group existed, individuals could apply to the association directly.

The entire membership of a state or district society could be admitted to the Association as a whole body, and the individual members of such a society would automatically become fellows or associates of the Association, *provided, however, that such members could individually qualify as fellows or associates in accordance with the provisions above.*

These provisions were complicated enough. They were an expedient compromise between the concept of a "qualifying body," as the old American Association had hoped to become, along the lines of the English model, and the idea of a federation of local groups regardless of the individual qualifications of members. While all members of the Federation were of necessity automatically taken into the Association, there was provision for the exclusion of members of state organizations subsequently affiliated with the Association if such members did not meet the practice requirements for admission as fellows individually. It is doubtful, however, that this provision was enforced.

Awkward as these arrangements appear, it is difficult to see how anyone could have done any better at the time. The profession was in a transitional stage. The numbers of public accountants were small; unity was obviously desirable; there was no national standard of qualification for professional accountants; the profession had already committed itself to the development of such standards through state legislation, but the legislation had not yet been enacted in many states. The state societies were influential in their respective areas, and their co-operation was essential if the profession was to move forward as rapidly as possible.

Inevitably, however, this patchwork organization would be subjected to strains and stresses.

Pressure for a National CPA Association

In fact, as early as 1907 a speech was made at the annual meeting, by C. M. Vollum of Pennsylvania, in which he contended that the mixture of CPAs and public accountants in the American Association did not sufficiently recognize the distinction between CPAs and those who had not availed themselves of the legislative recognition of the profession. He advocated formation of a national association of certified public accountants.

The consensus, of course, was that this idea was premature, since so few states had enacted CPA laws.

However, the Association did identify those of its members who were CPAs. In each of the yearbooks beginning in 1906 the lists of fellows and associates were published. Those who were certified public accountants had asterisks placed before their names. These asterisks grew more numerous year by year.

In 1910 Mr. Vollum renewed his proposal at the annual meeting, and called for action.

A resolution was introduced to the effect that a committee of five members of the Association who were CPAs be appointed to procure a charter under the laws of the District of Columbia for a corporation under the name of the National Association of Certified Public Accountants.

Speaking in support of the resolution, Mr. Vollum asserted that the Association had been organized principally by "foreign accountants." He said that the Federation, on the other hand, had organized societies of public accountants without regard to the standing of the individual members. Since the two organizations had joined together most of the members had become certified public accountants, as state after state had enacted CPA laws. He looked forward to the day when practice could be restricted to certified public accountants, but suggested that this could not be done as long as the national organization was known as the American Association of Public Accountants.

Another speaker suggested that the objective should be a national organization not under a local charter, but under federal recognition through a charter granted by the Congress.

A third speaker pointed out that only half the states had CPA laws, and advocated waiting until all the states had such laws before approaching the federal government for recognition.

A supporter of the resolution emphasized the need for explaining the difference between a public accountant and a certified public accountant. He didn't want to say to the public, "There are a lot of old fellows in the American Association who are not certified public accountants."

The pending motion was amended to provide that a committee of five members who were CPAs be appointed to consider the matter of obtaining a charter for a corporation under the name of the National Association of Certified Public Accountants; that the findings of the committee be reported to the board of trustees and that the board report on the matter to the next annual meeting.

As amended, the resolution was adopted.

However, nothing further was heard on this subject for some years, and in the meantime it became evident that the leaders had other ideas, one of which was to strengthen the Association and its influence.

Beginning of a Headquarters Staff

In 1909, President Sterrett had recommended that the Association secure permanent headquarters. Up until then the headquarters had shifted among the offices of volunteer officers. He had also proposed that the Association secure the services of a full-time executive officer. These steps, he recognized, would require increased revenues. Since an increase in dues would be difficult, he suggested that members subscribe to an annual fund to be used to supplement the income of the Association.

On the floor of the 1909 annual meeting there had been active discussion of the proposal to employ a full-time executive secretary—not necessarily an accountant. Strong feelings were expressed in opposition to the proposal, which was described as "a waste of money" and also an improper delegation of power to a salaried officer.

Others, however, supported the idea strongly, pointing out that in matters of publicity, legislation, and relations with bankers, for example, the presence of a full-time official could greatly expedite progress.

It was finally resolved that the executive committee be requested to look into the matter and make a recommendation later.

In his 1910 farewell address Mr. Sterrett repeated his recommendations. He said that the guarantee fund, which had already acquired $4,400, appeared to promise an early possibility of securing permanent headquarters and employing an executive officer.

At the 1911 annual meeting it was announced, without any request for specific approval of the membership, that an executive officer had been engaged. His name was not mentioned at the meeting, since the final details of the negotiations had not yet been completed.

It was stated, however, that his title would be "secretary," and that his work would be especially valuable in strengthening relations between the state societies and the Association. It was also reported that he would assume the position of editor of *The Journal of Accountancy* which, while it had attained a self-supporting status, had as yet not realized its full potential.

The need for more money was stressed. It was reported that the President of the United States had proposed a federal incorporation bill, and it was urged that this provided an opportunity for recognition of the profession in federal legislation —possibly through the inclusion of an audit provision. The need for funds to support such legislation was emphasized. After a good deal of argument it was decided to ask the state societies to contribute an amount equivalent to $2 for each of their members. Appeals were also made for support of the guarantee fund, raised by voluntary annual contributions of $25 each by individual members.

Some members opposed these indirect ways of raising money, and suggested increases in the dues. However, the dues were fixed in the constitution at $10 for fellows and $5 for associates, and it was said that the difficulty and delays involved in amending the constitution made this solution impracticable for immediate purposes.

The employment of the first full-time officer of the Association was an important step. A. P. Richardson, who was engaged as secretary in December 1911, made his first report at the annual meeting in 1912, which showed that the duties he was expected to perform were hardly within the capacities of any one man.

He had been in Washington frequently on federal legislative problems. He had assumed the editorship of *The Journal of Accountancy*. He also had responsibility for preparation of the *Yearbook,* for attempting to get speakers from the profession on the programs of business and financial organizations, for establishing the new headquarters office of the Association, for visiting the state societies, and for providing services to individual members.

When he took the job, Mr. Richardson was 34 years old. He had had a varied career. He attended the Lawrenceville School in New Jersey, but before entering college, he ran away from home and shipped as a sailor to South Africa. There he worked in the mines, taught school, and served as a newspaper correspondent during the Boer War. When he returned to this country, he became bond editor of *The Wall Street Journal*.

He had a fine command of the English language, and read widely. As a desk editor he wielded the blue pencil with superior skill. He was a man of principle, dedicated to high standards of conduct, with strong views of right and wrong, and on acceptable behavior.

During his years in South Africa, and in visits to England, Richardson had acquired great respect for English attitudes and methods. This was to have some bearing on the future course of the Association, in view of the mild undercurrent of anti-British feeling in some quarters. It was apparent that many of the Association's leaders regarded the Institute of Chartered Accountants in England and Wales as a model. But this view was not shared by some native American CPAs, who had a strong feeling for states' rights, and for the tradition that professional licenses should be issued under state laws.

Montgomery Becomes President

At the 1912 annual meeting, when Secretary Richardson first appeared, Robert H. Montgomery was elected president of the Association. He was 40 years old, the youngest president up to that time. But his record was already remarkable. Since he was to have a profound influence on the course of the profession in the years ahead, the remarks he made at the time of his election in 1912 seem especially significant:

> I am here today because I love the profession. . . . I have found among the accountants the highest type of men—men with whom I have been glad to ally my fortunes and friendship. . . . A few months ago I was offered an opportunity . . . and you will pardon this personal word, but it relates so deeply to my own feelings that I am going to give it to you in confidence, as my friends—I was offered a partnership in one of the largest banking houses of the world. To me that would have meant a fortune. To remain in the accounting profession does not mean a fortune. I tried myself, and I found that I would rather stand with you men, and go to the meetings and meet you than I would leave it for any consideration of which I could think. . . .
>
> And I hope, if it is true that progress cannot arise from contentment, that there will still be enough discontent with our standards, with our ethics, to press forward, to do more than we have ever done before. In such disagreements, if we work together, we shall continue to be friends, and we shall make of this profession something of which the country itself can be proud.

But while the leaders were working hard to realize their lofty ambitions for the profession, and were indeed accomplishing impressive results, there was evidence that they were losing touch with the rank and file.

In the October 1912 *Journal* an editorial on the 25th anniversary of the American Association said, "The progress that has been made has been principally due to the work of a very few men. A great majority of the membership takes little interest, or, if the interest is felt it is not displayed. A very small percentage of the total membership could honestly be described as active in association affairs."

By 1914 the total membership of the Association was only 1,170. The slow growth was partly due to the fact that only certified public accountants were eligible in those states which had passed CPA laws. The numbers of new certificates granted each year were small. In addition, many accountants had not been convinced of the advantages which membership in the national association would bring them.

A "Qualifying Body" Emerges

Secretary Richardson reported, "If . . . the profession could be placed upon a national basis, the jealousies between states and the chance of undesirable legislation would be reduced to a minimum. . . . It might be desirable to seek a charter for the American Association, whereby it would have authority to conduct examinations and to issue certificates whose recognition would be country-wide."

This report undoubtedly reflected the views of the executive committee.

But contrary sentiment among some members persisted. The proposal that the Association become a national organization exclusively of CPAs, and change its name accordingly, was renewed. However, after reconsideration of this proposal a special committee reported in 1915 that since some members of the Association were not CPAs, though the majority now were, it would be embarrassing to change the name of the organization to American Association of Certified Public Accountants. This report was accepted by the membership.

In the same year the membership declined for the first time in many years, from 1,170 to 1,157.

At the 1915 annual meeting the president, J. Porter Joplin, said that 39 states had enacted CPA laws, though he expressed regret that standards in some of the states were inadequate, and would, therefore, preclude CPAs of those states from applying successfully for admission to the Association:

> . . . how to bring about . . . uniformity of standards among account-
> ants when the laws enacted by the different states throughout the

country are so imperfect, and in many cases so poorly carried out, would seem to be a problem most difficult to solve.

A uniformity, however, of some sort will have to be established so that the need—the demand of the age—may be met. If we could within our organization establish such standards and a control to which the profession as a whole would subscribe and measure up, a vital step would be taken which would make for a lasting recognition in the community. . . . I would recommend that this matter be referred to a special committee to be appointed for the purpose.

The report of the secretary again referred to the slow growth of membership, the lack of uniformity of state legislation, the difficulty which applicants for CPA certificates encountered in certain states, and the inability of the Association to discipline its members:

It is frequently stated that the Association and the state societies have never disciplined a member, however flagrant may have been the offenses committed. While this is not absolutely true, it has a sufficient amount of truth in it to call for serious consideration by the American Association and by all its constituent societies.

The Association has come to a period in its career when it is impossible to accept things as they are. There must be such a readjustment of circumstances as will permit the Association to progress.

Spokesmen referred to the activities of the Federal Reserve Board as a reason for establishing uniformity in the standards for admission to the accounting profession. If the Board should require certified financial statements in support of applications for rediscount of commercial paper, it was quite soundly predicted, the qualifications of the certifying accountants would become of immediate interest to the federal government. It had been rumored that the Federal Reserve Board might make its own selection of accountants whose certificates on financial statements would be accepted—which would be most distasteful to the profession.

Sentiment was building up for a reorganization of the Association along the lines of a "qualifying body." The climax came in 1916.

The special committee appointed in response to President Joplin's recommendation at the 1915 annual meeting, to study means of achieving uniform standards, was headed by the tireless Joseph E. Sterrett, and included W. Sanders Davies of New York, Carl H. Nau, partner of a local firm in Ohio, Waldron H. Rand of Massachusetts, and Elijah Watt Sells of New York.

A New Institute Is Born

This special committee went to work immediately, and prior to the spring meeting of the trustees of the Association in April 1916, submitted to all the trustees a written plan of reorganization.

In presenting the plan for action at the trustees' meeting, Chairman Sterrett said:

> It does seem to me, looking into the future, that accountancy has in this country a marvelous opportunity, but at present we are not taking advantage of it, and as I see it we cannot fully take advantage of it while we are hampered by local conditions over which we have no direct control.
>
> So the central thought of the plan which is before you now for your consideration is that the control of the profession should be vested directly in the profession itself; and with the control placed there, it seems to me that it ought to be possible for us to develop an organization that is just as good and will stand just as high as it will deserve to stand in view of the men who compose the profession itself.

John F. Forbes of California, who would become president of the new Institute many years later, questioned the wisdom of "burning our bridges behind us," and entering upon a new and untried plan. He disapproved the intention of ignoring the CPA certificate in establishing the requirements for membership in the new Institute. He recalled the strenuous efforts that had been made to have CPA legislation enacted in 39 states.

He also expressed doubt about the desirability of cutting the national body loose from the state societies.

Mr. Forbes' position was supported by John B. Niven of New York, a chartered accountant of Edinburgh, and partner of Touche, Niven & Co. He said, in part:

> We have had our difficulties to meet, but at the same time, I can't see the thought of almost throwing overboard the CPA principle without some qualms of fear. ... I have seen the difficulties that have arisen through a multiplication of organizations. ...
>
> I am myself a member of the oldest society of all. I know that it made some very grave mistakes which it hasn't overcome to this day. If it had been a little more generous and a little more ready to take in the people whom it considered as outsiders ... there would have been fewer societies in Great Britain today than there are. There need only have been one if they had only gotten together in time. ... I think today we are in some respects better organized here than they are in Great Britain. ... I do think that we must try to carry the present state organizations with us in some form or another and have it so arranged that they may feel that they are absolutely part of the national body.

William F. Weiss of New York, who was also a member of the Association's executive committee, supported the views expressed by Messrs. Forbes and Niven. He said:

> We are coming up to the question of the recognition of the CPA certificate as compared to the certificate of examination of the Institute. Which will be the stronger of the two? Which shall have the bigger standing and the most recognition? That is the vital step in the entire organization. ... I think the CPA certificate, if it has any standing—and it was backed by our serious efforts since the Association has been organized ... that certificate should not be overlooked. It deserves recognition. We will undo much of what we have done if we do not give it recognition.

Responses to these arguments were made by a number of others. "The feeling in the committee," Mr. Sterrett said, "has been all through that we want to develop an organization that will include in its membership all of the accountants throughout the country. . . . We want to make them subject to the effective control of the national organization. . . ."

He repeated that the diversity among CPA laws and in their administration offered many difficulties. He said that if it were practicable, he would favor a requirement that the CPA certificate be in possession of applicants for membership in the new Institute. But he recalled that in New York many competent people had been unable to get CPA certificates through no fault of their own. When the CPA laws of certain states were operated in such a way as to discriminate against qualified men, he said, the profession itself should not add emphasis to the discrimination. He reminded the trustees also that no CPA laws as yet existed in some states.

Another speaker said it could be assumed that there would be direct and continuous contact between the state societies and the new national organization, and that the voice and weight of the state societies would still be apparent in the national organization.

Elijah Watt Sells informed the trustees that several large accounting firms had dropped the title "certified public accountants." He also stated that only 10 per cent of the candidates at a recent examination had passed, and that in some cases it had been less than 5 per cent.

W. Sanders Davies, who was to become the first Institute president, said:

> I'm sorry to say that it has become a fact in this state that it is getting to the point where a respectable man will not go in for the examination because duly qualified men, as Mr. Sells said, had been unable to succeed in it. . . . The American Association of Public Accountants years ago was more or less an admiration society because we were small and the men from the West did not come in and join us. We got down to the society organization finally as a step in the progress of the Association. We come now, I think, to what seems to me to be a broader step. . . .

At this point, Mr. Forbes made a prophetic remark. He suggested that there would be no difficulty in having the examinations prepared by the new national organization adopted in the states as the basis for the CPA certificate. This was the origin of the Uniform CPA Examination later to be established.

Carl H. Nau said that the CPA movement had been the nucleus around which much had been accomplished, but, he continued, "I'm also of the conviction that it has served its usefulness. It was a mere temporary expedient. It was an instrument that was valuable at a certain time in the evolution of our profession, and I think its usefulness has absolutely gone by.... Accountancy as a profession is not confined by any state lines.... The time has arrived when an attempt should be made at some solidarity in the profession, an organization of professional men that will be a law unto themselves."

At the conclusion of several hours of debate, a resolution approving the plan of reorganization was adopted with only two negative votes, those of Messrs. Forbes and Niven.

Anticipating favorable action by the annual meeting in the fall, it was resolved that three members be designated to incorporate the new Institute of Accountants in the United States of America under the laws of the District of Columbia.

The Annual Meeting Approves

The report of the special committee and the plan of reorganization were sent to the presidents of all state societies for discussion with their members prior to the annual meeting.

At that meeting, held on September 19 and 20, 1916, in New York, the report of the special committee was presented. It stated the background:

> The idea of a national organization controlling the profession from within was in the minds of the founders of the American Association of Public Accountants in 1887, but was soon in large measure discarded by the leaders of the profession for a form of state organization... although some hopes were entertained by a few that national

regulation of the profession might be secured by Congressional action substantially similar to that of the states.

As early as 1904, at the Congress of Accountants held in St. Louis, it was pointed out that some serious defects in the CPA laws had already been disclosed, one of which was the limitation upon the holder of a CPA certificate of one state practicing as such in another state. . . . Experience seems to have demonstrated that it is impracticable to secure by legislation adequate reciprocity between states, and therefore the hopes once entertained that the title "certified public accountant" would become the recognized designation of the practicing accountant in this country must fail of anything like complete realization.

The report recited the shortcomings of many CPA laws:

What then is needed is some form of yardstick which can be applied fairly to accountants in every part of the country. . . . The business public demands rightfully that upon entering the profession an accountant should have a sound education and should be adequately trained . . . and that his continued membership in the national body of accountants must be accepted as evidence that he has conducted himself with reasonable regard to his obligations as a professional man. . . .

Admission to membership in the American Association is based not upon a uniform standard, but upon 30 sets of standards, no two of which are altogether alike and some of which are lower than others. Moreover . . . the Association declines to recognize nine other sets of standards because they do not measure up to the lowest of the 30 accepted standards. Incidentally, there is excluded from membership in the Association a number of reputable practitioners who for one reason or another are unable to meet the requirements of the CPA laws. . . .

The history of the American Association during recent years has been marked by two highly unsatisfactory features. The first is the slowness of the growth in membership. In this country accountancy ought to go forward by leaps and bounds . . . but this progress is not fairly reflected in the membership list of the Association. . . . The second matter . . . is the lack of proper discipline. . . . The Association has been unable to act effectively . . . because it has been held generally that action must be taken, if at all, by the state society.

The report pointed out that other newly organized professions, such as architecture and engineering, followed a course

similar to that proposed in the plan of reorganization being submitted.

The name of the new organization, it was proposed, should be "The Institute of Accountants in the United States of America: the name 'Institute' has a dignity and educational significance which the more general name 'Association' does not seem to possess. And the term 'public accountant' is at best somewhat awkward. Moreover, it is submitted that the term 'accountant' is being more and more restricted in the public mind to those in public practice."

The plan contemplated an organization embracing within its membership all the reputable practicing public accountants in the United States. Members would be admitted as individuals, and by direct examination rather than through other societies. Through maintenance of proper standards it was envisioned that a substantial recognition of the profession could be secured from governmental and trade bodies.

The committee acknowledged that the plan was not necessarily the last word to be said on the subject, and that experience would demonstrate the need for changes as time went on.

At the 1916 annual meeting there was practically no opposition to the plan.

George Wilkinson, who had been active in the organization and conduct of the Federation of Societies of Public Accountants many years before, said: "It is the most important event that has happened in our profession in this country ever since there was a profession. We are going back to the old original idea of 1887, nearly 30 years ago, which was that the Association under our own control should have control of the profession. Twenty years ago, here in the State of New York, that idea was abandoned in favor of state legislation. . . . Now we are about to reverse that. We are about to go back and say that the national organization, the body under our own control, should have the examining of candidates for the profession. I believe it is right."

After discussion, the plan was approved, and a committee was authorized to receive suggestions for changes in the bylaws, and then to submit the proposed amendments to the entire membership for approval by mail ballot.

The meeting then proceeded with the organization of the new Institute. W. Sanders Davies was elected as the first president. Harvey S. Chase and Carl H. Nau were elected vice presidents, and Adam A. Ross was elected treasurer. A new Council, composed of 35 members in classes of seven, serving for staggered terms of five years each, was also duly elected.

The Council then elected A. P. Richardson as secretary, and an executive committee consisting of the president, the treasurer, and the following members of Council: Robert H. Montgomery, Waldron H. Rand, Elijah Watt Sells, J. E. Sterrett, and William F. Weiss. Five of the seven resided in New York.

The Council also elected a Board of Examiners and a committee on professional ethics under the new bylaws. Appointment of other committees was the prerogative of the president.

The constitution and bylaws of the new Institute provided that its membership would consist of members and associates. Members would include all fellows of the American Association at September 19, 1916, and all associates who had been in practice for five years next preceding the date of application; and other accountants who presented evidence of education satisfactory to the Board, who had been in practice on their own account for not less than five years immediately preceding the date of application, and who were recommended by the Board of Examiners *after examination* and elected by the Council.

Associates would include all associate members of the old Association at September 19, 1916; and thereafter all persons presenting evidence of satisfactory education, training and experience in public accounting, who *after examination* were recommended by the Board of Examiners and elected by the Council.

Only members had the privilege of voting.

After October 31, 1916, no applicant was to be admitted as a member or an associate without examination. The examinations could be oral or written, or partly oral and partly written, "and by this and such other methods as may be adopted the Board of Examiners shall determine the technical qualifications and the preliminary education and training of all applicants for membership before applications are submitted to the Council."

The governing body of the Institute was the Council.

The executive committee was empowered with all functions of the Council except election of officers and members, discipline of members, filling a vacancy in the executive committee and the adoption or alteration of a budget.

The committee on professional ethics was authorized to hear and consider any complaint preferred against a member or associate, and upon finding a prima facie case showing violation of any bylaw or rule of conduct of the Institute or conduct discreditable to a public accountant, the committee was required to report the matter to the executive committee, which would summon the member or associate involved to appear in answer at the next meeting of the Council sitting as a Trial Board.

The entire reorganization was approved by the membership by mail ballot. It was, indeed, a radical change. Yet in the light of the conditions of the time, it seemed a logical and constructive step.

Seeds of Dissension

The demands on the profession were increasing rapidly. As the federal government intervened more and more in the economy of the country, its needs were becoming of critical importance to the profession. A strong national organization, effectively representing the profession in Washington, was undoubtedly considered of high importance.

While no word was breathed of the English precedent, there is little doubt that the example of the Institute of Chartered Accountants in England and Wales was much in the minds of those who advocated the reorganization of the Association. The title, "Institute of Accountants in the United States of America," in itself suggested the parallel. The governing body of the new Institute was designated a "Council," as was the case in the English Institute, rather than as "trustees" which had been the term formerly used by the Association.

West of the Alleghenies, however, and in the South particularly, the states'-rights sentiment was strong. In many states strenuous efforts had been made by small numbers of dedicated men to obtain the enactment of CPA laws. They were not likely to view with pleasure a move that seemed to denigrate the CPA certificate which they had worked so hard to obtain.

It may be assumed also that some tensions were developing between the larger firms, which had established offices in a number of states, and the local firms, many of which were struggling for a foothold. Allusions to reciprocity and to the difficulties of interstate practice by certified public accountants indicated one motive for the change.

The seeds of discontent and opposition were being sown. While the proceedings of the 1916 annual meeting indicate no strong opposition to the reorganization, some of the delegates, like some of the trustees, must have had grave doubts about its wisdom.

The 1916 *Yearbook* showed the total membership of the American Association as 1,238 and the total membership of the new Institute of Accountants as 1,169, indicating that some of the Association members did not wish to identify themselves with the new body.

Yet as future events were to show, the new Institute was to have a strong and constructive influence on technical and ethical standards, and on the standards for the CPA certificate. After 20 more years of trials and tribulations, the organized profession of certified public accountants emerged stronger and better than it would have been if the reorganization had not taken place.

According to a study made in 1915, a total of about 2,000 CPA certificates had been issued in the states where CPA laws then existed. Nearly 700 had been issued by waiver, and only a little more than 1,000 by examination—the rest by reciprocity. These figures excluded 12 states from which no report had been received, in some of which it was known that waiver certificates had been issued more generously than in others.

All but a relatively few of the fellows of the Association who became members of the new Institute were certified public accountants, though among the comparatively few associates there were more non-CPAs.

In the November 1916 *Journal* the editor, who was also the Institute's secretary, discussed the status of state societies under the new conditions.

He predicted that most members of state societies would still feel that the welfare of the profession in their vicinity was dependent upon co-operative effort by accountants residing or practicing therein, and "while proud of their membership in the Institute of Accountants, they will feel that they have not only a duty but a privilege in the opportunity to continue on terms of society fellowship with their neighbors in the profession. . . . By virtue of the more independent character of the state societies it may be that membership will appeal to some men who have not felt much interest in national affairs. . . . Whatever may be the feeling of members it is to be hoped that all who are now members of state societies will retain that membership. . . . It will be necessary for accountants to keep a close watch upon the activities of legislators and be ready to prevent by every proper means the enactment of injurious legislation or what might be termed the amendment downward of existing laws. . . .

"The usefulness of the state society has not passed, as some accountants seem to feel. On the contrary, while there is apt to be a slight divergence of interest or activity between the national and the state bodies, there is continuing need for the existence of strong, representative organizations of accountants in every state."

With high hopes, much enthusiasm, and some uncertainty, the organized profession thus embarked on an unfamiliar course.

CHAPTER 9

New Challenges

THE new Institute had barely been organized when the profession began to confront a series of largely unforeseen problems.

At the first meeting of the new Council, held the day after the annual meeting at which the reorganization had been approved, an ominous letter was received from Edwin Hurley, chairman of the Federal Trade Commission.

Reference has already been made to Mr. Hurley's interest in uniform accounting for the several classes of industries, and to his discussions with a committee of the Association. It will also be recalled that spokesmen for the accounting profession had suggested that the Federal Reserve Board should require independently audited financial statements of companies whose commercial paper was accepted as a basis for the issuance of currency.

Mr. Hurley's latest letter indicated dissatisfaction, which

he said was shared by the Federal Reserve Board, with financial statements certified by public accountants. Special mention was made of the inadequacy of depreciation charges. Mr. Hurley suggested that consideration might be given to the possibility of developing a register of public accountants whose audit certificates would be acceptable to the Commission and the Board.

This letter had the effect of a bombshell on the Council.

It was recognized as improbable that a government registration of accountants could be confined to members of the new Institute. Naturally the prevailing sentiment in the Council was strongly opposed to a federal register, which could mean political control of the profession.

Said Joseph E. Sterrett, "It will mean that the control which we have sought to secure by the organization of this body will almost at once pass from us into outside hands, and that we will not be able to control our own standards and our affairs. . . . It would be most unfortunate to have the Federal Reserve Board in position to absolutely decide as to whether a member of this body, or a practicing accountant anywhere in the country, should be accepted by it. . . .

"It seems to me that the committee on federal legislation . . . should be directed to take up with the Federal Trade Commission the problem of working a relationship out in that way that will at once assure the government departments of the proper standards of accounting conduct, and at the same time will retain within the profession the effective control of the members of the organization."

Another Council member pointed out that Mr. Hurley's letter also suggested that the national organization of the profession should formulate a set of rules, which should express its judgment as to the manner in which "various contending principles or rather questions of unsettled position shall be handled, and that those rules shall be accepted. That was the inference accepted by the Federal Reserve Board. . . . It seems to me it would go a long way toward accomplishing what Mr. Hurley has in mind. Furthermore, accompanying those rules could be this, that this body would undertake to exercise supervision on various members, so that in case anything should happen with respect to any of its members which is contrary to its own expression of principles or ideas, discipline should be administered."

Secretary Richardson stated, in view of his personal knowledge of Mr. Hurley's attitude, that it might be possible to bring about a compromise which would be acceptable.

"When he originally suggested this idea of registration," Mr. Richardson said, "the federal legislation committee opposed it, and they asked him to hold up any such proposition until this Institute idea could be acted on by the American Association. Now this letter, I think, is directly due to his knowledge of the change that was to take place. That is the reason the letter is written to be brought before the new body, and I think I can read into that a desire to have the active assistance of this body. I think Mr. Hurley is perfectly honest, but I think he really means to do the best he can for the business of the country. I think he is trying to get into close touch with the accountants through this body."

It was finally resolved that the committee on federal legislation be directed to confer with the Federal Trade Commission and with the Federal Reserve Board, "advising them of the organization of this Institute, and giving them a knowledge of the plan and scope of the organization, with a view to deferring or perhaps, if possible, preventing the establishment of any governmental registration; assuring the Federal Trade Commission and Federal Reserve Board of the willingness of the Institute to co-operate in fullest manner with them in securing proper rules and regulations regarding the certification of statements for federal or other purposes."

The committee on federal legislation consisted of Robert H. Montgomery, chairman, George O. May, who had become senior partner of Price Waterhouse & Co., and Harvey Chase of Boston.

What happened is not all on the record. However, the evidence suggests that the Association's committee explained to

Mr. Hurley how the reorganization of the Association as the American Institute would strengthen the national organization's controls over its admission requirements and the ethical conduct of its members. This, it could have been argued, eliminated the need for a federal register of accountants, which would require a government agency to review the qualifications of applicants for such recognition.

What was needed, the Association's committee apparently urged, were guidelines for the conduct of independent audits which would meet the requirements of the Trade Commission and the Federal Reserve Board.

Actually Mr. Hurley was more interested in uniform accounting for various industry groups than in audited financial statements for credit purposes. The Federal Reserve Board, however, was keenly interested in the credit worthiness of organizations whose commercial paper was discounted by Federal Reserve banks. The Board, therefore, had an immediate and vital interest in the reliability of certified financial statements of such enterprises. The accountants, although they had co-operated with Mr. Hurley in his efforts, were not enthusiastic about uniform accounting. They did, however, recognize the need for authoritative audit guidelines in order to maintain a standard of performance that would strengthen public confidence.

The Famous Federal Reserve Bulletin

This was what emerged. Mr. May said, many years later, "As a result of discussions between the committee members and the government officials it was decided that the preparation of a pamphlet [on the independent audit of financial statements for credit purposes]would serve useful purposes."[1]

---

[1] *Memoirs and Accounting Thought of George O. May,* edited by Paul Grady, The Ronald Press Company, New York, 1962.

After an initial draft had proved unsatisfactory, Mr. May said, "...I turned over to the committee a document prepared, a few years previously, by John C. Scobie for internal use by Price Waterhouse. The other members of the Institute committee were favorably impressed with this document, and it was reproduced without a great deal of change in the pamphlet published by the Federal Reserve Board."

It must be assumed that Montgomery, as editor of the leading American book on auditing, had a hand in whatever changes were made.

In any event, the result was the historic *Federal Reserve Bulletin* of 1917, first entitled "Uniform Accounting."

The accountants may have taken advantage of some confusion in Mr. Hurley's mind as to the distinction between uniform accounting and standard audit requirements. The two concepts are rather curiously mixed in the first edition of the 1917 bulletin. The preface said, "The following tentative proposal for a uniform system of accounting to be adopted by manufacturing and merchandising concerns ... is now reprinted for more general distribution."

However, the text of the bulletin consisted mainly of recommended audit procedures, though suggested forms for a comparative profit-and-loss account for three years and a balance sheet appear at the end. Literally, the bulletin had nothing to do with uniform systems of accounting.

In 1917, perhaps even before the appearance of the bulletin, Mr. Hurley resigned his position with the Federal Trade Commission. A year later the same bulletin was reissued by the Federal Reserve Board under a different and more appropriate title, "Approved Methods for the Preparation of Balance Sheet Statements." The text was identical save for the *omission* from the preface of the reference to a uniform system of accounting. This supports the possibility that Mr. Hurley's interest in uniform accounting was catered to in the first edition.

The introduction in both editions refers to the courtesy of the Federal Trade Commission in making available to the Federal Reserve Board information related to financial statements of merchants, manufacturers, etc. Reference is also made to the Federal Trade Commission's enlisting the aid of the American Institute of Accountants in its studies, including a request that the Institute prepare a memorandum on balance-sheet audits. This memorandum was approved by the Council of the Institute and by the Federal Trade Commission, and then placed before the Federal Reserve Board for consideration. The Board, after conference with representatives of the Commission and the Institute, had given it provisional or tentative endorsement, and submitted it to bankers throughout the country for their consideration.

The text of the bulletin began with general instructions for a balance-sheet audit of a manufacturing or a merchandising concern. It then outlined specific instructions related to the audit of cash, notes receivable, accounts receivable, securities, inventories, cost of fixed property, deferred charges to operations, notes and bills payable, accounts payable, contingent liabilities, accrued liabilities, bonded and mortgage debt, capital stock and surplus; sales, cost of sales, gross profit on sales, selling, general and administrative expenses, net profit on sales, other income, deductions from income, net income—profit and loss, and surplus additions and deductions. It concluded with general comment and a suggested form of certificate as follows:

> I have audited the accounts of Blank and Co. for the period from . . . to . . . and I certify that the above balance sheet and statement of profit and loss have been made in accordance with the plan suggested and advised by the Federal Reserve Board and in my opinion set forth the financial condition of the firm at . . . and the results of its operations for the period.

This bulletin was sent to all members of the Institute. It had both an immediate and a lasting effect on auditing standards and procedures.

Through the years, of course, these standards and procedures were amended and refined in the light of experience and changing conditions, but the profession had set its feet on a path which was to lead to increased prestige and progress.

While it must be conceded that the initial effort was partly a response to outside pressure, the Federal Reserve Bulletin of 1917 marked the beginning of what has proved to be a remarkable achievement in self-discipline.

In England auditing standards had been largely developed through statutory and common-law channels. English textbooks on auditing were largely composed of analyses of court decisions dealing with auditors' responsibilities, and, of course, with the provisions of the successive amendments to the Companies Acts. But in the United States the profession seized the initiative, and over a period of more than 50 years continually refined and elaborated the guidelines which independent auditors should follow.

The Institute's successive pronouncements in this area have steadily improved the quality of auditing, to the great benefit of the public. They have also been admissible as evidence in court, and thus have served as a protection against unreasonable impositions of liability on auditors who follow the standards.

A Library and Information Bureau

However, it was recognized that improvement of the standards of accounting practice was not to be achieved entirely by official pronouncements. No profession can be practiced by "cookbook." Conceptual foundations are needed, and they emerge slowly, partly as a result of experience and partly by discussion and debate which build a professional literature. In addition, countless questions arise in the application of basic concepts and recommended procedures.

In 1917 it became clear to George O. May that the growing accounting profession needed urgently a central repository of its accumulated knowledge. He took the lead in the establishment of the Institute's library and bureau of information, whose importance in facilitating the rise of the profession can hardly be overestimated.

Among the remarkable number of able leaders who emerged in this small profession during its developmental period, Mr. May was surely among the most outstanding.

He had entered the London office of Price Waterhouse & Co. in 1897 at the age of 22, and only a few months later he was sent by the firm to join its New York staff. In 1902 he was admitted to partnership. Despite his comparative youth, he was soon put in charge of the St. Louis office.

In 1911 Dickinson retired as senior partner of Price Waterhouse and returned to England. May, who was returned to New York, became the senior partner of the firm.

He was a man of wide-ranging interests, including law, economics, music, literature, and travel. He was imaginative and far-seeing. He was thoughtful and highly articulate. He did not particularly care for official position—in fact, more than once he declined the presidency of the American Institute. But he was deeply interested in the technical and professional aspects of his chosen field, and his speeches, articles, and writings probably have had more influence on American accounting than those of any other man. Even the outstanding academic theorists, some of whom disagreed with his philosophy, respected his intellectual capacity and his skill as a debater.

Frequent mention of his activities will be made later in this book. However, his initiation of the Institute's library and bureau of information, though less dramatic than others, was one of his greatest contributions. It was typical of his approach to professional problems. He perceived that the profession could not advance without a repository of literature, so without delay he went ahead and created it.

It came about in this way.

The first president of the new Institute, W. Sanders Davies, in his report to the 1917 annual meeting, stated that Mr. May had made a splendid offer on behalf of himself and his partners.

The proposal was to raise a fund of $150,000, the interest

from which, together with an amount equal to the present rent of the secretary's office, would pay the rent of more desirable headquarters, and the salaries of a librarian and statistician. The library at the headquarters would be available to the members.

Through the headquarters staff, members could submit questions confronting them in their practice, the answers to which would be obtained and transmitted without disclosure of the name either of the inquirer or the member answering the inquiry.

Mr. May and his partners subscribed $25,000 to the new Endowment Fund. Elijah Watt Sells immediately subscribed an additional $15,000. The project was in being.

The committee on endowment, of which Mr. May was chairman, stated in its first report to the Council:

> Members should be notified as soon as possible that the machinery has been set in motion and that the facilities are available for use. It is hoped that all members of the Institute will take advantage of the privilege which will be offered. For some time there has been a feeling among accountants, particularly in distant parts of the country, that they had no actual interest or part in the development of the national organization. The bureau of advice will set at rest that objection, however ill-founded it may have been. Every accountant will be able to approach the offices of the Institute with assurance that his communications will be strictly confidential, if he so desires, and may obtain the advice of accountants representing the best thought in the profession. Neither advisor nor person seeking advice will know the identity of the other.

Thus began the library of the Institute, which became as complete as any accountancy library in the world. It has been of immense value to members and others, throughout this country and abroad, in supplying references to practicing CPAs, to students preparing for the examinations, to thesis-writing candidates for advanced degrees, and to many accounting professors in their research activities. It has also been of indispensable aid to the staff of the Institute in meeting its own research and reference needs. The vision of those who in

1917 conceived and supported the library and the related information service deserves the gratitude of all who have benefited from it.

By 1919 the goal of $150,000 had been reached.

The Institute had already moved to new quarters at One Liberty Street. Louise S. Miltimore had been employed as librarian.

Among the donations to the Institute was the copyright of a series of articles entitled "The Duties of the Junior Accountant," written by W. B. Reynolds and F. W. Thornton. These articles were published under the Endowment Fund in book form. A best seller for many years, it was the first of many books to be published under the auspices of the Institute.

The library began operations with 1,100 bound books and magazines, 1,300 unbound books, pamphlets and clippings, and 51 magazines and newspapers. Many of the books were donated, including a complete set of *Moody's Manual* and the *Commercial and Financial Chronicle*. All the items had been indexed on cards.

In its first year the bureau of information answered 120 questions from members, mostly from accountants outside New York.

Between 1920 and 1929 the librarians issued 33 special bulletins containing questions and answers on technical matters cleared through the library and bureau of information. The bulletins were carefully qualified as not having official status, and not "presenting the last word on any subject," but they nonetheless did represent the best thought as to the best practice at the time, and thus contributed to elevation of standards.

In 1921, the librarians produced the *Accountants' Index*, a mammoth volume listing all books and articles on accounting published in English up to that time. The items were listed by titles, by subject matter and by authors' names. This was an invaluable aid to practitioners and researchers. A supplement covering material published in the intervening two years was published in 1923, and additional supplements have appeared every two or three years since.

These quiet achievements of the library deserve a place of high honor in the annals of the profession. The implications of its work were more significant than could have been predicted. When it was founded, there was no place in the United States, outside the offices of a few large firms and perhaps the libraries of a few universities, where a public accountant could obtain information on technical questions which confronted him in his practice. The new library was at the service of the entire membership—and, indeed, of all persons interested in accounting. Not only did it provide references to published material bearing on a member's problem, and lend him a book if necessary, but if nothing relevant appeared in print the bureau of information would seek an answer from another member familiar with the subject matter.

There can be little doubt that even when the Institute's popularity was at its lowest ebb in some quarters a few years later, the library's service was a significant influence in holding the membership together. This suggests that an organization which gives individual members direct personal service—value for their dues dollars—can weather even severe political storms.

The statistics in the table on page 140 show the extent of the use of the library's facilities up to the end of the period covered in this volume, when the Institute's membership was somewhat more than 2,000.

The credit for this remarkable showing goes largely to Louise S. Miltimore, the first librarian. The library was largely her creation. She was wholly dedicated to its success. She worked fantastic hours to make it succeed. Some think she worked herself to death.

World War I

The efforts to build the new Institute were slowed down, though not entirely halted, by the first World War.

	Total Collection of Books, Pamphlets, Periodicals, etc.	Items Loaned to Members	Inquiries Answered
1918	2,451	—	120
1919	3,021	—	572
1920	3,522	—	831
1921	4,719	—	1,444
1922	6,148	—	2,630
1923	7,207	—	3,021
1924	8,084	1,146	3,603
1925	9,163	1,985	4,104
1926	10,530	2,303	4,694
1927	11,129	2,073	5,221
1928	11,176	1,500	5,373
1929	12,331	1,580	6,003
1930	12,816	2,087	6,043
1931	13,396	2,325	6,561
1932	13,803	3,204	7,554
1933	14,115	3,316	7,826
1934	14,419	3,371	8,146
1935	14,110	2,647	8,381
1936	14,405	2,006	8,401

The first reference to the war in *The Journal of Accountancy* was a remarkable one. It appeared in February 1915, shortly after hostilities had broken out in Europe, in an article, "A Plan for International Peace," by Elijah Watt Sells.

This article was a thoughtful, detailed prospectus for a world tribunal to adjudicate differences between nations, with an armed force available to enforce its decisions or suppress hostilities between nations. It seems worthy of note that three years before the League of Nations was proposed, one of the leading accountants should have shown such a deep interest in world affairs as to devise a complete plan for a similar world organization.

At the 1916 annual meeting reference was made to the war raging in Europe, in which the United States was to find itself a participant in one short year.

The president of the Association, J. Porter Joplin, said, "So that this Association might not be considered behind the times in connection with matters which are of paramount interest to our country's welfare, the opportunity was embraced of bringing to the attention of the chairman of the Industrial Preparedness Committee the desirability of co-operation on the part of accountants in the work of industrial preparedness. . . . There is much that could be done in time of national crisis by the members of this profession through their national body, provided the nature of the need was made known to the Association and opportunity thus afforded for service along lines wherein our members excel."

Shortly thereafter the opportunity was afforded. It was to absorb much of the profession's energies for the next two years.

Before the United States actually declared war on Germany, during the period of "preparedness," the Institute offered its services to the Naval Consulting Board and the Council of National Defense.

An Institute committee on national defense conferred with both bodies. As a result, the Institute committee was constituted as a subcommittee of the Council of National Defense, and later a subcommittee of the General Munitions Board.

The work of the Board was largely concerned with the purchase of emergency supplies. The accountants' subcommittee arranged things so that at least two of its members would be in attendance at all times in the offices of the Board. These members investigated the provisions of all contracts for the purchase of supplies of an emergency nature, and also advised on numerous questions which arose from day to day.

On April 6, 1917, the United States declared war on Germany. This, President W. Sanders Davies said in his report to the 1917 annual meeting, "has changed the whole trend of our national life and given us but one object . . . the overwhelming of the enemy."

The Institute immediately requested its members to signify their ability and readiness to take government work. Replies were received from approximately half the membership, and many of these members were referred by the Institute to war agencies in response to requests for accounting aid. By the fall of 1917 over 100 members were employed by such agencies.

A notable example of the need for accountants was the supervision of audits of costs and other accounting work connected with the construction of cantonments. Twelve members of the Institute were appointed division auditors from as widely separated points as Portland, Oregon, and Jacksonville, Florida. They drew up a manual for the use of cantonment auditors, and generally supervised the accounting of all cantonments built for the conscript army, and later for the National Guard. These 12 members employed great numbers of other accountants and clerical assistants. The magnitude of the job is indicated by the fact that cantonments were constructed to house from 20,000 to 40,000 inhabitants in as short a time as three months.

The Institute refused to seek deferment from the draft of accountants as a class, but suggested to the government that the example of Great Britain be followed: that accountants of long experience and mature years be exempted from military duty, in the light of the fact that their numbers were few and their services were essential to both the civilian and military economies. A ruling was secured that accountants were not members of a non-essential vocation.

During the war years *The Journal of Accountancy* was filled with articles on such subjects as Navy Yard cost accounting, construction records and accounts, the determination of costs for contract purposes, wartime taxes, and similar matters.

In 1918 the War Committee reported an estimate of from 12 to 15 per cent of the entire membership as engaged in war service. Mr. Sterrett was vice chairman of the Excess-profits-tax Review Board. Lieutenant Colonel Robert H. Montgomery was the representative of the War Department on the

Price-fixing Committee of the War Industries Board. Arthur W. Teele, of Patterson, Teele and Dennis, one of the Institute's strong leaders, was the civilian member of a committee appointed by the Quartermaster's department to consider the determination of property accountability. Charles S. Ludlam, of Haskins & Sells, was to represent the government in the determination of its responsibilities created through inter-allied transactions.

At the 1918 annual meeting a motion was adopted expressing the Institute's appreciation of the service rendered by Mr. Sterrett to the profession and to the nation.

Speakers at the informal banquet included Colonel Montgomery, who had received his commission for service to the War Department (and who later said he had donned a uniform only under compulsion!), and Major J. Lee Nicholson, who had also received his commission for wartime service.

The secretary reported that 40 members and two associates of the Institute were wearing the uniform of the United States or its allies, and that in the civilian ranks 72 members and three associates were serving the United States or allied governments in war work. He said:

> Early in the struggle the War Committee of the Council of National Defense was the official mouthpiece of the profession, and largely because of its efforts the Institute was able to impress upon the government departments the importance of the utilization of the best accounting ability in the country. The enormous volume of cost-plus contracts, with its concomitant necessity to determine cost, and the thousand-and-one activities in which the knowledge and training of the accountant were essential had compelled the government and its agencies to rely to an unprecedented degree upon members of the Institute and other accountants of ability and standing.... The Institute's office has become a clearing house of accounting personnel.

While the Institute naturally took pride in its war activities, which were indeed significant in relation to its resources, in retrospect it must be conceded that its contribution was modest in relation to the total national effort. Nevertheless, what it was able to do added to the stature of the profession as a whole. Important and powerful people were brought into close association with accountants, some for the first time—and learned to respect them. Friendships were formed which eased the profession's access to Washington in later years.

Increasing Visibility of Auditors

The United States emerged from the war a creditor nation for the first time in its history. Then began a period of unparalleled growth and prosperity, characterized by industrial expansion, mergers, holding-company empires—and, unfortunately, some unsound financial practices. This period ended abruptly in 1930.

From 1916 to 1930, however, accounting practice boomed. Between 1921 and 1928 the number of common stocks listed on the New York Stock Exchange increased by more than half. The issuance of new securities, the purchases, mergers and consolidations, brought many special engagements to accounting firms—not only the so-called "national" firms, but many others of moderate size.

Corporations issuing securities were not required to have independent audits until the early 1930's, and there were no well-defined standards governing financial reporting. The leading corporations, however, voluntarily engaged independent auditors, and a substantial proportion of the companies listed on the New York Stock Exchange were publishing audited financial statements long before they were required to do so. The best accounting firms of all sizes maintained their own high standards, based partly on British practice, the 1917 Federal Reserve Bulletin, the professional literature, and their own common sense.

At the other extreme, however, were some inexcusable practices. In January 1919, the editor of *The Journal of Accountancy* predicted efforts to sell all manner of securities to a gullible public: "Yet it is a remarkable fact that an offering of securities supported by an accountant's statement is a rare exception." He urged the Congress to legislate requirements that would correct this situation.

In 1920 the editor said, "In these days of secret reserves and hidden surpluses on the part of companies...one wonders whether complete publicity as to the destination of every dollar of profit would not do much to bring us to our senses."

Prospectuses sometimes contained statements that the accounts of the company had been audited by such-and-such an accounting firm—but without presenting the financial statements and the auditor's certificate. One prominent accounting firm found it necessary to print the following note on every report it issued: "The publication of any condensation or modification of statements herein contained, or the use of our certificate detached from its context, or the use of our name in connection with the sale of securities or other publicity will not be sanctioned unless first submitted for our approval."

Some accountants were certifying statements in which certain assets and liabilities were presented in amounts which would be appropriate if proposed financing arrangements became effective. Usually such revised balance sheets contained such notices as "after giving effect to proposed financing."

Commercial bankers also were beginning to press for audited financial statements from loan applicants. As business expanded, the personal relationship between borrowers and lenders became attenuated. "Character loans," and loans based solely on previous experience with borrowers became less popular. The auditing procedures recommended in the Federal Reserve Bulletin encouraged banks to rely more and more on financial statements audited by certified public accountants. This trend was accelerated by co-operative relationships established between the Robert Morris Associates (bank credit officers) and the Institute. Audits for credit purposes added greatly to the volume of practice of local CPA firms, as well as the larger, multi-office firms.

Growth of Advisory Services

Rising tax rates, during and after the war, and the increasing complexities of the tax laws and regulations added enormously to the demand for accountants. Not only did tax work augment the practice of existing accounting firms, but it provided opportunity for the establishment of new firms and individual practices in all parts of the country. Small businessmen and private individuals who had never bothered much about keeping records found that with Uncle Sam as a silent partner it paid to have good accounts, good advice, and a good representative when the revenue agents came around.

The impact of taxes on accounting practice will be more fully discussed in Chapter 12.

Auditing and tax practice did not, however, constitute the entire area of accounting practice. Advisory services were beginning to grow in importance, although they were not generally identified as a separate type of service, and were often rendered in conjunction with audits.

The scope of advisory services in the early days is indicated by a report dated June 8, 1910, submitted to the Westinghouse Electric and Manufacturing Company by "Marwick, Mitchell & Co., Chartered Accountants." The accountants had been engaged to investigate the company's organization, its cost and general accounting systems, its production methods and its employee incentives.

The report covered the following matters among others: (1) cumbersome organization of certain departments—elimination of some middle-management positions was suggested; (2) disagreement with management's attempt to transfer responsibility for cost records from controller to manager of works—centralization of cost accounting was recommended, and simplified forms were suggested; (3) opportunities for improvement of production methods—for example, in routing of materials and in providing better machinery and equipment; and (4) adjustment of compensation and incentives to improve morale of employees at various levels.

All this appeared to be regarded both by client and accounting firm as a natural and proper field of service by professional accountants.

Public accountants in the United States had taken pride for many years in their competence in cost accounting—a field in which they felt superior to their British colleagues. The cost-plus contracts commonly used in World War I had given an additional boost to cost accounting, not only among accountants, but among businessmen as well. Public accountants were among the organizers of the National Association of Cost Accountants in 1919. Some accounting firms began to go into cost accounting in a big way, even bringing in industrial-engineering talent to assist in time and motion studies, work-flow studies and related measurement techniques.

The "scientific management" movement had begun to attract attention years before the war, and the public accountants, who had staked out a claim in the fields of systems and cost accounting, did not ignore it. An editorial on scientific management appeared in the *Journal* for May 1911, and in the June issue of the same year remarks by Frederick Winslow Taylor, one of the fathers of scientific management, were reprinted.

Clinton H. Scovell, of Scovell, Wellington & Co., Boston, one of the pioneers in the field now described as "management services," advocated a combining of accounting and engineering skills to increase clients' efficiency and profitability.

Spokesmen for the accounting profession inveighed against "charlatans" calling themselves "industrial engineers," who advertised in circular letters that they could increase production without adding to costs, and increase profits by reducing selling expenses.

CPAs began to complain about work solicited by management consultants in the areas of systems and procedures, which the accountants claimed could have been done better by themselves, and for which the consultants received fees greatly in excess of those ordinarily obtained by accountants. However, criticism also traveled in the opposite direction.

Yet more and more, as time went on the accountant *was* being consulted, and his advice was being adopted in the general control of business undertakings. He was beginning to be looked upon, it was said, as a "business physician." His work was extending to fields which a few years before would have been considered outside his legitimate sphere of action.

The advisory services of the time were summed up in a paper presented at the annual meeting of the Institute in 1920, entitled, "Advisory Accountancy," by William B. Gower. Mr. Gower listed the following matters on which accountants were being asked for advice:

1. Finance, such as an original investment or purchase, or a subsequent acquirement of an interest, or the financing of a contemplated expansion of the business, or a temporary financing necessitated by growing inventories, or the payment of cash or stock dividends.

2. Business policy, such as expansion of the enterprise, or embarking on new lines of trade or manufacture, acquisition of properties, volume of output and its relation to overhead expenses, cessation or curtailment of unprofitable lines, accumulation of inventories, work in process, or finished goods, the question of branches and departments, and the policy of credits and discounts.

3. Management and administration, economical production, the prevention of waste, extravagance and useless expense, and questions of personnel.

Practice Units

In 1930 the president of the Institute announced that more than 900 firms and individual practitioners were represented in the Institute, and estimated that this was a "goodly percentage" of all the practice units in the country. Since the Institute included only about a quarter of all the CPAs in the country, to say nothing of the numerous non-certified public accountants and "tax experts" who had sprung up in great numbers, it may be surmised that the "goodly percentage" was less than half. While there are no readily available statistics indicating the number of practice units in 1916, it would not be surprising to find that they had tripled between then and 1930.

Despite the long head start of the older accounting firms which had been established about the turn of the century, some of which had grown to national scope, it was not too late for other firms to begin, to flourish, and to grow.

Scores of new firms were established in the 20-year period from 1916 to 1936, some of which have attained national scope, others regional coverage, and still others strong local positions.

The fascinating stories of the development of some of these firms demonstrate that it is never too late to start an accounting practice, and there is no limit to the size to which an accounting firm can grow if its partners have the energy, competence and determination to succeed.

The "Busy Season"

Most of the time, in fact, there has been more accounting work to be done than there were competent accountants to do it. But the difficulty of getting it done was compounded for many years by the prevalent practice of closing books at the end of the calendar year.

Year-end audits were heavily concentrated in a period of

several months. Income-tax returns were due March 15. Accountants worked their heads off from December to April, and then sank back exhausted.

Efforts to alleviate this condition took two forms: persuasion of businesses to close their books at times other than December 31; and pleas to the Bureau of Internal Revenue to grant extensions of time for filing tax returns. Both were partially and sporadically successful.

The best time for a business to close its books is when its annual operating cycle is completed—when inventories and receivables are at their lowest point. This date marks the end of its "natural business year." In the 1920's the Institute launched a campaign to inform the business community of the advantages of adopting natural business years.

Existing information on the subject was reviewed. It was found that approximately 85 per cent of the clients of some firms closed their books on December 31. This required the employment of temporary staff accountants who were dropped in the spring, and this in turn served as a barrier to the attraction of desirable young men to public accounting practice.

Questionnaires were mailed to members of the Institute asking for data on changes by clients from the calendar year to a natural year. A newspaper item was prepared on the basis of this information which received wide publicity. A magazine article on the advantages of natural business years was published in *System Magazine*. A committee of the Robert Morris Associates endorsed the natural business year. A circular letter was mailed to 200 trade associations on the subject, enclosing the *System* reprint.

By hammering away at the subject the profession began to make some progress. The Institute's efforts encouraged individual firms to press their own clients to change to natural years.

Through research and analysis a formidable body of propaganda on natural business years was developed.

In the 1930's the effort was enlarged by the creation of a Natural Business Year Council, consisting of representatives of the Institute, the National Association of Credit Men, the Robert Morris Associates, the American Management Association, the National Association of Cost Accountants, American Trade Association Executives, and Dun & Bradstreet. This Council issued educational material which was widely circulated among business organizations.

The Institute did most of the Council's work, but the co-operation of the other organizations added authority to the movement and provided direct access to many business audiences.

After a decade of effort the results became visible. Many companies had changed to natural fiscal years, and many new companies had adopted natural years from the beginning. To be sure, many others, perhaps more than half, stayed with the calendar year, but the peak load on the accounting firms had been lightened to an extent that made the effort worthwhile. Later other means were devised to spread the work more evenly through the year.

The efforts to get extensions of time for filing tax returns were successful in some years and unsuccessful in others, depending on the attitude of the Commissioner of Internal Revenue who happened to be in office. Rarely were blanket extensions granted. Sometimes it was easy to get extensions in specific cases. In other years even this was difficult.

Unsuccessful attempts were made to persuade the Bureau of Internal Revenue to stagger the filing dates, by permitting different groups of taxpayers to file returns in successive months. Finally, the Institute did succeed in having the filing date for individual returns moved forward to April 15, while March 15 remained the date for corporations.

Personnel

The uncertainty of continuous employment was a serious barrier to the attraction of able young people to the profession. Firms generally preferred staff men who had bookkeeping experience. Staffs were augmented largely from applicants who approached the firms on their own initiative, or came through employment agencies. Heavy dependence was placed on temporary staffs—"temps" or "floaters"—men who were content to work for public accounting firms during the busy season and to pursue other occupations during the remainder of the year.

These conditions were a tremendous handicap in efforts to persuade college-trained men to enter public accounting as a career. The fear of layoff in idle periods was a great deterrent.

Before the First World War a young man wrote a pathetic letter to the *Journal*:

> The present attractions which public accounting has to offer—for the junior, even for the experienced junior, the junior who puts all his effort into the work to make good—are excessively hard work, poor pay, and poorer appreciation of one's efforts than the laborer secures from the gang boss. Often I have worked until the wee small hours of the morning, gone home for some three hours of rest, and was the first one back on the job at the regular time the next day. Many an uncompleted task I took home with me, to work on it most of the night so I could turn in a completed paper the next morning, and then, when I asked for a raise, what happened? I was told my work was not satisfactory. I would never make an accountant. I was lazy and was retained merely out of charity or pity.

Extensive travel was also the lot of most staff accountants, as well as partners. It was not unusual for men to be away from home on audits for a month or two at a time. This did not please most wives.

There was also much complaint about the difficulty of obtaining a position with an accounting firm. One young man referred to the fact that he couldn't get a job because he had no accounting experience, but asked how he could get the experience unless he got a job!

It took a long time to change working conditions and compensation levels to the point where professional accounting became fully competitive with other vocations in seeking recruits. But after World War II these levels were attained, and in some cases exceeded. Then began the great influx of college graduates into the profession.

Women in Accounting

Despite frequent complaints about the shortage of good staff personnel, women were generally considered unavailable for public accounting prior to World War II.

The number of women studying accounting was increasing, but the majority found their way into employment as bookkeepers in corporations. Those imbued with ambition to enter public accounting were frequently discouraged.

An editorial in the December 1923 *Journal* said, "the fact of the matter is that women are not wanted as accountants on the staff of practicing public accountants." The reasons for this reluctance were cited: that staff accountants traveled widely, and that they did a great deal of overtime work, including night work "in places of difficulty and inconvenience. Large numbers of men are sent to work, but any attempt at heterogeneous personnel would hamper progress and lead to infinite embarrassment." Further, it was said, many businessmen were still living in the age when a woman's place was in the home, and would be shocked if their accounting firms were to send a woman to audit their accounts.

There were several women at that time who were members of the Institute, conducting their own practices, but the range of their activities was said to be restricted.

Despite these prejudices, a number of women were tenacious enough to secure a foothold in public accounting. In 1933, the American Women's Society of Certified Public Accountants was organized to encourage and assist women in entering the profession, and in improving their professional proficiency.

In 1934 this Society made a survey indicating that at January 1 of that year, 105 women held certificates as certified public accountants. Of those who answered the Society's questionnaire, 55 per cent were in public practice: 17 on their own account, eight in partnerships, and 12 as staff assistants.

The Society's report on the survey said, "Opinion ranges all the way from the woman who thinks there is little future in the profession to the one who says, 'the surface has hardly been scratched.' By far, the majority are optimistic, and many express themselves as believing that the field will grow as more women enter it, demonstrate their ability, and help to educate the public to the idea." These predictions proved true.

The Depression

The stock-market crash in 1929 and the subsequent depression meant hard times for accountants, as for many others. The Securities Act of 1933 and the Securities and Exchange Act of 1934 potentially increased the accounting and auditing work required by companies whose securities were publicly traded. But there was not much new financing during those chilling years of the early 1930's.

Arthur Andersen & Co., in its history of the firm, *The First Fifty Years,* states, "The decade of the 1930's was a period of challenge and testing in common with practically all professional and industrial enterprises. The firm saw its business curtailed and its profits drastically reduced during the depression years. Fees which had aggregated $2,023,000 in 1929 sank to a low of $1,488,000 in 1932."

Thomas G. Higgins, in his privately published autobiography, cites similar figures for Arthur Young & Co., as follows:

Chargeable hours (in thousands)

1929	599.4
1932	477.7

Most accounting firms, large and small, suffered comparable declines in volume. Some clients failed. Others had to cut fees. Retraction replaced expansion.

Few new staff accountants were employed in the early and middle 1930's, and many were laid off or took salary cuts. The lack of new recruits during this period left a void which was hard to fill when the depression was over, and the rapid growth of accounting practice began again.

Nevertheless, all the well-established accounting firms survived the depression and its aftermath. Even in a time of economic disaster there was much accounting work that had to be done. And after World War II the profession was to enjoy the greatest prosperity and growth that it had yet experienced.

CHAPTER 10

The Drive for Better Financial Reporting

Except for a brief recession in 1920, the postwar wave of prosperity mounted steadily until the stock-market crash in 1929.

The Harding, Coolidge, and Hoover Administrations leaned toward *laissez faire*. Big business had a fairly free hand. High tariffs were enacted, immigration was restricted, and for a time the country enjoyed unparalleled economic well-being.

New industries, like automobiles and aviation, were developing rapidly, carrying in their train a host of contributory activities—such as extensive construction of highways and airports.

Demands for capital mounted, and new securities were issued on an unprecedented scale.

In the absence of any regulation of the securities markets, abuses were inevitable. Samuel Eliot Morison describes the period as "the greatest orgy of speculation and over-optimism since the South Sea Bubble of 1720." Unbridled speculation in the stock market had pushed prices to fantastic heights. Almost everyone thought that "a new era" had dawned, and prosperity would continue forever.

Concern Among Accountants

Thoughtful members of the accounting profession were aware that financial-reporting practices were not all they should be, and that the responsibilities of independent auditors had not been clearly defined. There were no generally accepted accounting principles, nor well-defined standards of disclosure.

The Institute, on its own initiative, made sporadic efforts to plug some of the gaps.

With the backing of the bank credit officers represented in the Robert Morris Associates, a special committee of the Institute on co-operation with bankers, headed by William B. Campbell, produced a report outlining rules to be followed in the certification of balance sheets giving effect to transactions consummated at a date later than the date of the balance sheet. This was the first substantive matter dealt with by these co-operating groups. These rules were unanimously approved at the Institute's 1923 annual meeting. The Council ordered that the report be printed as a pamphlet and distributed to the entire membership, as well as being printed in the *Yearbook*.

These rules were the forerunner of a later Council resolution, and ultimately a rule of professional conduct, prohibiting association of a member's name with estimates contingent upon future transactions in a manner which might lead to the belief that the member vouched for the accuracy of the forecast.

Brokers' Accounts

Until 1922 the New York Stock Exchange had not required its member firms, the brokers, to furnish information about their financial affairs. In that year, however, the Committee on Business Conduct of the Exchange issued a questionnaire to registered firms requiring information as to their financial status at a specific date.

This was hailed by accountants as a step to protect the investing public. Information called for included total bank balances, total money borrowed and total value of collateral, market value of negotiable securities in box and in transfer, total ledger debit balances in customers' accounts and the value of securities deposited as collateral against them, partners' accounts, including capital accounts, profit-and-loss accounts, and other accounts.

It was not then required that the brokers' financial data be subject to independent audit, but it was evidently assumed that accountants would be called upon to assist brokerage firms in complying with the new requirements. A commentator in *The Journal of Accountancy* said, "The preparation of the foregoing figures is, in effect, an internal audit of the assets and liabilities of the firm at a specific date. . . ."

Earned Surplus

In 1926 a special committee on definition of earned surplus was appointed, headed by Arthur Andersen, head of the firm bearing his name, which had been formed only 13 years before, but was growing rapidly. In 1930, after the stock-market crash, this committee proposed the following definition:

> Earned surplus is the balance of the net profits, net income, and gains of a corporation after deducting losses and after deducting distributions to stockholders and transfers to capital-stock accounts.

Collateral definitions of the following terms were presented: surplus, capital surplus, paid-in surplus, revaluation surplus, net profits, net income and gains. The report also presented a recommendation on presentation of surplus accounts.

At the meeting of Council on September 15, 1930, it was resolved that this report be considered further at the Council meeting in April 1931, and meanwhile that the report be printed in the *Yearbook,* with a statement that it must be regarded as tentative, not yet having the approval of the Institute. It was never approved.

Revision of the Federal Reserve Bulletin

In 1929 a new edition of the 1917 Federal Reserve Bulletin was published. The new version bore the title, "Verification of Financial Statements." The revision had been undertaken in 1928—well before the stock-market crash—by a special committee of the Institute headed by Arthur Teele, in recognition of radically changed conditions during the intervening 11 years.

The 1917 version was largely a straightforward audit program, with little conceptual background, and no reference to internal check and control. It stressed balance-sheet items, as was natural in that day when commercial bankers, whom the bulletin was mainly intended to serve, were more interested in liquidity than earning capacity. Furthermore, the 1917 version made no reference to income taxes, which had not yet become a material item of expense.

The 1929 revision stressed reliance on the system of internal control, and on the use of tests instead of detailed verification when internal controls were reliable.

The new bulletin stated, for the first time officially, that testing and sampling would not necessarily disclose defalcations, or every understatement of assets concealed in the records of operating transactions or by manipulation of the accounts.

The detailed instructions in the revision were somewhat more extensive than in the original bulletin, including a section on taxes.

The form of audit certificate suggested in 1929 was as follows:

> I have examined the accounts of . . . . company for the period from . . . . to . . . .
>
> I certify that the accompanying balance sheet and statement of profit and loss, in my opinion, set forth the financial condition of the company at . . . . and the results of operations for the period.

Forms of balance sheet and profit-and-loss statement were appended, which in the text were said to be forms suitable for credit purposes, whereas more condensed forms were customary for general distribution.

It was most fortunate that the profession had developed this statement, with the Reserve Board's approval, prior to the crisis of the early 1930's, since the revised bulletin provided an authoritative foundation for consideration of the auditor's responsibilities.

Stock-Exchange Concern

The New York Stock Exchange as early as 1922 showed uneasiness about some prevalent financial practices. The president of the Exchange, Seymour L. Cromwell, made a speech in that year advocating full publicity in connection with the issuance of securities, and full information about the status of issuing companies, in line with the English practice. He proposed a requirement that "sworn statements" be filed prior to the issuance of securities, and semi-annually thereafter, including adequate information on the financial position of the issuing companies, as well as their operations and earnings.

Apparently there had been some talk about the possibility of new legislation to regulate the issuance of securities.

In commenting on the Cromwell speech, *The Journal of Accountancy* said: "What can and should be done by legislation and effective public administration is to throw a light of publicity upon the issuance of securities that will enable investors to judge for themselves whether a given security is sound and to what extent it is speculative."

The editor further advocated provisions similar to those of the English Companies Act, including independent audits of financial statements—a point which Mr. Cromwell had apparently overlooked.

This was 11 years before the "Truth in Securities Act" of 1933, which might have been unnecessary if the business and financial community had disciplined itself in time.

But no action was taken in response to these and many other criticisms. The stock market was zooming, corporations were merging, and holding companies in the utility field were developing vast empires, financed by issue after issue of common stock.

Public Criticism

Perceptive critics began to break into print.

Professor William Z. Ripley of Harvard began to make speeches and write articles sharply criticizing current financial practices, including financial reporting. His writings were brought together in 1927 in a book entitled *Main Street and Wall Street*, which attracted wide public attention. He wrote with zest of "the docility of corporate shareholders permitting themselves to be honeyfugled;" and about "the hoodwinking of the shareholders," in the field of public utilities—much of his criticism supported by references to specific situations involving specific companies.

"The accountants," he wrote, "are enabled to play ball with figures to an astounding degree." Referring to Institute proposals for independent audits in accordance with British practice, he said, quite inaccurately, that the accounting profession in Great Britain was standardized by statute which prescribed qualifications and performance, while in the United States, "with the credentials of competence emanating from 48 conflicting and competing state legislatures, sheer independent audit would be no better than management audit as we have it at the present time."

However, Professor Ripley advocated full publicity about corporate affairs, and turned his wrath on many current financial reporting practices. State legislation, he concluded, held out little promise. He expressed the belief that under existing legislation the Federal Trade Commission had the power to deal with the problem, and implied that this power should be exercised.

The Profession Responds

One of the early Ripley articles appeared in *The Atlantic Monthly* of September 1926. The annual meeting of the American Institute was held in Atlantic City later that month, and George O. May took the opportunity to reply.

While expressing disagreement with the professor on many points, Mr. May said, "I would rather express my gratification at the success with which he has attracted the attention of the public to the subject, and consider what we, as accountants, can do to bring about that improvement in the information furnished to stockholders and potential stockholders of corporations for which his article is a plea. . . . I am not sure that auditors have done their full duty in this respect in the past. . . . I think the time has come when auditors should assume larger responsibilities, and their position be more clearly defined."

Mr. May said that 90 per cent or more of industrial companies listed on the New York Stock Exchange were independently audited; that the powers and duties prescribed for auditors under the English Companies Acts had resulted in a fully satisfactory situation; and that similar results might be achieved in the United States through co-operation with the accounting profession on the part of the stock exchanges, the investment bankers and the commercial banks.

Through agreements among these groups, he said, standards might be established for balance sheets and income statements, and he discussed in general terms the possible nature of such standards. He urged the Institute to take the initiative in such a co-operative effort.

In the next few years Mr. May proceeded to follow his own suggestion.

It happened that in November 1926, a few months after making this speech, Mr. May relinquished his administrative duties as senior partner of Price Waterhouse, in order to devote more time to economic studies and to the broader problems of financial and business affairs. It was fortunate for the profession that this brilliant man acquired the freedom of time and of action which permitted him to lead the profession in some urgently needed reforms.

An Approach to the Stock Exchange

Early in 1927 an effort was made by the Institute to follow Mr. May's suggestion that co-operative relations with the New York Stock Exchange be established to consider requirements for more comprehensive financial reports from listed companies.

However, the Institute's secretary reported to Council that efforts to assist the stock exchanges "had not yet borne fruit"— though the secretary hoped confidently that in the near future "there would be a greater inclination on the part of Exchange authorities to assist accountants in their attempts to insist upon full and frank disclosures of financial facts."

This was somewhat over-optimistic. In fact, an offer from the president of the Institute, William H. West, of West, Flint & Co., New York, to the president of the New York Stock Exchange, to initiate co-operative efforts to improve financial reporting had been rather peremptorily rejected. Disappointed and somewhat resentful of the brush-off, the Institute officially maintained a dignified silence, until Mr. May, not the least of whose qualities was tenacity, breached the Exchange's indifference from another direction.

In 1926, J. M. B. Hoxsey had been named executive assistant to the Committee on Stock List of the New York Stock Exchange, a full-time salaried position which carried no great authority but did provide direct access to that powerful committee. While not a CPA, Hoxsey had some knowledge of accounting, and May cultivated his acquaintance. Hoxsey was wholly in accord with May's objective to make financial statements of listed companies as informative and reliable as possible, and consulted May informally on technical questions.

When the president of the Exchange rejected the Institute's offer of co-operation, Hoxsey inquired of May whether Price Waterhouse & Co. would accept a retainer as consulting accountants to the Exchange. As an alternative May suggested a committee of the Institute to co-operate with the Exchange. However, the Stock List Committee preferred to have its own advisers, and the firm therefore accepted the appointment. This gave May direct access to the committee, and he constantly urged improved financial reporting, clearly perceiving that the speculative boom, if not checked, would collapse. It did.

The Crash

The stock-market crash in the fall of 1929 was a catastrophe beyond the worst predictions of the most pessimistic observers.

The financial community was in a state of shock. Thirty billion dollars of quoted value of securities vanished in less than a month. Banks failed, and in some states were closed. Financial paralysis gripped the country. Public reaction was bitter, and a critical review of the processes of the financial market, including financial-reporting practices, became an obvious political necessity.

The severity of the reaction is vividly illustrated by the changes in stock prices between 1929 and 1932. American Telephone & Telegraph sold as high as 310¼ in 1929 prior to the crash—and as low as 69¾ in 1932. Electric Bond and Share went from a high of 189 to a low of 5; General Electric from 403 to 8½; General Motors from 91¾ to 7⅝; Radio Corporation of America from 114¾ to 2½; Remington Rand from 57¾ to 1; United States Steel from 261¾ to 21¼.

The Stock Exchange suddenly showed an eager interest in reform, and a desire to co-operate with the Institute in improving financial reporting.

Mr. Hoxsey was dispatched to the annual meeting of the Institute at Colorado Springs in September 1930, to make his famous speech, "Accounting for Investors." He recited some of the important areas of financial reporting in which there were variations in practice that needed attention—depreciation, consolidated statements, disclosure of sales, distinction between operating income and other income, surplus, stock dividends, over-conservatism in accounting.

In conclusion, Hoxsey said that the Stock Exchange would welcome, "should you see fit to do so," the appointment of an Institute committee to co-operate with the Exchange for the consideration of all such problems.

The invitation was promptly accepted.

A special committee on co-operation with stock exchanges was appointed, and George O. May was made chairman. The committee went to work promptly, and was able to report progress a year later.

The committee said that it had had discussions and correspondence with the Exchange, and that the officers of the

Exchange recognized their obligation to see that companies whose securities were listed made reasonable disclosures to the public. The Exchange desired the co-operation of auditors in this venture. The Exchange had also expressed the view that there was considerable uncertainty regarding the extent of the responsibilities assumed by auditors in the ordinary audit of accounts for publication in companies' annual reports, and suggested the advisability of defining and possibly adding to those responsibilities. No details were suggested in 1931.

Piecemeal Efforts

Following the Hoxsey speech in 1930 the Institute also hastily created a special committee on accounting procedure, to consider "a number of technical questions that had been raised." The first subject to which it turned its attention was accounting for stock dividends—a topic to which Hoxsey had devoted much space in his speech. However, the new committee, without referring to its earlier intention to deal with stock dividends, submitted in 1932 a comprehensive memorandum on the treatment of foreign exchange in the accounts of American corporations. This was considered a matter of vital importance, due to the exceptional foreign-exchange conditions arising from abandonment of the gold standard by Great Britain and other countries.

The committee also reported that it had under consideration the possibility of the profession's adopting a standard form of auditors' certificate, but doubted the necessity of a formal recommendation, since substantial uniformity seemed to be emerging as a matter of evolution.

While it was no doubt true that firms auditing listed companies tended to use similar language in their "certificates," there was nothing to prevent variations in language which the reader would have to interpret for himself. Particularly vulnerable to criticism was the practice of stating, for example, "we certify that, in our opinion, they (the financial statements) correctly set forth, subject to the foregoing, the financial position . . ." The "foregoing" might deal with such significant factors as the adequacy of depreciation or the reserve for bad debts, the omission of certain audit steps, or any combination of comments. There was, in short, no standard language from which deviations could be considered as having special significance.

A reflection of this state of affairs appeared in a jingle which it amused CPAs to quote to one another. It went as follows:

> We have audited this balance sheet and say in our report
> That the cash is overstated, the cashier being short;
> That the customers' receivables are very much past due;
> That if there are some good ones they are very, very few;
> That the inventories are out of date and principally junk;
> That the method of their pricing is very largely bunk;
> That, according to our figures, the undertaking's wrecked,
> But, subject to these comments, the balance sheet's correct.

In the light of hindsight, it seems clear that fragmented efforts to solve difficult technical problems through different committees were doomed to failure. There was no agreement as yet on a basic philosophy—a conceptual framework within which each specific problem could be dealt with consistently.

However, the resources of the Institute, with only about 2,000 members, were limited. There was no full-time technical staff to aid the committees. The members, with such help as they could commandeer within their own firms, did all the work. There was some rivalry among the large firms, and differences of opinion arose on almost all controversial accounting questions. In the circumstances, it is no wonder that progress was slow.

The Pecora Investigation

The U.S. Senate Committee on Banking and Currency instituted a lengthy investigation of the securities markets. Ferdinand Pecora was counsel to the committee, and its proceedings were popularly referred to as the "Pecora Investigation," in the course of which the Securities Act of 1933 and the Securities Exchange Act of 1934 became law.

The legislative ardor was heightened by the collapse of the Kreuger and Toll international empire in 1932. When the Swede, Ivar Kreuger, known as "the match king," committed suicide, it was revealed that he had falsified accounts, forged documents, and concealed misappropriation of funds in enormous amounts by an intricate system of interrelated corporations among which he was able to manipulate transactions in secrecy.

The Senate Committee engaged in extensive inquiries about the Kreuger and Toll collapse, including questions about independent audits, the method of selection of auditors, the responsibilities of auditors and related matters.

The principal accounts of Kreuger and Toll had been audited by Swedish accountants; only the United States subsidiary had been audited by an American firm. But American investors had suffered losses, and indignation again reached a high pitch. The press was full of news about the Kreuger scandal, and *Fortune* published a long article on the subject, including references to inadequate accounting and auditing safeguards.

An example of the pressure for accounting reform was a statement by the American Management Association in 1932 advocating "such action as may be necessary to secure the appointment, by the leading professional accounting societies, of a joint committee on accounting standards, which committee shall be charged with the formulation and periodical revision of the accounting rules necessary to safeguard against recognized errors and misrepresentations in corporate reports and statements."

This declaration was submitted to the New York Stock Exchange. The Committee on Stock List requested an opinion from the Institute's co-operating committee as to the lines along which the policies of the Exchange should be developed in relation to the accounts of listed corporations. The Institute committee submitted a memorandum in response, but did not believe it proper to make it public at that time.

The committee reported, however, that it believed the prescription of complete standard accounting rules for corporations would be impracticable and undesirable. It recommended that any formulation of rules which might be attempted should be restricted to a statement of a relatively small number of established principles upon which there was no substantial difference between reputable accountants and corporations. This committee further suggested that in regard to other matters, such as inventory valuation, on which legitimate differences of opinion and practice existed, it was preferable to recognize the right of corporations to use those methods best adapted to their requirements so long as the methods were reasonable and were properly disclosed.

Exchange Requires Audits

As one step in the direction of reform, the Exchange in 1932 adopted a policy under which corporations applying for listings were asked to sign an agreement stipulating that their financial statements would bear the certificate of accountants "qualified under the laws of some state or country."

The Institute's committee on co-operation with stock exchanges pointed out that these developments required auditors to accept a larger responsibility to stockholders, and "to display courage and independence when their approval is sought for accounts which are either clearly inadequate or misleading, even if technically accurate. The committee believes that a full acceptance of this responsibility in the difficult times through which we are passing will do much to enhance the position of the profession for the future."

More Pressure

The pressure for legislation to protect investors was heightened in 1932 by the publication of *The Modern Corporation and Private Property*, by Adolf A. Berle, Jr., and Gardiner C. Means. Berle was a professor of law at Columbia University, and was soon to become a member of President Franklin D. Roosevelt's "brain trust"—a group of young liberals assembled to advise the President on how to recover from the depression and how to prevent a recurrence.

The Modern Corporation and Private Property may well have been a blueprint for the Securities Acts. Significantly, in the preface, Berle gave credit to William Z. Ripley, "who must be recognized as having pioneered this area."

Berle and Means analyzed the "concentration of economic power" in a relatively small number of large corporations. The book showed how the dispersion of stock ownership enabled management to control corporate finances, including the distribution of earnings. The authors criticized the inadequacy of information given to investors.

On the latter point, in discussing prospectuses, the authors said: "A statement, for example, that the average income during the past five years has been thus and so, may hide the fact that the income is steadily declining. Accountants of the highest grade decline to certify to such statements . . . but enough of it still goes on to raise questions whether the law should not itself take cognizance of the situation." The same complaint had been voiced by a banker as early as 1912 (see p. 78).

Berle and Means went on to point out methods of "accounting manipulation" which could be used to show abnormal profits, through inventory valuations, depreciation, issue of bonds with stock or stock warrants (resulting in lower than normal interest charges against income), overvaluation of assets, charges to surplus that should go against income, elimination of "non-recurring expenses" from income accounts, and crowding of sales into the last period.

"Capable accountants of a high degree of integrity will

catch these situations as they arise," said the authors, "and will usually make the necessary corrections before permitting the use of their name. . . . The integrity of the accountant and the soundness of his method are the greatest single safeguard to the public investor. . . . But rules of accounting are not as yet fully recognized rules of law. . . . In fact, the failure of the law to recognize accounting standards is probably due to the lack of agreement among accountants. . . ."

This 382-page book had great influence. Prepared under the auspices of the Columbia University Council for Research in the Social Sciences, acting on behalf of the Social Science Research Council of America, it was the first scholarly and authoritative analysis of the modern corporation, its position in society, and its relation to stockholders and investors.

In view of the magnitude of the problems to be solved, the temper of public opinion, the lack of any statutory powers vested in independent auditors, and the limited resources and influence of the Institute, its efforts to adjust to the new environment seem in retrospect like trying to bail out the ocean with a teaspoon. But to do them credit, the profession's leaders kept trying, and in the end, considering everything, they were surprisingly successful.

The Profession's Dilemma

The dilemma in which the profession found itself was well expressed in the report of the Institute's president, Charles B. Couchman, in 1932. Mr. Couchman was a partner of Barrow, Wade, Guthrie & Co., and author of *The Balance-Sheet*, a widely read text. He said, in part, with a note of barely concealed desperation:

> A constant problem of the accounting profession lies in the development of procedures to keep pace with changing economic conditions. It must be remembered that the fundamentals of accountancy were built up during a period when commercial transactions were simple

and direct. Within the past few decades the whole status of business organizations has changed. Transactions have become complicated beyond the conception of the businessman of the nineteenth century. These complexities were not scientifically planned in advance; they grew step by step as expediency dictated.

The accountant called upon to record these operations has had to adapt the established rules to the particular cases. As complexities grew, this adaptation of simple rules has become increasingly difficult and complicated. In the 20 years from 1910 to 1930 there was never a pause sufficient to allow a careful scientific devising of methods adequate to meet the changing conditions. Any attempt at this found that before such rules could be established business had already devised new complications....

Small wonder that accountants trying to record the results of these transactions should have been extremely puzzled to find a logical solution.... The accountant has faced a more difficult task throughout these years. The laws which he attempts to interpret as to their application to specific transactions have not even been enacted in any set form. He has been compelled to apply the variable laws of economics and the fundamental bases of accountancy rules to transactions which were beyond the contemplation of the businessman or the economist of a decade before.

Development of Accounting Principles

Mr. Couchman was succeeded as president of the Institute in 1932 by John F. Forbes of San Francisco.

Soon after his election, President Forbes appointed a new special committee on development of accounting principles with George O. May as chairman; May also continued as chairman of the committee on co-operation with stock exchanges.

The latter committee had been cautious in reporting the results of its work, pending final decisions on a number of matters by the New York Stock Exchange itself. However, in 1933, the committee reported, "The passage of the Securities Act seems to your committee to make a clearer definition of the responsibilities of auditors more imperatively necessary."

This conclusion was reinforced by a paper on "Public Interest in Accountancy" by the same A. A. Berle, Jr., who had co-authored *The Modern Corporation and Private Property*. His paper was presented at the 1933 annual meeting of the Institute, approximately four months after enactment of the Securities Act of 1933.

While Mr. Berle had accepted an invitation to speak at the annual meeting, other commitments had forced him to forgo a personal appearance at the last minute, and his paper was read by Walter A. Staub of New York.

The paper emphasized the growing importance of accounting in the economy. "It becomes plain," Berle said, "that accounting is rapidly ceasing to be in any sense of the word a private matter."

He then raised questions about several accounting practices: the cost-or-market method of valuing inventories in certain circumstances; the inclusion of non-recurring credits or charges in the income statement; changes in accounting methods between years, which might distort comparisons.

He stressed the desirability of comparisons of the results of one company with others in the same industry.

He continued, "How then should we handle the consistent development of principles of accounting, bearing in mind that these are likely to be subjected to the test of public opinion and public desirability as well as to their effectiveness in specified private transactions? For accountancy is now coming of age; there is no mistake about it."

Mr. Berle suggested that the first approach must be made by accountants themselves, acting through such organizations as the American Institute. But he questioned whether the job could be done by accountants alone—whether individual accountants could maintain completely impartial minds when under the instructions of a client. He predicted that a bureau would be set up, presumably in the Department of Commerce, to standardize accounting practices in various industries.

The speech was something of a shock to the Institute audience.

Mr. Staub, who had read the paper, also led the discussion.

He contended that the accounting practices which Berle questioned had already been generally eliminated, either through the efforts of the accounting profession itself or the Stock Exchange, or were in process of elimination through the co-operative efforts of the Institute and the Stock Exchange, the results of which were to be published in the near future.

Objecting to the proposal that accounting practices be standardized by a government agency, Mr. Staub alluded to the unsatisfactory experiences with government control of accounting under the Interstate Commerce Commission, in the utility field and under the bank regulatory agencies. Mr. Staub also challenged Mr. Berle's doubts about the independence and impartiality of public accountants.

Other members, however, urged the Institute to take affirmative action. One of these was Frederick B. Andrews of Chicago, who was head of his own local firm, highly articulate, idealistic and an independent thinker. Mr. Andrews said: "...unless the profession works out for itself something along the line that is suggested in Professor Berle's paper, the government may, and probably will." He urged official pronouncements by the Institute on the many phases of accounting procedure which were not yet crystallized "because different views are expressed by different accountants of equal standing . . . and there is no place where those views are finally reconciled. . . I hope. . . there may come to be a body of officially recognized promulgated views on what constitutes proper accounting procedures in certain directions."

The Stock-Exchange Correspondence

Soon after this discussion came a breakthrough of historic significance.

In 1934 Mr. May reported on behalf of both the special

committees on co-operation with stock exchanges and development of accounting principles.

The long negotiations with the Stock Exchange had been completed. Under date of January 21, 1934, the Institute published a pamphlet entitled "Audits of Corporate Accounts," containing the correspondence between the Institute's committee and the Committee on Stock List of the Exchange, with supplementary material. This document was circulated to all members of the Institute and given a wide general distribution. It marked a long step forward in the development of accounting principles and clarification of the responsibilities of auditors.

The document was signed by the six members of the Institute committee: Mr. May, as chairman, of Price Waterhouse & Co.; Archibald Bowman, of Peat, Marwick, Mitchell & Co.; Col. Arthur H. Carter, of Haskins & Sells; Charles B. Couchman, of Barrow, Wade, Guthrie & Co.; Samuel D. Leidesdorf, of S. D. Leidesdorf & Co.; and Walter A. Staub, of Lybrand, Ross Bros. & Montgomery.

The text of the document began with a letter from the Institute committee to the Exchange's Committee on Stock List, dated September 22, 1932 (16 months before its publication). This letter, after discussing the nature of accounting and the widespread misunderstanding of its significance and limitations, stressed the importance of the earning capacity of an enterprise as contrasted with the valuation of assets.

There followed a discussion of accepted alternative methods of accounting for depreciation and inventories, as examples.

The importance of judgment in accounting was stressed, as was the importance of the income account as contrasted with the balance sheet.

Alternative ways of improving the situation were considered: (1) selection by a competent authority, from presently accepted methods, of a detailed set of rules binding on all corporations of a given class; or (2) permission to corporations to choose their own methods within reasonable limits, but with disclosure of such methods and with consistency in their application from year to year.

The arguments against the first alternative were considered overwhelming. The second was strongly advocated.

Finally, a change in the form of audit certificate was recommended, so that auditors would specifically report whether the accounts were prepared in accordance with the methods of accounting regularly employed by the company, as filed with the Exchange and available to the public.

In an exhibit accompanying this letter five broad principles of accounting were proposed, as follows:

1. Unrealized profit should not be credited to income account of the corporation either directly or indirectly, through the medium of charging against such unrealized profits amounts which would ordinarily fall to be charged against income account. Profit is deemed to be realized when a sale in the ordinary course of business is effected, unless the circumstances are such that the collection of the sale price is not reasonably assured. An exception to the general rule may be made in respect of inventories in industries (such as the packing-house industry) in which owing to the impossibility of determining costs it is a trade custom to take inventories at net selling prices, which may exceed cost.

2. Capital surplus, however created, should not be used to relieve the income account of the current or future years of charges which would otherwise fall to be made thereagainst. This rule might be subject to the exception that where, upon reorganization, a reorganized company would be relieved of charges which would require to be made against income if the existing corporation were continued, it might be regarded as permissible to accomplish the same result without reorganization provided the facts were as fully revealed to and the action as formally approved by the shareholders as in reorganization.

3. Earned surplus of a subsidiary company created prior to acquisition does not form a part of the consolidated earned surplus of the parent company and subsidiaries; nor can any dividend declared out of such surplus properly be credited to the income account of the parent company.

4. While it is perhaps in some circumstances permissible to show stock of a corporation held in its own treasury as an asset, if adequately disclosed, the dividends on stock so held should not be treated as a credit to the income account of the company.

5. Notes or accounts receivable due from officers, employees, or

affiliated companies must be shown separately and not included under a general heading such as Notes Receivable or Accounts Receivable.

Another exhibit illustrated the nature of the statement which a corporation would file with the Exchange, disclosing the accounting methods it followed.

The Institute committee's recommendations were in general approved by the Stock Exchange and put into effect in 1933 —with one important exception. Listed companies were not required to disclose the accounting methods they followed.

Instead, the Exchange took two steps in January 1933. It required independently audited financial statements to be filed with listing applications and to be published annually thereafter. The Exchange also asked listed companies to secure from their auditors and furnish to the Exchange information as to the scope of their audit; the audit of subsidiaries; the auditor's access to essential information; whether the form of the financial statements was such as fairly to present the financial position and results of operations; whether the accounts reflected consistent application of the company's regular accounting system; and whether such system conformed to accepted accounting practices and was not inconsistent with the five broad principles proposed by the Institute committee (quoted above).

Nine large accounting firms responded jointly on February 24, 1933, to the inquiries on these six points, with the objective of further clarifying the responsibilities of the auditor. In this letter special reference was made to reliance on internal check and control, the primary responsibility of management for accounting judgments, and the concept of materiality.

In October 1933 the Committee on Stock List addressed a formal letter to the Governing Committee of the Exchange, enclosing the communication from the nine accounting firms. The letter recommended that the "five broad principles" of accounting be regarded "as so generally accepted that they should be followed by all listed companies." The letter then discussed further the appropriate scope of independent audit, and suggested development of a form of "audit report or certificate" more informative than those currently in use. The governing committee immediately approved these recommendations.

Throughout this correspondence were references, with general approval, to the revised Federal Reserve Board bulletin, published in 1929 under the title "Verification of Financial Statements."

The accountants pointed out that this bulletin was "framed to fit the case of borrowers engaged in business on a relatively small or medium-sized scale," and that in larger corporations, with effective systems of accounting and internal control, less extensive detailed checking was required by the independent auditor.

In a letter to the Exchange dated December 21, 1933, the Institute's committee stated that if "a defalcation should occur and escape detection, the accountants cannot be expected to accept any financial responsibility, but only to accept such blame as may attach to a possible error of judgment on their part with respect to their review of the methods and extent of the internal check and control. The effect on the reputation of a public accountant, arising from such an error of judgment, is serious and quite sufficient to ensure care on his part."

The Institute committee agreed with the Exchange, however, that the auditor should "accept the burden of seeing that the income received and the expenditures made are properly classified insofar as the facts are known to them or are ascertainable by reasonable inquiry."

A standard form of "accountants' report" (instead of "certificate") was then suggested by the Institute committee on cooperation with stock exchanges, which after modification was approved by the Controllers Institute of America and the Committee on Stock List. It read as follows:

To the XYZ Company:
  We have made an examination of the balance sheet of the XYZ Company as at December 31, 1933, and of the statement of income and surplus for the year 1933. In connection therewith, we examined or tested accounting records of the Company and other supporting evidence and obtained information and explanations from officers

and employees of the Company; we also made a general review of the accounting methods and of the operating and income accounts for the year, but we did not make a detailed audit of the transactions.

In our opinion, based upon such examination, the accompanying balance sheet and related statement of income and surplus fairly present, in accordance with accepted principles of accounting consistently maintained by the Company during the year under review, its position at December 31, 1933, and the results of its operations for the year.

Notes

1. It is contemplated that before signing a report of the type suggested, the accountant should have at least made an examination of the character outlined in the bulletin, "Verification of Financial Statements," as interpreted in the communication of the Committee on Stock List to the Governing Committee dated October 24, 1933.

2. The report should be addressed to the directors of the company or to the stockholders, if the appointment is made by them.

3. The statement of what has been examined would, of course, conform to the titles of the accounts or statements reported upon.

4. In the second sentence, any special forms of confirmation could be mentioned: e.g., "including confirmation of cash and securities by inspection or certificates from depositaries."

5. This certificate is appropriate only if the accounting for the year is consistent in basis with that for the preceding year. If there has been any material change either in accounting principles or in the manner of their application, the nature of the change should be indicated.

6. It is contemplated that the form of report would be modified when and as necessary to embody any qualifications, reservations or supplementary explanations.

All the material described above was included in the pamphlet, "Audits of Corporate Accounts," sent to all members. The "five basic principles" of accounting were approved by the Council of the Institute on October 15, 1934—more than a year after passage of the Securities Act of 1933.

Eight years had elapsed since George O. May first proposed voluntary action to deal with some of the same problems which that legislation was designed to solve.

The Securities Exchange Act of 1934 was approved June 6, 1934. Among other things this law created the Securities and Exchange Commission, to which was entrusted administration of both the 1934 Act and the Securities Act of 1933, which had first been administered by the Federal Trade Commission.

It is now appropriate to review briefly the accounting profession's involvement in these two vitally important pieces of legislation.

CHAPTER 11

Government Intervention in Accounting

THE downward plunge of securities prices in 1929 upset the banking and credit structure, and triggered the Great Depression of the 1930's. In both severity and duration it was the worst economic period the country had known.

Employees were laid off in droves; salary cuts were common. Jobs were almost impossible to find. Men sold apples on street corners. Mortgages were foreclosed on homes and farms. Breadlines and soup kitchens appeared in the land. Some banks failed, and depositors lost their money.

The people were in an ugly mood. Farmers rioted. The attitude of labor unions was ominous. To many intellectuals, especially the disenchanted young, Russian communism looked inviting.

The election of Franklin D. Roosevelt in 1932 marked a turning point. To rescue the economy the new President took steps which seemed radical in comparison with the policies of the three preceding administrations. The federal government took charge of the economy to a large extent. Some businessmen called the President "a traitor to his class," and his

"New Deal" was attacked as socialism. But Samuel Eliot Morison correctly says, "It was American as a bale of hay—an opportunist, rule-of-thumb method of curing deep-seated ills. Probably it saved the capitalist system in the United States."

Loose accounting practices had contributed to the debacle. *Laissez faire* had prevailed in broad areas of accounting practice as in the rest of the economy—though the Institute, with the backing of the Federal Reserve Board, had established authoritative guidelines in the field of auditing.

The indifference and caution of the New York Stock Exchange, prior to Hoxsey's involvement, had unduly delayed fruition of George May's farsighted plan to establish basic standards of corporate financial reporting. However, the Institute's correspondence with the Exchange, even before its publication in 1934, was made known informally to the Federal Trade Commission and to the Securities and Exchange Commission, and had a helpful influence on their administrative decisions. But publication of "Audits of Corporate Accounts" was a year too late to temper the harsh provisions of the Securities Act of 1933.

Among the masses of reform laws enacted in Roosevelt's first hundred days was this "Truth in Securities Act." It was the first federal law providing for independent audits of private corporations issuing securities in interstate commerce—though similar legislation had existed in Great Britain for nearly a century.

More significant, however, was the new Act's delegation of administrative authority to prescribe accounting principles and methods. The British Companies Acts had never gone that far.

The Securities Act of 1933

Despite William Z. Ripley, despite Berle and Means, despite the Pecora investigation, despite public demand for reform of the securities markets, the Institute had made no effective preparation to deal with legislation directed to that end.

When bills were introduced in both Houses of Congress—only a few months before final enactment of the Securities Act of 1933 on May 27 of that year—they came as something of a surprise to the profession. No policy positions, no strategy for dealing with such legislation, no constructive proposals for inclusion in such legislation had been worked out. The correspondence with the New York Stock Exchange was in midstream, and since final agreements were not to be reached until a year later, the Institute's suggestions could not be released, although some of them had been drafted in 1932.

Consequently, instead of having a hand in the drafting of the Securities Act, the profession had to react to drafts prepared by others.

When word came that legislation was expected, the Institute immediately created a committee to deal with it, and made arrangements with legal counsel in Washington, J. Harry Covington, to keep close watch over the bills to be introduced.

On this and on many other occasions the profession was fortunate in having the guidance of Judge Covington. He was a highly respected citizen of the nation's capital. He was an extremely able lawyer, of unimpeachable integrity. He also had access to influential members of Congress and of the executive branch.

Perhaps at Judge Covington's advice, the Institute did not appear formally at the hearings on the securities legislation. After all, the profession's record in developing standards of financial reporting was not impressive. Even the basic philosophy outlined in the Stock Exchange correspondence was not yet available for public reference. If official representatives of the Institute had testified at hearings, they might have been subjected to hostile questioning. This could have resulted in further adverse publicity, and possibly even more punitive legislation than that proposed.

In any case, the Institute's committee did study intently various drafts of the bill, exchanged correspondence among its

183

members, and held several meetings. The committee reported, with characteristic caution, that it had transmitted certain recommendations "through various channels . . . to persons influential in the administration and in Congress."

The Audit Provision

The first draft of the bill introduced in both houses contained only one reference to examinations by independent accountants. These were provided for only in case the Federal Trade Commission (which was originally designated to administer the legislation) desired to initiate an investigation of the affairs of any company about whose eligibility for registration there appeared to be any doubt upon the basis of the statements submitted with the application.

On the day following the publication of this draft, the Institute dispatched a letter to the appropriate Congressional committee, suggesting that it might be desirable to extend the provision for independent audit to all financial statements filed for purposes of registration. The letter explained that many reputable issuers of securities were already subjected to independent audits, either voluntarily or through stock-exchange requirements, and that the omission of such a provision from the "Truth in Securities" bill might be an advantage to less reputable issuers, over whom the government evidently desired particularly to exercise supervision. This letter—possibly followed by informal communications by Judge Covington—apparently made an impression on the House Committee on Interstate Commerce, since its bill was amended to include the audit provisions which finally became the law.

Meanwhile, Colonel Arthur H. Carter, who had become senior partner of Haskins & Sells, and was then president of the New York State Society of Certified Public Accountants, decided to testify at hearings before the Senate Committee on Banking and Currency.

Colonel Carter was a West Point graduate, a man of action and of military mien. He may not have been aware of what the Institute was doing, or he may have felt it was not enough. Although he had served for some years as a member of the Institute's executive committee, he was not one of the Institute's inner circle in 1933. He and Colonel Montgomery were both ardent advocates of policies which were highly unpopular with the majority of the Institute's Council at that time. Consequently the two Colonels were not in close touch with the Insitute's policymakers.

For whatever reason, on March 30, 1933, Carter dispatched a telegram to the chairman of the Senate Committee, congratulating him on the legislation, and offering the assistance of the New York State Society. He suggested in the telegram, among other things, that financial statements included in prospectuses should be certified by "accountants qualified under the laws of some state." As a result of this telegram Colonel Carter was invited to appear before the Senate Committee. On this occasion, the following fascinating exchanges took place:

MR. CARTER. At the end of subsection 4—A of section 5 on page 8 I would suggest that the following be added after the words "actual business":

"The accounts pertaining to such balance sheet, statement of income and surplus shall have been examined by an independent accountant and his report shall present his certificate wherein he shall express his opinion as to the correctness of the assets, liabilities, reserves, capital and surplus as of the balance sheet date and also the income statement for the period indicated."

That is, three years.

SENATOR BARKLEY. How much more and additional employment would that give to certified accountants?

MR. CARTER. Eighty-five per cent of the companies that are listed on the exchanges in New York today are examined.

SENATOR REYNOLDS. Do you think it proper to insert in there that these independent public accountants should be privileged to state their opinion as to the value of securities or the condition of the company?

MR. CARTER. We are unable to express an opinion as to the value of securities. I think the impression generally prevails that one who reads a balance sheet and an income statement regards the figures in such a statement as a defensible definitely ascertainable fact, whereas, as a matter of fact in reality it can only be an opinion based upon certain accounting assumptions which must be applied to the opinion of some individual as to values. . . .

SENATOR BARKLEY. In other words, after the statement has been filed by the officers of the company you want an independent organization to go over it and then report to the Federal Trade Commission whether that is correct or not?

MR. CARTER. I mean that that statement itself should have been the subject of an examination and audit by an independent accountant.

SENATOR GORE. Before filing?

MR. CARTER. Before filing.

SENATOR GORE. Is that patterned after the English system?

MR. CARTER. Yes, sir.

SENATOR REYNOLDS. Together with an opinion.

MR. CARTER. That is all they can give; that is all they can give. That is all anyone can give as to a balance sheet.

SENATOR WAGNER. Well, basically, are not these facts that have got to be alleged rather than an opinion?

MR. CARTER. Under the terms of the bill it has to be given under oath. I do not see that anyone can certify under oath that a balance sheet giving many millions of dollars of assets is as a matter of fact correct. He can state his opinion based upon a thorough investigation.

SENATOR BARKLEY. In other words, before the officers of the company that is issuing stock shall file that statement that is contained in this bill with the Federal Trade Commission the company must call in outside independent accountants and give them the job of going over it and passing on whether they have told the truth or not. Well, I am not for your amendment, I will say that now. . . .

MR. CARTER. . . . But there is in the bill a provision which gives the Commission a right to demand such an investigation and demand such a report as a result of such investigation. My point is to put that in the application in the beginning.

SENATOR BARKLEY. Do you not think it is more in the interest of the public that is to buy these securities, if there is to be any checkup or any guarantee as to the correctness, that it be done by some government agency rather than by some private association of accountants?

186

Mr. Carter. I think it is an impractical thing for the government agency to do it effectively.

Senator Reynolds. Why?

Mr. Carter. Because it involves such a large force. It involves the question of time.

Senator Reynolds. Well, it would not require any more time on the part of the government officials to make a checkup and audit than it would by private individuals, would it?

Mr. Carter. I think the public accountant is better equipped to do that than the average government agency would be able to do that. . . .

Senator Barkley. Is there any relationship between your organization with 2,000 members and the organization of controllers, represented here yesterday with 2,000 members?

Mr. Carter. None at all. We audit the controllers.

Senator Barkley. You audit the controllers?

Mr. Carter. Yes; the public accountant audits the controller's account.

Senator Barkley. Who audits you?

Mr. Carter. Our conscience.

Senator Barkley. I am wondering whether after all a controller is not for all practical purposes the same as an auditor, and must he not know something about auditing?

Mr. Carter. He is in the employ of the company. He is subject to the orders of his superiors.

Senator Barkley. I understand. But he has got to know something about auditing?

Mr. Carter. Yes.

Senator Barkley. He has got to know something about bookkeeping?

Mr. Carter. But he is not independent. . . .

Senator Reynolds. Why should your members ask that they be permitted and empowered to check these accounts?

Mr. Carter. Because it is generally regarded that an independent audit of any business is a good thing.

Senator Reynolds. All right. Then, after it goes to the Commission they have to check up to see who is right; they have to go through and audit again. There has to be a government audit, as suggested by Senator Barkley. Would it not be creating more difficulty and more expense and more time for the government if auditing organizations interest themselves in these various and sundry corporations? . . . Could they do it more economically than the government?

Mr. Carter. I think so.

Senator Gore. There would not be any doubt about that.

Senator Reynolds. Why?

Mr. Carter. We know the conditions of the accounts; we know the ramifications of the business; we know the pitfalls of the accounting structure that the company maintains. You have got every kind of business to deal with.

Senator Reynolds. Suppose that we decide in the final passage of this bill here to employ five or six hundred auditors from your organization, that would be all right, then, would it not?

Mr. Carter. I do not think the government could employ five or six hundred independent accountants.

Senator Reynolds. Why could they not?

Mr. Carter. I do not think the type of men that are in the public practice of accountancy would leave their present practice to go in the government employ....

Senator Adams. How much of a burden is this going to put on the comparatively small company? You were speaking a while back of the companies whose stocks are listed being independently audited. Now coming under the control of this bill are going to be thousands of small companies putting out an issue for their original financing. How much of a burden and cost is that going to put on them?

Mr. Carter. Very little measured in value to the investor and to them.

Senator Gore. What would be the range?

Mr. Carter. My experience would be that the average company pays around $500 or $600 or $700 for its auditing, that is, taking the large and small together.... And the largest organizations of our country do it and have been doing it for the last 15 years.

Senator Gore. Have had these independent audits made?

Mr. Carter. Have had these independent audits made, yes.

Senator Gore. But they have not been available for any public authority to examine and afford no safeguards?

Mr. Carter. They have been published in their annual reports and distributed to all of their stockholders, to the newspapers and anyone who calls for them.

Senator Gore. And have not done any good?

Mr. Carter. Yes, sir; I think they have.

Senator Gore. We have had all this debacle here in spite of that....

Mr. Carter. Eighty-five per cent of all the companies listed on the New York Stock Exchange have independent audits....

The Chairman. This bill covers all of them, those listed and those not listed.

MR. CARTER. Those are the ones that should be independently audited.

SENATOR REYNOLDS. Which ones?

MR. CARTER. Those that are not listed.

SENATOR REYNOLDS. All right; the ones that are not listed are the little fellows, are they not?

MR. CARTER. Yes, sir.

SENATOR REYNOLDS. Could they pay you $75 a day to go into their books? . . .

MR. CARTER. It does not cost them $75 a day.

SENATOR REYNOLDS. How much do you charge a day, then?

MR. CARTER. It would cost them an average of, I should say, $25 a day.

SENATOR KEAN. What big companies charge $25?

MR. CARTER. That is about an average.

SENATOR KEAN. Marwick, Mitchell & Co. cost more than that.

MR. CARTER. I am giving you an average.

SENATOR KEAN. Waterhouse & Co. cost more than that. What companies do you know of that charge only $25 a day?

MR. CARTER. I said that was an average for all. The rates range from $100 a day for a partner down to $15 and $20 a day for a junior. The average scale of rates that are charged are $35, $30, $25, $20, and $15, depending upon the class of men. . . .

SENATOR GORE. Don't you think we have got to establish some sort of standard of bookkeeping for different lines of industry before we can make any comparison?

MR. CARTER. I think it is very hard to establish a standard of bookkeeping. You can rely upon principles of accounting. . . .

SENATOR GORE. I mean the bookkeeping would be standard there so that you could compare one with another, and if they are not standardized give this Commission the power to require them to conform to it?

MR. CARTER. Take the automobile industry. You could have the reports of the various companies and you could find a great similarity in their bookkeeping.

SENATOR GORE. I know, but unless there is a substantial similarity I do not see how any comparison could be made. You take the textile companies: I presume they may have standards now that they all conform to, but if they do not, don't you think it would be necessary?

MR. CARTER. I think you would have to take each industry itself and . . . provide a system in which they would set up their accounts peculiar to that particular industry.

SENATOR GORE. That is what I mean, some sort of standard or set of principles so that each industry and individual instances in each industry could be compared with each other. . . . Is this mandatory in England, the requirement that an independent accountant shall check up?

MR. CARTER. All companies in England are required to be audited by an independent accountant, who is present at the stockholders' meeting and is available to answer any questions the stockholders wish to put to him. . . .

The House bill, which was finally enacted into law, contained an audit provision and additional provisions of vital interest to the accounting profession.

With a registration statement it was required that the following financial statements be filed:

(25) A balance sheet as of a date not more than 90 days prior to the date of the filing of the registration statement showing all of the assets of the issuer, the nature and cost thereof, whenever determinable, in such detail and in such form as the Commission shall prescribe (with intangible items segregated), including any loan in excess of $20,000 to any officer, director, stockholder or person directly or indirectly controlling or controlled by the issuer, or person under direct or indirect common control with the issuer. All the liabilities of the issuer in such detail and such form as the Commission shall prescribe, including surplus of the issuer showing how and from what sources such surplus was created, all as of a date not more than 90 days prior to the filing of the registration statement. If such statement be not certified by an independent public or certified accountant, in addition to the balance sheet required to be submitted under this schedule, a similar detailed balance sheet of the assets and liabilities of the issuer, certified by an independent public or certified accountant, of a date not more than one year prior to the filing of the registration statement, shall be submitted;

(26) A profit-and-loss statement of the issuer showing earnings and income, the nature and source thereof, and the expenses and fixed charges in such detail and such form as the Commission shall prescribe for the latest fiscal year for which such statement is available and for the two preceding fiscal years, year by year, or, if such issuer has been in actual business for less than three years, then for such time as the issuer has been in actual business, year by year. If the date of the filing of the registration statement is more than six months after the close of the last fiscal year, a statement from such

closing date to the latest practicable date. Such statement shall show what the practice of the issuer has been during the three years or lesser period as to the character of the charges, dividends or other distributions made against its various surplus accounts, and as to depreciation, depletion, and maintenance charges, in such detail and form as the Commission shall prescribe, and if stock dividends or avails from the sale of rights have been credited to income, they shall be shown separately with a statement of the basis upon which the credit is computed. Such statement shall also differentiate between any recurring and nonrecurring income and between any investment and operating income. Such statement shall be certified by an independent public or certified accountant.

If the proceeds, or any part of the proceeds, of the security to be issued is to be applied directly or indirectly to the purchase of any business, a profit-and-loss statement of such business certified by an independent public or certified accountant, meeting the requirements of paragraph (26) of this schedule, for the three preceding fiscal years, together with a balance sheet, similarly certified, of such business, meeting the requirements of paragraph (25) of this schedule of a date not more than 90 days prior to the filing of the registration statement or at the date such business was acquired by the issuer if the business was acquired by the issuer more than 90 days prior to the filing of the registration statement.

These provisions reflected reactions to some of the financial-reporting practices criticized by Ripley, Berle and Means, and others.

Of special concern to the accountants were the following provisions authorizing the Commission to prescribe accounting rules:

> Among other things, the Commission shall have authority, for the purposes of this title, to prescribe the form or forms in which required information shall be set forth, the items or details to be shown in the balance sheet and earning statement, and the methods to be followed in the preparation of accounts, in the appraisal or valuation of assets and liabilities, in the determination of depreciation and depletion, in the differentiation of recurring and nonrecurring income, in the differentiation of investment and operating income, and in the preparation, where the Commission deems it necessary or desirable, of consolidated balance sheets or income accounts of any person directly or indirectly controlling or controlled by the issuer,

or any person under direct or indirect common control with the issuer; ...

Most alarming of all were the liability provisions.

These provisions, it must be remembered, were enacted in a punitive atmosphere. They were, and continue to be, a cause of grave concern to the profession for several reasons: first, they put the burden of proof on the defendant-accountant rather than on the plaintiff-investor; second, the plaintiff need not prove reliance on the statements alleged to be false and misleading; and third, no limitation is placed on the amount of damages for which a defendant-accountant might be held liable— conceivably it could be the total amount of an issue of securities.

In commenting on these harsh provisions, George O. May said:

> I cannot believe that a law is just or can long be maintained in effect which deliberately contemplates the possibility that a purchaser may recover from a person from whom he has not bought, in respect of a statement which at the time of his purchase he had not read, contained in a document which he did not then know to exist, a sum which is not to be measured by injury resulting from falsity in such statement. Yet, under the Securities Act as it stands, once a material misstatement or omission is proved, it is no defense to show that the plaintiff had no knowledge of the statement in question or of the document in which it was contained, or that the fall in the value of the security which he has purchased is due, not to the misstatement or omission complained of, but to quite different causes, such as the natural progress of invention, or even fire or earthquake. The Securities Act not only abandons the old rule that the burden of proof is on the plaintiff, but the doctrine of contributory negligence and the seemingly sound theory that there should be some relation between the injury caused and the sum to be recovered.

On the other side of the question was a remark by James M. Landis of the Federal Trade Commission, one of the early administrators of the Securities Act. He said at a meeting of the New York State Society of Certified Public Accountants, late in 1933:

It has been said, and very rightly in my humble opinion, that accounting is after all a matter of opinion rather than anything else. But though this may be true I have still to see the case of a prospective investor being offered a balance sheet and having it carefully explained to him that this or that item is merely an opinion or deduction from a series of other opinions mixed in with a few acknowledged facts. But the fact is that accountancy has paraded too largely as being an exact science. Accountancy, as distinguished from law, has generally been portrayed as an exact science, and its representations have been proffered to the unlearned as representations of fact and not of opinion. If it insists upon such fact representations, it is, of course, fair that it should be burdened with the responsibility attendant upon such a portrayal of its results.

Administration of the Act

Following enactment of the 1933 Act, close co-operative relations were established by the Institute with the Federal Trade Commission, which initially had responsibility for administration of the law. The Commission was glad to have the help of experienced accountants in dealing with some of the technical problems confronting it, and the Institute had considerable influence on the regulations dealing with the form of financial statements, the form of accountants' certificates and related matters.

The Securities Exchange Act

A little more than a year after the 1933 Act became law, the Securities Exchange Act of 1934 was approved on June 6, 1934. It created the Securities and Exchange Commission, which was charged with administration of the 1933 Act as well as the subsequent one.

When the 1934 Act was under consideration by Congress

the American Institute of Accountants submitted a memorandum brief for incorporation in the record of the hearings.

The memorandum objected to the liability provisions of the proposed legislation, particularly the "immeasurable liability" to which an accountant would be exposed.

The memorandum also questioned the proposal that quarterly reports be certified by independent public accountants. It suggested that annual independent audits should be sufficient, and pointed out that quarterly statements could not be as accurate as those for longer periods of time.

In addition, the Institute challenged a provision giving the Commission power to prescribe uniform accounting for industry, pointing out that attempted uniformity in the accounting of public utilities and railroads had not resulted in more dependable financial statements in those industries; on the contrary there had been a greater advance in the accounting practices of representative unregulated companies.

In the law as enacted certified quarterly statements were not required. Every listed company was required to file "such annual reports, certified if required by the rules and regulations of the Commission by independent public accountants, and such quarterly reports, as the Commission may prescribe."

The Commission did choose to require certification of annual reports by independent auditors.

However, the power of the Commission to prescribe accounting methods was retained. The liability provisions were somewhat less harsh than those of the 1933 Act.

The SEC and the Institute

The Institute immediately appointed a special committee on co-operation with the new Securities and Exchange Commission.

The committee waited upon Joseph P. Kennedy, the Commission's first chairman, to offer its co-operation, and was cordially received.

Another member of the SEC was James M. Landis, who had moved over from the Federal Trade Commission, and who was to become chairman when Mr. Kennedy resigned in the fall of 1935.

In the first years, the administrators of the two acts were preoccupied with organizational problems, the development of rules, forms and procedures, prosecution of flagrant violators of the law, and encouragement of public acceptance of the new state of affairs.

Institute members had long sessions with the SEC staff, working on regulations, forms and procedures.

Speeches by SEC spokesmen were conciliatory. In October 1933, Mr. Landis told the New York State Society of Certified Public Accountants that misconceptions about the Securities Act seemed to abound. He suggested that the liability provisions of Section 11 were not as terrifying as commonly supposed, that exposure to liability equivalent to the total offering price of an issue was more theoretical than real, and that no extraordinary principle of legal liability had been introduced in the new law.

Although in some quarters there was a disposition to exercise the Commission's authority by prescribing accounting principles and methods, it was finally decided—partly due to the persuasiveness of Institute representatives—not to do so. Rather the Commission adopted a policy of gradual improvement, leaving to the accounting profession the initiative in proposing preferred accounting principles to the extent to which it was able and willing to do so.

In January 1935, SEC Commissioner George C. Matthews addressed the Illinois Society of Certified Public Accountants. He, too, was reassuring. Most of his talk consisted of interpretation of the Commission's rules, forms, and instructions.

Significantly, he stressed that the SEC had "carefully avoided requiring uniformity of accounting either as to matters of classification or as to matters of principle."

On the question of independence, he said that "a nominal

stock holding which obviously would not influence the judgment of an accountant, would not, I believe, affect the accountant's independence. . . I think it would be clear that the mere holding of a small interest does not destroy the independence of the accountant. . . ."

Disclosure of Sales

Of special interest, from an historical point of view, was a recommendation by the Institute's committee that the regulations should not require disclosure in detail of sales, cost of sales, and gross profit in all cases. Actually the Commission did include in its regulations a provision that any information might be kept in the confidential files of the Commission if the company concerned showed reason why public disclosure of the data might injure it.

The Institute committee's objections to disclosure of sales information were that it might be detrimental to the interests of investors, and that the information itself might be misleading. The first point was supported by an argument that companies would be at a competitive disadvantage if their sales and profit margins were known to foreign competitors, or to other companies not subject to the same disclosure requirements. It was also asserted that disclosure of sales volume and profit margins might attract competition detrimental to the stockholders of companies which were pioneering in certain fields.

The fear that sales and profit information might be misleading was supported by the argument that it would be impossible to give stockholders data on such points as individual sales policies, selling prices, seasonal businesses and other factors which might underlie what seemed to be a sales trend. In some industries, it was said, larger sales might be shown in a year in which less business was actually transacted.

The Institute committee also raised the question whether selling and administrative expenses should be required to be disclosed: "The important disclosure, after all, is the profit arising from the normal or ordinary operation of the business of the particular company." The committee suggested that the interests of investors would be best served by permitting listed companies the following three alternatives:

1. Show sales, and combine cost of goods sold with selling, administrative and general expenses;

2. Show sales first as a memorandum only, and then begin the statement with the net operating profit from the normal or ordinary operation of the business of the company;

3. Show as the first item the gross profit and deduct therefrom the selling, administrative and general expenses.

Today this seems an astonishingly conservative position, but it also serves as a bench mark from which to measure the extraordinary progress that has been made in financial reporting and disclosures to investors in the United States.

Hundreds of companies requested confidential treatment of sales information, but after extensive hearings the SEC denied such requests. The requirement for public disclosure of sales soon became universally accepted.

Independence

The fact that the Securities Acts provided for certification of financial statements by "an independent public or certified accountant" explicitly introduced into law for the first time the concept of independence. This concept had long been accepted in professional literature and in the practice of most CPA firms, but it had never been clearly defined.

The Federal Trade Commission's first regulations under the 1933 Act provided that an accountant would not be considered independent with respect to any person (registrant) in whom he had *any* interest, directly or indirectly, or with whom he was connected as an officer, agent, employee, promoter, underwriter, trustee, partner, director, or person performing similar function. [Emphasis supplied.]

When the Securities and Exchange Commission was formed in 1934 and assumed administration of the two Securities Acts, it apparently was persuaded that the provision with respect to financial interest was a little harsh. As Commissioner Matthews observed in his Illinois speech, ownership of a few shares in a client corporation would not necessarily impair an accountant's independence. In regulations issued in 1936 the rule was changed to proscribe any *substantial* interest, direct or indirect.

In addition the amended regulations provided that in determining whether an accountant might, in fact, be not independent with respect to a particular registrant, the Commission would give appropriate consideration to all relevant circumstances, including relationships between the accountant and client not necessarily confined to the relationships existing in connection with the filing of reports with the Commission.

Interpretation of "substantial," however, caused some difficulty. In Accounting Series Release No. 2, issued May 6, 1937, it was stated that an accountant could not be deemed to be independent if he held an interest in a registrant that was significant with respect to its total capital or his own personal fortune. The criterion of a significant or substantial interest was held in a test case to be more than one per cent of an accountant's personal fortune.

This evoked some grumbling among accountants who felt that independence was a state of mind and the equivalent of integrity, and that a small financial interest in a client corporation would not affect a CPA's judgment. But the SEC's rules on independence were to be tightened even more in the years ahead, as will be reported later in this book.

A Chief Accountant Appointed

Numerous questions arose during the early years of the 1933 and 1934 Acts requiring interpretation of their provisions and the related regulations. Since many of these involved accounting questions, the Commission decided to create the office of Chief Accountant.

Carman G. Blough was appointed to this new post. He had served in the SEC as security analyst and as assistant director of the registration division. He held CPA certificates of Wisconsin and North Dakota, and had served at one time as a member of the Wisconsin State Board of Accountancy. He had taught accounting at several universities, and was head of the accounting department at the University of North Dakota for four years. For more than five years he was a member of the staff of the Wisconsin Tax Commission, and for two more years was secretary of the Wisconsin State Board of Public Affairs, in charge of budgeting and auditing for all state departments. He was destined to have great influence on the technical standards of the profession in the years ahead.

Honeymoon Ends

In January 1935, Mr. Landis spoke before the New York State Society again, and once more he was conciliatory. He praised the CPA organizations for the help they had given the Commission in drafting corporate-reporting regulations. This co-operation, he said, was vastly different from the kind of "co-operation" involving only the pretense of joint effort and not its real content: "Instead, the story is one of long days and long nights of work."

He pleased the audience by saying that the SEC did not prescribe the form of the accountant's certificate: "Instead we ask for a certificate that shall be illuminating both as to the scope of the audit and the quality of the accounting principles employed by the registrant."

Mr. Landis defended the requirement that gross sales and cost of goods sold be disclosed—to which the Institute had taken some exception. However, he softened his defense by recognizing that in unusual circumstances non-disclosure of those items might be justified, due to the extraordinarily competitive nature of the registrant's business.

In closing this speech, Mr. Landis exhorted the accounting profession to continue its earnest co-operation with the Commission: "You will still be more than welcomed at Washington for both your help, your criticisms and your inquiries . . . we need you as you need us. . . you must, for your own good, come when we need you."

Some eight months later, in October 1935, shortly after his appointment as chairman of the SEC, Mr. Landis addressed the American Management Association in New York, and won the applause of this audience by stressing the efforts of the SEC to reduce the expense of registration.

In the course of these remarks, he said, "Accounting costs have already shown a significant decline. American business generally seems now to have accepted the theory of the independent audit. . . . Our continuing discussions with the accounting profession have brought us to grips with the question of what additional tasks must be assumed by accountants as a consequence of the requirements of the Securities Act. Certain initial costs will inevitably be incurred where independent auditing has not in the past been the customary practice of the corporation." But even here, he said, where other checks or safeguards were available, so far as past financial statements were concerned, exceptions could be made.

Everything seemed to be going well, so far as the accounting profession was concerned. The SEC seemed friendly, tolerant and flexible. The Institute was pleased and proud to have such a sound working relationship with the Commission. But apparently the attitudes of some accountants in dealing with actual cases before the SEC were irritating its members. In a speech to the Investment Bankers Association of America on December 4, 1936, Mr. Landis spoke of accountants in less endearing terms:

> The impact of almost daily tilts with accountants, some of them called leaders in their profession, often leaves little doubt that their loyalties to management are stronger than their sense of responsibility to the investor. Such an experience does not lead readily to acquiescence in the plea recently made by one of the leaders of the accounting profession that the form of statement can be less rigidly controlled and left more largely to professional responsibility alone. Simplicity and more adequate presentation is of course an end much to be desired, but a simplicity that misleads is not to be tolerated. The choice here of more or less regulation is an open one for the profession. It is a "Hobson's choice" for government.

This blunt expression of disenchantment evoked a response from the Institute's special committee on co-operation with SEC.

Rodney F. Starkey, of Price Waterhouse, the committee's chairman, telephoned Mr. Landis, saying that his remarks had created considerable disturbance; that if he was right the Institute's committee "had a job to undertake," but that if he was wrong, in all fairness he should avoid undue criticism in the future.

Mr. Landis expressed a desire to be helpful, and suggested consultation with the Commission's Chief Accountant. The result was an arrangement under which Carman Blough would refer to the Institute's committee major accounting questions on which the SEC felt that it should take issue with the accountants who had signed the statements.

Mr. Starkey subsequently reported that, although even after this arrangement SEC spokesmen had made speeches critical of accountants, Mr. Blough had indicated a desire to co-operate with the Institute, and had submitted several questions which had arisen in actual cases, to which the Institute committee had responded.

While the short-lived honeymoon was over, co-operation on

brass-tacks problems was taking the place of expressions of mutual esteem.

In the years ahead SEC spokesmen alternated between praise of the profession's substantive contributions to improvement of corporate reporting, and frank criticism of the profession's failures of omission or commission. The criticism was sometimes mingled with thinly veiled threats that the Commission might exercise its latent powers to prescribe accounting principles and methods if the profession did not move forward more rapidly.

The influence of the SEC on accounting and auditing standards and practice was tremendous. Without doubt the Securities Acts strengthened the position of independent auditors in insisting that clients follow sound principles and make adequate disclosures. The Commission's requirements also greatly increased the volume of auditing engagements. And it must be conceded that the SEC's goad prodded the profession to make improvements both in accounting and auditing that otherwise might have taken longer to achieve.

At times, the Commission's words and actions have seemed unnecessarily harsh. The liability provisions of the 1933 Act are regarded to this day as punitive and inequitable. But in spite of all the tensions, interspersed with truly constructive and friendly co-operation, corporate accounting and professional auditing remain in the private sector.

The Institute's Stance on Accounting Principles

As mentioned earlier, at the 1934 annual meeting of the Institute Mr. May reported not only for the committee on co-operation with stock exchanges, but also as chairman of the special committee on development of accounting principles. In the latter report the committee made the following six points:

1. Principles of accounting cannot be arrived at by pure reasoning, but must find their justification in practical wisdom.

2. The Institute should proceed with caution in selecting from among various commonly employed methods those which should be accorded the standing of principles or rules of accounting.

3. It was desirable to secure the acceptance of any rules or principles laid down by the Institute also by the courts or by independent bodies having some regulatory powers or authority.

4. The concurrence of the Federal Reserve Board and the Federal Trade Commission in the definition of the scope of a balance-sheet or financial audit and the agreement on principles reached in the correspondence between the Institute and the New York Stock Exchange constituted precedents which the committee proposed to follow as far as possible.

5. Under the Securities Acts, the SEC had wide powers to prescribe methods of accounting, and close co-operation between the Institute and that Commission was desirable.

6. The Stock Exchange had approved the five general principles submitted by the Institute's committee on co-operation with that body, and these "rules or principles" should be adopted by the Institute. (The Council formally approved these principles, and the members at the 1934 annual meeting approved all acts of the Council.)

In the same report, the committee further recommended that the Institute should go on record as to the treatment to be applied to a series of interrelated transactions, comprising (1) the issue of capital stock of a corporation ostensibly for property; (2) the donation of a part of such stock to the corporation; (3) the sale of a part of the donated stock for cash by the corporation.

The committee said that in the past it had not been uncommon to charge to property account the par value of stock issued, and credit to surplus the cash received from the sale by the corporation of the stock donated to it. "It is clear, however, that such a procedure results in an overstatement of the property account and of the surplus account." The committee, therefore, recommended that formal approval be given to the following statement:

> If capital stock is issued nominally for the acquisition of property, and it appears that at about the same time, and pursuant to a previous agreement or understanding, some portion of the stock so issued is donated to the corporation, it is not permissible to treat the par value of the stock nominally issued for the property as the cost of that property. If stock so donated is subsequently sold, it is not permissible to treat the proceeds as a credit to surplus of the corporation.

The Council also approved this statement, and the Council's action was approved by the members at the annual meeting.

A start had been made by the accounting profession—none too soon—in establishing rules and principles governing corporate financial reports. The need for continued effort in this direction was stressed by John Forbes in his final address as president of the Institute at the 1934 meeting:

> Everywhere we find questions arising of the utmost importance having to do with accounting principles, which by reason of no particular thought being given to them by an authoritative body, are vexing us frequently. . . . The committee on professional ethics has been confronted by some of the most awkward questions, questions which cannot be solved by a mere technical committee for the reason that custom has made many solutions acceptable, and the most desirable solution would be largely a matter of opinion. These questions must be studied and must be solved, and I very much feel that if we do not take the matter in hand forthwith governmental and other agencies will usurp the prerogatives which are certainly our own. I ask that your best thought be devoted to this very serious situation.

Efforts to develop technical standards did continue at an

accelerated pace, though for the next few years they were unco-ordinated and somewhat sporadic.

Another Revision of the Federal Reserve Bulletin

In 1935 a special committee, headed by Samuel J. Broad, of Peat, Marwick, Mitchell & Co., undertook another revision of the Federal Reserve Bulletin, the second edition of which had appeared six years earlier. An introductory section was inserted, dealing with the general philosophy of accounts, their significance, limitations and basis, much along the lines of the correspondence with the Stock Exchange. Reasonable elasticity in application of the audit program outlined was said to be permissible. A section was added indicating modifications usual in examinations of larger companies, with adequate systems of internal check and control, as contrasted with examinations of smaller companies with less extensive systems of internal control.

A draft of the revised bulletin was approved and sent to representative accountants throughout the country, which resulted in numerous suggestions.

This work was completed in 1936. A second draft of the bulletin was submitted to the Securities and Exchange Commission and the Federal Reserve Board. It was suggested that this latest edition should not be issued under the sponsorship of the Federal Reserve Board, but be published by the Institute itself. This proposal was agreeable to the Federal Reserve Board, and a letter was received from the secretary of the Board acknowledging that the latest bulletin, issued under the title "Examination of Financial Statements by Certified Public Accountants," superseded the 1929 edition.

Twenty-six thousand copies of the new bulletin were distributed to members, state societies, and others interested.

Accounting Terminology

Accounting terminology had been a matter of concern for decades. Successive committees struggled sporadically to produce definitions of the hundreds of words and phrases in the accountant's vocabulary.

In 1921, a new special committee on terminology was created to carry on this effort. This committee first selected between 2,000 and 3,000 words and phrases which seemed to require definition. Then it proceeded to define them. As definitions were agreed on, they were published from time to time in *The Journal of Accountancy,* in the hope of attracting comment and criticism.

When it is considered that all this work was done by volunteer committee members, without compensation and without any technical staff assistance, it is not surprising either that progress was slow or that the results were not universally acceptable.

It was not until 1929 that anything approaching a "final" report was prepared.

In that year the special committee on terminology, then headed by Walter Mucklow (one of whose members was William B. Franke, who later became Secretary of the Navy), assembled in a pamphlet the tentative definitions which had been published in the *Journal* through the years. The pamphlet was exposed for comment and criticism by members of the profession.

It took two more years to give effect to suggestions received, to fill in gaps, revise and refine.

In 1931 the long-awaited book on accounting terminology was published by The Century Company under contract with the Institute. The introduction made it clear that the definitions were purely tentative and were in no sense an official pronouncement of the Institute. Said the executive committee, "The book has aroused a good deal of comment and the

Arthur Lowes Dickinson

Group including officials of 1904 International Congress of Accountants at St. Louis. Seated, far left, George Wilkinson; second from left Robert H. Montgomery; center Arthur Lowes Dickinson; standing rear, far right, George O. May.

George O. May

W. Sanders Davies
President, 1897- 1898 and 1916- 1918

Frederick H. Hurdman, President, 1928-1930

John F. Forbes, President, 1932-1934

Robert H. Montgomery
President, 1912-1914 and 1935-1937

Officers of Federation of Societies of Public Accountants in the United States, 1902. Front row, left to right, George Wilkinson,
Secretary; J. MacRae, President; Robert H. Montgomery, Treasurer.

sale has been encouraging." Not all the comment was favorable, but at least a start had been made.

Savings and Loan Audits

In 1936 a special committee on savings and loan accounts, after a conference with the Federal Home Loan Bank Board, undertook to draft a proposed program of audit and form of auditor's certificate for use in conjunction with audits of savings and loan associations insured by the federal government. This was the first of a series of audit programs and audit guides for special industries.

Inventories

A special committee on inventories, which had been in consultation with the American Petroleum Institute's Committee on Uniform Methods of Oil Accounting since 1933, presented a lengthy report in 1936, reciting the effort to bring about a desirable degree of uniformity in valuation of oil companies' inventories.

The Institute committee's conclusion was that the "last-in, first-out method for the valuation of oil-company inventories constitutes an acceptable accounting principle for those companies which apply it consistently from year to year; . . . It is important however that full and clear disclosure, in their published financial statements, be made by the companies adopting it, both as to the fact of its adoption and the manner of its application, including information as to the period adopted for the unit of time within which the goods 'last in' are deemed to be the 'first out,' that is, whether the fiscal year or shorter or longer period."

A Changed Approach

In the 20 years from 1916 to 1936 the accounting profession's approach to technical standards underwent a radical change. From a permissive, subjective, every-man-for-himself approach, there was a strong movement toward acceptance of responsibility for the promulgation of standards of general application.

To be sure, the change was partly a reaction to outside pressures—with the notable exceptions of the 1929 and 1936 revisions of the 1917 Federal Reserve Bulletin. These were undertaken at the Institute's initiative, and they stood the profession in good stead shortly after their completion: the 1929 version in the negotiations with the Stock Exchange, and the 1936 version a few years later when public criticism was again at a high pitch.

Admittedly, efforts to deal with specific accounting problems were slow and fragmentary. Numerous volunteer committees worked on various technical questions without overall planning or co-ordination.

However, it must be recalled that even in 1936 the Institute's membership was only about 2,500. By present standards its financial resources were pitifully small. It had no technical staff whatever. And it had only modest influence either in Washington or in the financial community.

In these circumstances the achievements of the second decade of this period, particularly, are impressive. A comparatively small number of able leaders virtually reshaped the accounting profession and set its sights on new and higher goals.

CHAPTER 12

The Burgeoning Tax Practice

W HILE auditing and financial reporting occupied the center of the accounting stage, the tax practice of certified public accountants was growing steadily.

The wartime excess-profits tax and rising income-tax rates rapidly increased the demand for skilled assistance in the preparation of returns of corporations and individuals, and even more in representation of taxpayers in disputes with the Bureau of Internal Revenue, as it was then called.

Few of the creators of the income-tax law had any conception of the difficulty of measuring business income for short time periods. Most people, then as now, thought of income and expense in terms of cash receipts and disbursements. The accrual concept was not readily grasped, even by most lawyers or by many of the legislators and administrators of the law. This blind spot was clearly evident in the 1909 Corporation Excise Tax Law, and it persisted in the later income-tax legislation.

The result, inevitably, was a tangle of controversy between taxpayers and the government, mostly over questions which only accountants could resolve. The law said that the tax was to be based on methods of accounting normally employed by taxpayers unless such methods did not clearly reflect net income. This obviously left a large door wide open for differences of opinion. Taxpayers preferred accounting methods which minimized or deferred the tax. The Bureau assumed that methods which clearly reflected net income were those that yielded the most tax most quickly.

In the early years there were no well-established precedents to go by. Regulations and court decisions had to be built up by trial and error. The Bureau itself at first was hesitant and cautious. William A. Paton, who served for a time as head of the Special Assignment Section of the Bureau's Income-Tax Unit, has written: "Back in 1919 the Bureau of Internal Revenue was in a relatively humble mood, and was really trying to learn something about good financial and accounting practice. At one time I had a group of seven or eight (including a couple of CPAs) out on a field trip of several weeks, with the objective of learning how top executives and their accounting staffs regarded such special problems as officers' salaries, amortization of war facilities, inventory valuation (including the handling of various classes of manufacturing overhead), depreciation, bad debts and other special problems."

While the rules were being formulated tax practice was largely a free-for-all. Small businessmen who had never felt the need for sound bookkeeping suddenly found the absence of good records costly when tax time came around. Bookkeepers and accountants in industry quit their jobs and opened offices as public accountants to take advantage of the demand for tax service. Installing bookkeeping systems, and sometimes "writing up" the books monthly, preparing financial statements and tax returns, and arguing with revenue agents who proposed additional assessments, constituted a type of accounting practice that offered a good living—and even an occasional "killing" if a big case could be won on a contingent-fee basis.

Many revenue agents saw that there was more money in working for taxpayers than for the government, and they too became public accountants.

Large numbers of these practitioners became CPAs in order to enhance their status. Over the years many of the more ambitious were also admitted to the Bar, in order to handle legal aspects of taxation, and to represent their clients in court as well as at the administrative level. In time these CPA-lawyers —sometimes called "dual practitioners"—reached significant numbers.

Many of the accountants practicing as individuals, or in very small firms, serving the small-business community mainly in the tax field, had little interest in the auditing and financial-reporting problems which were of vital importance to the larger accounting firms—both local and national—whose clients issued securities to the public or borrowed habitually from banks. Thus there developed a dual orientation in the profession, many members becoming engrossed with taxes and general accounting services—with a strong inclination toward "advocacy" of the clients' interests—and many others mainly concerned with independent audits for third-party use, which required maintenance of independence and objectivity.

This is not to say that the larger accounting firms, local and national, were not also concerned with the tax problems of their corporate clients. They were. Some of their partners specialized in taxes. But most of the large firms were controlled by partners trained as auditors, and their tax practice was secondary.

Proposed Attestation of Tax Returns

It was one of these men, Edward E. Gore, head of his own flourishing local firm in Chicago, and later to become president of the Institute, who first suggested an adaptation of the auditor's approach to tax returns.

As early as 1917, at the fall meeting of the Institute's Council, Mr. Gore proposed consideration of a plan whereby the Treasury Department might rely on statements of accountants in respect of income-tax and excess-profits-tax returns. He suggested that if such returns were certified by accredited accountants, the Internal Revenue might not have to conduct audits, which would save the government a considerable amount of money, and also alleviate the acute shortage of manpower. One method of accomplishing the desired result, he suggested, would be to have accountants sworn as officers or employees of the government.

Mr. Gore's plan was opposed on a number of grounds: first, that it might lead to a federal register of accountants, such as suggested in 1916 by Mr. Hurley of the Federal Trade Commission. The Institute's committee on federal legislation had killed this idea. Second, it was asserted that under Civil Service Commission rules it would be impossible to appoint practicing accountants as employees of the government. George O. May stated that he had discussed the same question with a former Commissioner of Internal Revenue, who had expressed the wish that it were feasible for him to accept reports by accountants, but had concluded that it was altogether impracticable.

The matter was referred to the executive committee for further consideration, from whence it never again emerged.

From time to time in later years, however, the idea of CPAs' attesting to tax returns was revived, always to be buried under the opposition of a vast majority of CPAs in tax practice who preferred to regard themselves as "advocates," and their relations with the Internal Revenue as "adversary proceedings."

In the course of time, incidentally, the government did require attestation by practitioners who prepared claims for refund or protests, regarding their knowledge of the facts.

Growing Complexities

Before long the Institute's committee on federal legislation found itself preoccupied with tax matters almost to the exclusion of anything else.

New technical provisions involving complicated accounting questions were continually introduced in the tax system—for example, the installment method of accounting; the provision against unreasonable accumulation of surplus; the undistributed-profits tax; excess-profits taxes with the required determination of invested capital and special relief provisions; the unjust-enrichment tax, and the determination of earnings and investment for purposes of calculating March 1, 1913, values.

The Institute's committee tried to help the Treasury Department and the Congress to frame such technical provisions in workable form. The practicing CPAs had to struggle with their application.

The difficulty of tax practice was increased by the centralization of tax administration in Washington, where all protests against revenue agents' reports were filed and heard. Many CPAs, from all parts of the country, became virtual commuters to the nation's capital.

A perennial problem was the difficulty of getting all returns completed by the required filing date. Most companies and most individuals automatically adopted the calendar year as their fiscal year. March 15 was the date when all tax returns were due. The amount of work which had to be done in two-and-a-half months was then, and always has been, too great to be completed satisfactorily.

For the first time in 1918, and almost annually thereafter, the Institute formally requested the Commissioner to grant extensions of time for filing returns. The 1918 request was granted, but in later years, depending in part on circumstances and in part on the attitudes of successive commissioners, similar requests met with varying degrees of success and failure.

In 1920, for example, the Institute's committee on federal legislation reported that continuing efforts were being made to persuade the Bureau of Internal Revenue to give extensions of time for filling tax returns due in March. "If the Commissioner would let it be known . . . that tentative returns will be accepted on March 15 to be followed by final returns later, a great burden of anxiety would be removed from taxpayers, especially accountants, upon whom rests the duty of preparing most of the complicated returns."

Extensions were being granted, but never until the last minute. The committee addressed a letter to all members of the Institute to acquire statistics, which indicated that on March 1, 100 offices had 7,404 returns yet to be filed, of which 953 were corporation returns calling for consolidated statements.

Many suggestions have been made to solve this problem once and for all—such as staggered filing dates—but for one reason or another none has proved acceptable.

Ethical Problems

Ethical problems developing in tax practice also required attention.

In 1919 the president, Waldron H. Rand, in his address at the annual meeting, said, "Probably there were never before so many and such strong temptations besetting the citizens of this country in their determination of net income and of balance sheets—temptations to twist and to turn, to magnify and to minify, in attempting to decrease the amount of indebtedness to the government. Professed ignorance of the law's meaning and professed inability to understand the forms for returns prepared by government have furnished a multitude with excuses for doubtful and wrongful returns. Comparisons by government examiners frequently require a demand for explanations, and then there comes an increased dependence upon the public accountant to straighten things out. Not infrequently, this proper care results in great saving to the taxpayer who previously had been depending only upon his own office staff."

However, Mr. Rand referred to a disposition by some accountants—especially some so-called "tax experts" whose ideals and ethics were not in keeping with those of the profession—to adopt a practice in regard to fees which was open to criticism. "Our minds must be set against contingent fees, so-called, as unprofessional and reprehensible."

Perhaps as a result of President Rand's exhortation, a rule against contingent fees was adopted with this qualification: "This rule shall be construed as inhibiting only service in which the accountant's findings or expert opinion might be influenced by considerations of personal financial interest in alternative findings or opinion." This left open the question whether tax matters were included in the prohibition, and, as a matter of fact, contingent fees continued in wide usage in tax practice.

The Treasury Acts

At the 1921 annual meeting of the Institute, a representative of the Treasury Department spoke on problems involved in the enrollment of accountants, attorneys, and agents to practice before the Department. He expressed concern about the qualifications of some taxpayers' representatives, and particularly criticized advertising and solicitation of business by enrollees.

He announced that Treasury regulations on ethical conduct would be promulgated in the near future, patterned on the codes governing the learned professions.

He also said that the American Bar Association had recently adopted a resolution inviting the Treasury Department's Committee on Enrollment and Disbarment to query state and local bar associations regarding the fitness of any lawyer applying for admission to practice before the Treasury. The speaker suggested that similar co-operation from the Institute would be welcome.

The Council lost no time in responding. The committee on federal legislation was authorized to advise the Treasury that the Institute would co-operate fully. It was essential that the status of CPAs before the Treasury continue to be equal in all respects to that of lawyers.

In April 1922, Treasury Department Circular 230, which governed admission and conduct of practitioners before the Department, was amended in several respects. Advertising by such persons was restricted to simple statements of name, address and brief description of practice. Solicitation of claims or other business before the Treasury Department was forbidden, and any advertising or solicitation suggesting any special connection with the Treasury Department was emphatically prohibited. Violations were stated to be cause for suspension or disbarment.

Institute spokesmen applauded these steps, though it was not until a few months later that the Institute's rule against advertising was adopted—partly, perhaps, as a result of the Treasury's action.

Under date of August 15, 1923, Circular 230 was amended again. One of the new features was to incorporate by reference the codes of ethics of the American Bar Association and the American Institute of Accountants, making them applicable to all attorneys and agents practicing before the Department. The new circular also prohibited the use of titles which might imply official status or connection with the government, such as "federal tax expert" or "federal tax consultant."

These actions pleased both lawyers and CPAs, since "agents"

who were neither were subjected to the same restraints as members of the two professions.

In 1923 also the Department required disclosure of contingent-fee arrangements and the details thereof.

Procedural Matters

In addition to technical and ethical questions, procedural matters in tax practice also received the Institute's attention.

For example, suggestions were made for improvement in the form for corporation tax returns.

The Institute claimed some credit for persuading the Bureau of Internal Revenue to publish special bulletins reporting income-tax rulings.

In 1920 the Commissioner was asked to explain a new requirement that the names of persons preparing returns for taxpayers be disclosed. This was the precursor of the affidavit, or "jurat," to be executed by return-preparers. The Institute committee wanted clarification of the responsibility of accountants whose names were thus disclosed. The Commissioner sidestepped the question, suggesting that an accountant who assisted a taxpayer might prepare a memorandum indicating the responsibility he assumed, which could be filed with the return. Some CPAs followed this advice—others did not. But the responsibility of return-preparers was to come to the fore again years later.

In 1923 it was noted that revenue agents were attempting to examine accountants' working papers. The power of the Commissioner to require accountants to submit to this procedure was questioned. Accountants generally refused to make their working papers available without the consent of the client. In the face of this challenge, the Bureau apparently abandoned the effort, except when subpoenas were obtained.

The Board of Tax Appeals

Among both taxpayers and tax practitioners dissatisfaction had been growing because of the relatively disadvantageous position of the taxpayer vis-a-vis the Bureau of Internal Revenue.

Many revenue agents were zealous in pursuit of additional assessments when examining taxpayers' returns. Such assessments were often considered arbitrary and unfair. The taxpayer's only recourse was to appeal an agent's finding to a higher level within the Bureau itself—a conferee or the technical staff, later called the Appellate Division.

However, these higher officials were part of the organization whose duty it was to "protect the revenue," and their objectivity was sometimes questioned. The taxpayer who lost his case at the highest level in the Bureau, but remained convinced of the justice of his cause, had only one last resort— to pay the tax demanded by the Bureau, and sue for refund in a United States District Court. This was an expensive and time-consuming procedure, economically practicable only when substantial amounts were involved.

Public demand increased for a tribunal independent of the Bureau, where a taxpayer could seek resolution of differences with the Bureau before he had to pay the additional tax in controversy.

For a brief period, the Bureau attempted to meet this demand by creating a Special Committee on Appeals and Review within the Bureau itself. But taxpayers were not persuaded, regardless of the merits, that such a committee could be as independent and objective as they thought was desirable.

The pressure for a wholly independent tribunal finally resulted in Title IX of the Revenue Act of 1924, which created the Board of Tax Appeals as an independent agency in the executive branch of the government. The Board's members were appointed by the President, with the advice and consent of the Senate. While not a part of the judiciary, the Board's function was quasi-judicial. Its members, with rare exceptions, were lawyers. Formal rules of practice were adopted, including adherence to rules of evidence.

The first chairman of the new Board was Charles D. Hamel, a lawyer who had served as chairman of the Committee on Appeals and Review. He was instrumental in organizing the new Board, and in drafting its rules, which included a provision for admission of certified public accountants as well as lawyers to practice before it.

Judge Hamel was a speaker at a number of Institute meetings, and many of its members enjoyed close personal relationships with him. He was helpful to the accounting profession in many ways.

Restriction of admission to practice before the Board of Tax Appeals exclusively to attorneys-at-law and certified public accountants was a great morale builder for the CPAs. While they had always been admitted to practice before the Treasury Department as "agents," so had noncertified accountants and former revenue agents. Being coupled with lawyers as the only practitioners eligible to practice before the Board was a prestige symbol of which the CPAs were extremely proud. It was, in fact, the first official recognition of certified public accountants as a class by an agency of the federal government.

Edward E. Gore, who had become president of the Institute, had testified before the House Ways and Means Committee on the proposal to create the Board of Tax Appeals.

The Secretary of the Treasury had proposed that the Board be a part of his office. Mr. Gore had been instrumental in having the Chamber of Commerce of the United States pass a resolution to the effect that the Board of Tax Appeals should be an independent body appointed by the President. Mr. Gore's testimony, and that of other members of the Institute who accompanied him at the hearings, seems to have been influential in persuading the Ways and Means Committee that the Board should be independent of the Treasury.

It was reported to the Council that Mr. Gore had been given more than the allotted time to respond to questions by members of the Ways and Means Committee, and that some of the Congressmen expressed a desire to have him stay in Washington to assist them in framing the legislation.

Not All Lawyers Were Happy

The increasing influence of the accounting profession on tax legislation and administration, and the increasing stature of CPAs in tax practice did not go unnoticed by members of the Bar—and not all of them approved.

In 1909, 1913, and even 1916, not many lawyers thought of income taxation as a field for profitable employment of their talents. It was generally assumed that income taxes were a matter for accountants to handle. Rates were low, and the extent of tax controversies was not widely foreseen. Probably many lawyers thought that determination of income taxes was merely a matter of arithmetic anyway.

By the end of World War I, with its excess-profits tax and higher income-tax rates, it was clear that tax practice was a highly lucrative field, and that accountants were enjoying most of it.

As long ago as 1920, some lawyers had taken umbrage at statements in *The Journal of Accountancy* to the effect that no one could be expected to prepare income-tax returns as well as accountants. In defense of his position, the editor wrote, "Our critics say that income-tax law is law, and therefore should be interpreted by lawyers," and then quoted from testimony before a British Royal Commission on income tax, indicating that English accountants knew much more about income-tax law than the lawyers did, and that income-tax questions depended more on accounting than on any principle of law. This authority from across the Atlantic, however, did not seem to persuade the American lawyers.

A controversy between the two professions in the United

States was beginning to take shape. For the next 12 years steam built up without erupting. But in 1932 the Institute was confronted with events that developed into one of the most serious conflicts in which it would ever be called upon to engage.

Information was received that the American Bar Association, through its Special Committee on Unauthorized Practice of the Law, was giving consideration to the activities of public accountants which lawyers felt might encroach upon the field of law—notably in tax practice. A special committee of the Institute was appointed to confer with the chairman of the Bar Association's committee.

At the conference, the Institute's representative declared it most unlikely that members of the Institute would do anything which might be construed as practicing law. It was agreed that the Bar Association would refer to the Institute any complaint of alleged improper activity which might be directed against a member or associate of the Institute. Reference was made to Rule No. 5 of the Rules of Professional Conduct, which prohibited activity incompatible with public accounting, and the accountants said that under this rule the Institute could discipline any member or associate who wandered off the reservation.

These assurances, while politely received, did not induce the Bar Association committee to turn its attention to other matters. There was trouble ahead.

In 1933, without warning, the American Bar Association made an effort to have certified public accountants excluded from practice before the United States Board of Tax Appeals. The Institute, with the aid of legal counsel, opposed this move. The Board took no action.

From the West Coast, the Washington Society of Certified Public Accountants reported with alarm that the state bar association had applied for an injunction to prevent CPAs from engaging in some areas of tax practice which the bar believed constituted the practice of law. Institute counsel was enlisted to advise the Washington Society. Nothing happened.

In 1935, Senator Wagner of New York introduced Senate Bill 2944, which would have prohibited anyone except an attorney from representing another person before any governmental department or agency in a matter involving construction of statutes of the United States. It seemed clear that this bill would have prevented certified public accountants from representing taxpayers before the Bureau of Internal Revenue in many cases. Possibly the activities of CPAs before other governmental departments would have been curtailed.

The Institute vigorously opposed this legislation. It rallied to the cause members in states represented on the Senate Committee on Judiciary, to which the bill had been referred. The Institute formally requested an opportunity to testify if hearings were held. However, there were no hearings, and the Senate committee ultimately rendered an adverse report on the bill, which died.

Representatives of the American Bar Association assured the Institute that the Association was not actively supporting the bill. It was said to have been sponsored by the Federal Bar Association. There was not much comfort in this for CPAs, however.

Deeply disturbed by all these developments, the chairman of the Institute's committee on federal legislation, with other representatives of the Institute, met with spokesmen for the American Bar Association in Washington to discuss the whole subject of relations between accountants and lawyers in tax practice. The discussions were friendly, but inconclusive. Later, the president of the Institute appointed a special committee to co-operate with the American Bar Association.

This committee met from time to time with the Bar Association's Committee on Unauthorized Practice of the Law, which applied increasing pressure for concessions by the Institute, which would have had the effect of requiring CPAs to associate themselves with lawyers in dealing with complex tax matters.

These pressures were firmly resisted, but they continued— though for the time being the Bar committee seemed willing to seek a resolution of the disagreement by negotiation.

The 20-year period from 1916 to 1936 saw the accounting profession firmly established in the new and important field of tax practice. The profession's prestige was greatly enhanced through recognition of CPAs by the Treasury Department and the Board of Tax Appeals. The Institute's constructive recommendations on tax legislation and administration strengthened the profession's relations with the federal government. But warning signals were coming from some elements of the legal profession, and the CPAs were faced with a fight to hold the ground they had gained.

CHAPTER 13

Ethics and Self-Discipline

N o GROUP can claim professional status without meaningful standards of ethical conduct.

One of the main reasons for the formation of the new Institute in 1916 was the fact that the old American Association of Public Accountants was powerless, as a practical matter, to promulgate and enforce rules of ethics.

Members of the new Institute were directly responsible to the disciplinary authorities of the national organization itself. Under the old regime membership in an affiliated state society generally carried with it membership in the Association also. Discipline of Association members, therefore, had to be imposed for the most part through the state societies. Few of them at that time were large enough or strong enough to carry out this difficult and delicate task.

Immediately after formation of the Institute, however, its

ethics committee moved vigorously to discharge its responsibilities.

At the April 1917 meeting of Council—the first regular meeting following the reorganization—eight rules of professional conduct proposed by the committee were approved.

There was debate as to whether the Council had the power to adopt rules of conduct binding on the membership, or whether such rules should be submitted for membership approval, as required in the case of amendments to the bylaws. After discussion, it was concluded that the Council did have the necessary authority, under the bylaw provision that the Council exercise "all powers requisite for purposes of the Institute."

For many years thereafter the Council adopted rules and amendments to the rules without reference to the membership, although this procedure was again challenged unsuccessfully in 1922. Ultimately, however, the members at an annual meeting rose up and voted to take this power away from Council. Subsequently it was required that rules of conduct, like amendments to the bylaws, must be submitted to the entire membership for vote.

The Institute's First Rules of Conduct

The eight rules adopted in April 1917 were printed and distributed to the membership. They covered the following matters:

1. Use of the title "Members of the American Institute of Accountants"
2. Certification of statements containing essential misstatements of fact or omissions
3. Practice by others in the name of a member
4. Commissions or brokerages to or from the laity

5. Occupations incompatible with the practice of public accounting

6. Certification of statements not prepared under satisfactory supervision

7. Notice to the Institute of participation in efforts to secure legislation.

8. Solicitation of clients of other members

A Trial

The ethics committee also lost no time in exercising its disciplinary powers.

It preferred charges against two members of the Institute which were heard in 1917 by the Council sitting as a Trial Board.

The charge against both members, practicing as a partnership, was that they had knowingly certified to a consolidated balance sheet in which certain contingent liabilities were suppressed, and that balances owing by subsidiary companies were included in the current assets without disclosure of the relationship of the debtors.

The two members were admonished and suspended for 30 days.

An important precedent had been established: the rules were to be enforced.

Advertising

One of the most controversial questions facing the ethics committee was what to do about advertising. The widespread practice of seeking clients by means of direct-mail circulars had always been a source of humiliation to many of the profession's leaders. But even in the governing group there was stubborn resistance to curbs on advertising of any kind, on the ground that such restraints would be an unfair handicap to young men starting their own practices.

The crude and vulgar quality of much of the advertising material, however, was a visible contradiction of claims to professionalism. CPAs liked to compare themselves with lawyers and doctors. Yet it was well known that members of these professions were not permitted to advertise their services. Nor were British chartered accountants allowed to "tout for business."

In 1918 the committee on ethics took a cautious step forward. It recommended that a standing committee be appointed with power to censor circulars and other advertising matter to be issued by members.

In its report, the committee said:

> The committee feels that something should be done to discourage the practice of circularizing, particularly in its more unethical phases. Some letters and circulars are so repugnant to any sense of good taste and notions of decency, or to any conception of what constitutes a proper attitude of mind and seemly conduct in a professional man, that the circular itself defeats the purpose for which it was issued and only reflects discredit upon the professional organization which tolerates the offender among its membership.
>
> Other circulars are informative, dignified in tone and unobjectionable, and it therefore seems advisable to differentiate between circulars that contain professional information and those which constitute nothing but commercial drumming for business. . . .
>
> The committee has considered the formulation of a rule of professional conduct . . . but it has found the subject beset with so many difficulties that it has not attempted to present any concrete rule.

The members at the 1918 annual meeting approved the recommendation that a standing committee be established to censor advertising material. This resulted in a new rule of conduct, No. 9, adopted by the Council in 1919, as follows:

> For a period not exceeding two years after notice by the committee on ethical publicity no member or associate shall be permitted to

distribute circulars or other instruments of publicity without the consent and approval of said committee.

This, however, was not enough.

In 1920 the ethics committee reported that complaints about undignified advertising and circularization were continuing. At the spring Council meeting the committee on ethical publicity had recommended, and the Council had resolved, to invite members and associates to enter into a voluntary agreement to abstain from advertising and circularizing. The ethics committee warned that unless a marked improvement resulted it would be necessary to suggest a rule prohibiting such advertising.

Meanwhile, the Treasury Department was indicating displeasure with the advertising and solicitation practices of accountants enrolled to practice as "agents" before the Department. Since CPAs were practicing on an equal basis with lawyers in the tax field, it was obviously important to demonstrate that the ethical standards of the accounting profession were as high as those of the Bar.

In 1921, another committee of the Institute—the committee on professional advancement—recommended adoption of a rule prohibiting any member of the Institute from circularization and advertising in the public prints, and any other methods of publicity which would be deemed unethical by the other learned professions. The committee's report had been printed and distributed to all members prior to the annual meeting.

There was a lengthy debate on the floor of the meeting, with strong opposition to this proposal from some quarters. Finally, a resolution was offered that the publication or circulation of "ordinary, simple business cards" was not improper, but that solicitation, by circulars or advertisements or personal communications or interviews not warranted by personal relations, was unprofessional and should not be permitted. The resolution further provided that the Council was authorized to formulate rules for the guidance of members in this area.

Following more discussion, the motion was carried by 150 in favor to 68 opposed.

A motion was then adopted encouraging the Institute to conduct an educational campaign by advertisement, and to appoint a committee to investigate ways and means of giving publicity to the accountancy profession by educational advertising matter.

In 1922 the Council adopted an additional rule of professional conduct, prohibiting advertisement of a member's professional attainments through the mails, in the public prints or by other written words, with the single exception of a "card" indicating only the name, title and address of the advertiser without further qualifying words or letters. The size of the card permitted was specified in the rule.

Thus the long argument about advertising, which had continued from the beginning of the organized profession in 1887 until 1922, finally came to an end—but not without some tensions.

At this same annual meeting, it was proposed again that existing provisions for submission of amendments to the constitution and bylaws to the entire membership for vote by mail be extended to rules of professional conduct. It may be inferred that this proposal was supported by members opposed to the rule against advertising. However, the proposal was put to a vote and lost, leaving the power to amend or add to the rules of conduct in the hands of the Council.

The real test came at the meeting of Council in the fall of 1923. Resignations from membership in the Institute were received from A. C. Ernst and two of his partners in the firm of Ernst & Ernst, which he had founded in Cleveland in 1903, and which had grown to national scope. It was announced that complaint had been lodged against these three members for alleged violation of the rules against soliciting and advertising, and that they had been summoned to appear before the Council as a Trial Board. In responding to these notices the three members tendered their resignations.

It was resolved that the resignations be accepted, and that

a statement of the circumstances be reported to the annual meeting of the Institute, and also be published in the bulletin of the Institute. This was done.

A. C. Ernst had made no secret of the fact that he was philosophically opposed to restrictions on soliciting and advertising. The refusal of his firm to comply with the new Institute rule was a test of the organization's strength. The Council's willingness to lose the members of a large and influential firm on a question of principle was an important precedent. Some 13 years later, partners of the firm of Ernst & Ernst rejoined the Institute, with assurance that the firm would comply with all the rules of conduct. A. C. Ernst, however, never consented to rejoin.

The rule against advertising was never seriously challenged again, and it has always been rigorously enforced.

Offers of Employment

With little discussion the Council in 1919 adopted another rule of conduct, prohibiting an offer of employment to an employee of a fellow member without first informing that member.

Since all members of Council were employers it may be assumed that they welcomed this much protection against raids on their staffs.

The rule has been criticized by staff assistants, however, as an obstacle to their efforts to secure better positions.

Contingent Fees

A highly controversial question was whether contingent fees were proper. There was general agreement that it was improper for a CPA who certified financial statements to be used in an offering of securities or in an application for a bank loan, for example, to accept a fee based on a percentage of the proceeds. Obviously such an arrangement might appear to tempt the auditor to acquiesce in statements putting the most favorable possible light on his client's affairs.

In tax practice, however, lawyers commonly accepted contingent fees, and many CPAs saw no reason why they should not do likewise.

Accordingly in 1919 the Council attempted to cover both types of situations by adopting the following somewhat ambiguous rule:

> No member shall render professional service, the anticipated fee for which shall be contingent upon his findings and the results thereof. This rule shall be construed as inhibiting only services in which the accountant's findings or expert opinion might be influenced by considerations of personal financial interest.

The second sentence was confusing. It appeared to limit the application of the first sentence, but since a large fee certainly involved a "consideration of personal financial interest" the purpose of the apparent limitation was puzzling.

Accordingly, the Council in 1920 amended the rule by eliminating the second sentence. The resulting one-sentence rule was later construed to mean that since in tax cases the "findings" were those of the government, rather than those of the accountant, the prohibition did not apply to tax practice at all.

But this was not a satisfactory solution either. The justification for contingent fees was the contention that many taxpayers could not afford to fight for their rights if they had to pay their professional representatives regardless of the outcome. Such taxpayers, it was argued, were happy to have their cases handled on the understanding that the fee would be a percentage of the amount of tax saved or recovered—and nothing at all if the case was lost.

Yet abuses could occur. Some contingent fees were said to

run to 50 per cent, which could result in enormous rewards to lawyers and accountants when large claims were successful.

The rising income-tax rates, the growing complexities of the law, and the absence of established precedents in many areas led to numerous claims for refund, abatement and reconsideration. Many claims were of doubtful merit. There were tax practitioners who would accept almost any case on a contingent basis. This tended to burden the administration and the courts. President Waldron Rand's objections to this situation have already been cited.

The Treasury Department also decided that the situation was unsatisfactory.

In March 1923, the Department issued a letter to its staff and to attorneys, agents and others practicing before it, requiring disclosure of whether taxpayers' representatives were appearing before the Department on a contingent-fee basis, together with a description of the arrangements regarding compensation.

The Council of the Institute adopted a resolution approving this action, calling attention to the Institute's rule on contingent fees (though as construed this rule was not precisely in point), and offering to co-operate with the Treasury Department to insure compliance with its order.

Treasury Department Circular No. 230, governing practice before the Department, was subsequently amended to require disclosure of contingent-fee arrangements.

Thus the government took the burden from the shoulders of the professions. The Institute might well have prohibited its members from accepting contingent fees in tax cases if it had not been that lawyers and other "agents" were permitted to accept them.

As a matter of fact, in 1933 the ethics committee, under the chairmanship of Frederick B. Andrews, again raised the question whether contingent fees in tax cases were appropriate, despite the Treasury Department's tolerance of them. The committee recognized that since in tax cases the findings were ultimately those of the Internal Revenue, the acceptance of contingent fees in tax matters would not be regarded as a violation of the Institute's existing rule.

Nevertheless, the committee felt that a broader question was involved: whether it was ethically proper for a member to use his persuasive skills either in tax or other matters with the understanding that his fee was partly or wholly contingent on the degree of success achieved in final settlement. The committee urged clarification of the rule. The Council, however, did not act on this suggestion.

No doubt the majority of the Council considered the Treasury Department's disclosure requirement a satisfactory solution of the matter.

As it happened, just three years later, the Council did clarify the rule—in the opposite direction from that suggested in 1933 by the ethics committee. Recognizing the facts of life, Council amended the rule by adding the following wholly unambiguous sentence:

> This rule does not apply to cases such as those involving federal, state or other taxes, in which the findings are those of the tax or other similar authorities and not those of the accountant.

Responsibility to Investors

There had never been any disagreement about the vital necessity of maintaining public confidence in financial statements certified by professional accountants.

Among the first eight Rules of Professional Conduct adopted by the Council in 1917 was the following Rule No. 2, which evoked no opposition:

> The preparation and certification of exhibits, statements, schedules, or other forms of accountancy work, containing an essential misstatement of fact, or omission therefrom of such a fact as would amount to an essential misstatement shall be, ipso facto, cause for expulsion, or for such other discipline as the Council may determine,

upon proper presentation of proof that such misstatement was either wilful or was the result of such gross negligence as to be inexcusable.

In 1920 this rule was strengthened by inserting the clause, "or a failure to put prospective investors on notice in respect of an essential or material fact not specifically shown in the balance sheet itself," in conjunction with the provisions making essential misstatements or omissions of facts cause for discipline.

This rule, however, did not specifically cover a practice which bankers were criticizing: the certification of balance sheets "giving effect" to transactions to be consummated at a date later than the date of the balance sheet. These were called "pro forma" balance sheets, giving effect to proposed future transactions.

As noted earlier, the Institute's committee on co-operation with bankers and a corresponding committee of the Robert Morris Associates finally agreed on rules to be followed in dealing with statements of this kind, which were approved at the 1923 annual meeting, and were distributed in pamphlet form to the entire membership.

Apparently this action did not result in complete elimination of the undesirable practices.

In 1931 the ethics committee proposed a new rule of conduct, providing that no member or associate should sign or certify an estimate of earnings contingent upon future transactions, or permit his name to be used in conjunction with such forecasts in any manner which might lead third parties to believe that he vouched for their accuracy. The proposal was referred for consideration to Council which, in the following year, adopted this resolution:

Whereas estimates of earnings contingent upon future transactions should always be clearly distinguished from statements of actual earnings evidenced by definite records, and

Whereas an accountant may properly assist a client in estimating the results of future transactions, so long as no one may be led to believe that the estimates represent certainties,

Be it resolved, That no public accountant should permit his name to be used in conjunction with such an estimate in a manner which might lead anyone to believe that the accountant could vouch for the accuracy of the forecast; and

Be it further resolved, That violation of this dictum by a member or an associate of the American Institute of Accountants be considered by the committee on professional ethics as cause for charges under the provision of Article V, Section 4(e) of the bylaws, or Rule 2 of the Rules of Professional Conduct of the American Institute of Accountants or both.

This resolution was printed beneath the Rules of Professional Conduct as reproduced in the 1932 *Yearbook*. Later its substance was to be incorporated in the rules themselves.

Enforcement Problems

In 1933 the ethics committee reported that a number of complaints had been filed with the committee involving alleged violations of Rule 2, relating to essential misstatements or omissions in financial statements. In these cases, the committee stated, the omissions which it believed amounted to essential misstatements had had such widespread sanction by usage as to make it unfair for the accountants involved in these cases alone to be brought to trial. The committee urged an authoritative pronouncement in the form of a Council resolution covering four points:

1. Disclosure of large charges or credits direct to surplus or reserve accounts, in connection with the income statement

2. Disclosure in the balance sheet of differences between the stated value of capital stock and the amount received therefor

3. Disclosure of elements of surplus arising from sources other than undistributed net income

4. Direct annotation of items in financial statements to footnotes explaining such items

The Council decided, after consideration, that it would be

impracticable to enumerate specific causes of complaint under Rule 2, and that each individual case must be dealt with on its merits. Some of the four points were at the time under discussion with the New York Stock Exchange, and it may have seemed unwise for the Institute to act unilaterally on them.

Independence

Despite frequent references in professional literature to the independence of auditors in certifying financial statements, the word "independence" had not yet appeared in the Rules of Professional Conduct, nor was there any rule specifically addressed to the subject.

Implicitly, to be sure, the rules on misleading statements, contingent fees, and commissions from the laity were designed to buttress independence. However, the subject of relationships with clients which might impair independence, or appear to do so, had not yet been discussed.

After the stock-market crash in 1929, when public attention focused on the accounting profession more sharply than ever before, the profession began to engage in some self-examination.

At the 1931 annual meeting in Philadelphia, Frederick H. Hurdman, immediate past president, delivered an address on relations of client and accountant. Mr. Hurdman was one of the remarkable men who rose to leadership positions in the profession's early days. Born in Ottawa, Canada, he came to the United States at the age of 20, and became a citizen a few years later. After a year on the staff of Haskins & Sells he opened his own office, which developed into the firm of Hurdman & Cranstoun, a prominent local firm in New York.

In conjunction with his 1931 address, Mr. Hurdman introduced the following resolution:

> Whereas the relations between a client, in the form of a corporation, and the auditor for that corporation should be one of entire independence, and

Whereas it does not appear to be practicable for the auditor consistently to hold a dual relationship, as an auditor and executive of the corporation, and

Whereas the public interest and confidence will best be preserved by a complete separation of these two functions, therefore be it

Resolved, That the maintenance of a dual relationship, as director or officer of a corporation, while acting as auditor of that corporation, is against the best interests of the public and the profession and tends to destroy that independence of action considered essential in the relationship between client and auditor.

It was moved and seconded that the resolution be adopted. Following are some excerpts from remarks made by individual Council members in the discussion:

- We have too many rules already.

* * *

- I agree with the spirit of that resolution but I think it is far too broad and sweeping. I think if it has any force at all it is dangerous because it would prevent, or tend to prevent, a perfectly proper relationship that might come under it ethically.

* * *

- If there was some other way this rule could be enforced, or if it could be done in really worthwhile cases, then I am for it. But, do not let us have any more rules that would hamper the small man. . . .

* * *

- I think if we want to continue our profession on a strictly professional basis and have this independence of action, it is a mighty good thing for us to stand aloof and apart from the clients in our professional work.

* * *

- I think this resolution should be adopted. It is a splendid one and I thought years ago that it should have been adopted, and I still think it should have been adopted sooner.

* * *

- I think that should also extend to the ownership of any stock in the corporation that the auditor is auditing.

* * *

- Personally, I think to put over a resolution which excludes ownership of stock would be absurd. . . . You might be the auditor of some concern in which you held shares. I do not think it is sound to carry things of this type to an extreme.

* * *

• I think we are doubtless all agreed that the accountant should certainly keep himself in a position where he has no entangling alliances, but it seems to me that we are confronted with a situation of giving proper expression to that principle without getting ourselves into a straitjacket.

Finally, it was proposed as an amendment that the last paragraph read:

Resolved, That the maintenance of a dual relationship, as director or officer of a corporation, while acting as the *public* auditor of that corporation, is *in general* against the best interests of the public and profession and tends to destroy that independence of action considered essential to the relationship between client and auditor. [Emphasis supplied.]

A substitute motion was then offered that the proposed resolution be referred to the committee on professional ethics, with instructions to report back to the annual meeting in 1932. The substitute motion was carried.

In 1932 the ethics committee brought in a resolution expressing disapproval of joint service as auditor and director of a corporation. It was defeated after a debate which clearly indicated a lack of enthusiasm for too many restraints on the members' freedom of action.

The profession had missed a chance to take a forward step voluntarily. A year later the Securities Acts became law, and the Federal Trade Commission, under date of July 6, 1933, issued regulations including the rule on independence cited earlier, covering not only joint service as auditor and officer or director, but also financial interest of an auditor in a client corporation.

Mr. Hurdman's proposed resolution and the subsequent recommendations of the ethics committee show that some members of the profession were alert to the necessity of clarifying the independent auditor's role in the light of mounting public criticism. In its 1932 report the ethics committee frankly said, "The committee has felt a particular responsibility to the profession on account of the increasing public attention which is being focused on accountants' certificates and reports."

But the Council and most members were slow in recognizing the need for greater self-discipline. As a consequence, on this and other occasions the changes were ultimately made under pressure, when they could have attracted public applause by being made voluntarily at the initiative of the profession itself.

In 1933, as the result of a trial involving members of the Institute who had invested in securities of a client company, the ethics committee was requested by the Council to draft a rule covering such circumstances. In 1934 the committee presented a resolution, which the Council adopted, "that no member or associate shall certify the financial statements of any enterprise financed in whole or in part by the public distribution of securities if he is himself the actual or beneficial owner of a substantial financial interest in the enterprise or if he is committed to acquire such an interest."

By this time, however, the action might have seemed to outside observers only an echo of the SEC's requirements on independence.

Competitive Bidding

Competitive bidding for professional accounting engagements had long been deplored.

The editor of *The Journal of Accountancy* inveighed against the practice from time to time. In June 1921, for example, he quoted a letter written by an eminent accountant to the audit committee of a national bank, in response to a request to make a bid for an audit of the bank. The letter stated that "no reputable firm of high standing will make a competitive bid for a professional engagement," and pointed out that professional services based on price were likely to be unsatisfactory to the client.

But no official action on the subject was taken until the depression's economic pinch made bidding more and more prevalent. The pressure for some restraining measure mounted.

Accordingly, on recommendation of the ethics committee the Council in 1934 adopted a resolution which declared "that the Council of the American Institute of Accountants regards competitive bidding for professional accounting engagements as contrary to the best interests of members' clients and of the public generally, and urges members of the Institute to endeavor by all means at their disposal to eliminate the practice of competitive bidding."

This resolution, together with other resolutions of the Council on ethical questions, was published in the 1934 *Yearbook* as an appendage to the Rules of Professional Conduct. Later, the substance of all these resolutions was incorporated in formal rules.

Audit Companies

Growing concern had been expressed for many years about the activities of "audit companies"— corporations performing independent audits whose stock was held in part by non-accountants. In some cases the latter might even have a controlling interest.

In 1919 the Council adopted the following resolution:

Resolved, That there be submitted to the general meeting of the Institute a proposition that within three years from this date no member of the Institute be permitted to continue his membership if he be an officer, director or responsible manager of an audit company or other corporation or other company maintaining a department organized for the purpose of carring on a general accounting and auditing practice, unless all the stockholders and directors and officers of such corporation be and continue to be practising public accountants.

This was duly submitted to the annual meeting of members, where resistance developed.

It was first resolved that consideration of the proposal be deferred until the next annual meeting.

A motion to reconsider was then seconded and carried.

The following resolution was then presented and adopted unanimously:

Resolved, That it is the sense of this meeting that audit companies and similar organizations are detrimental to the best interests of the accounting profession.

This was obviously weaker—and no doubt deliberately so—than the Council's proposal. However, it was a step in the direction of a later rule of conduct prohibiting practice in corporate form.

Commissions From the Laity

One of the earliest ethical rules was a prohibition against acceptance of commissions from "the laity," offered to accountants for assistance in the sale of goods or services. Stationers offered compensation to accountants for the sale of business and accounting forms. Appraisal companies provided commissions to accountants who enlisted their services on behalf of clients. As late as 1923, a concern which offered to buy accounts receivable, trade acceptances, warehouse receipts, personal notes, etc., offered accountants a commission of 6 per cent for arranging for the sale of such commercial paper by the accountants' clients to the organization which purchased them.

Acceptance of this offer would, of course, have been a direct violation of the Institute's Rule No. 4 as it then existed. However, offers of this nature became less and less frequent as the commercial world gradually learned that accountants were ethically forbidden to accept them.

Proprietary Schools

In 1929 a rule of conduct was adopted by the Council, providing that no member or associate might be an officer, director, stockholder, representative, agent, teacher, or lecturer, nor participate in any other way in the activities or profits of any university, college or school which conducted its operation, solicited prospective students, or advertised its courses by discreditable methods. This was the result of the trial of a member associated with a proprietary school whose activities had been the subject of complaint.

Incompatible Occupations

The ethics committee asked the executive committee in 1929 whether engaging in the business of flotation of securities conjointly with public accounting was permissible. The executive committee resolved that such a business was not compatible or consistent with the professional practice of a public accountant. This was an interpretation of what was then Rule No. 5 of the Rules of Professional Conduct.

In response to a similar request, the executive committee expressed the opinion that a practicing accountant could, with propriety, act as a notary public.

Enforcement

Promulgating rules and resolutions is one thing. Enforcing them is another and more difficult task. Yet the Institute faced up to this part of its job, and acted on complaints without fear or favor, summoning partners of some of the largest firms before the Trial Board, as well as erring members from smaller organizations.

From 1917 onward, hardly a year passed when complaints against members were not heard by the Council sitting as a Trial Board. The members began to realize that the Institute meant business in requiring compliance with its ethical rules. Many infractions, of course, never resulted in trials, since the offenders were let off by the ethics committee on assurance that they would not repeat the violations.

As the years went on, the general level of behavior in the profession improved remarkably. A truly professional quality of conduct was gradually being achieved.

The Institute was learning, however, as most democratic institutions learn, that the path to self-discipline is not strewn with roses. Most people react negatively to suggestions that they impose restraints on themselves—and accountants are no exception.

In the 1930's, however, it was also becoming clear that in areas involving the public interest the only alternative to self-discipline in the long run is discipline imposed by the public through government.

The task of leadership in a professional organization, whose members are highly individualistic and cannot be coerced, is to explain and persuade: explain the relationship between self-imposed rules and the maintenance of public confidence; persuade the members to adopt such rules before they are compelled to do so by external authority.

CHAPTER 14

The Courts Begin to Take Notice

Closely related to technical and ethical standards is legal liability. Evidence of prevailing technical standards—via official pronouncements, professional literature, or expert testimony—is admissible in court in cases involving accountants. Theoretically, at least, if an accountant has complied with all the standards, with a degree of skill commonly possessed by his colleagues, and in good faith, he should not be held guilty of negligence: he should not be held liable for honest errors of judgment.

The technical pronouncements of the Institute, and its Code of Ethics, therefore, may thus serve as a defense for accountants who comply with them—but may also be used as a weapon against those who have not.

Thus, as the legal liabilities of professional accountants in the United States have seemed to be extended by court decisions and legislation, the Institute has become increasingly aware that pronouncements or rules which encourage higher standards of performance might be used against its members unfairly in the courts. The natural impulse to assume greater responsibility is met by warnings to hold back.

The evolution of judicial theory governing accountants' liability is well set forth in Saul Levy's useful book, *Accountants' Legal Responsibilities,* published by the Institute in 1954.

British Precedent

In Great Britain, where the profession was well developed some decades before its American counterpart, court decisions involving questions of accountants' liability date back to the 1890's. According to Levy, the 1951 edition of Dicksee's *Auditing,* a leading English text, devoted almost 300 pages of fine print to some 57 cases, while numerous other cases were mentioned and discussed elsewhere in the book. A study of court decisions apparently was part of the chartered accountants' technical equipment. The courts, not the profession, were setting auditing standards.

Some of the early English decisions have become classics and have been cited in American cases.

For example, in the *London and General Bank* case in 1895, it was said:

> An auditor, however, is not bound to do more than exercise reasonable care and skill . . . He is not an insurer; . . . he does not guarantee . . . that his balance sheet is accurate. . . .

In the famous *Kingston Cotton Mill* case of 1896, the court said:

> An auditor is not bound to be a detective . . . to approach his work with suspicion or with a foregone conclusion that there is something wrong. He is a watchdog, but not a bloodhound. . . .

These and similar judicial expressions were comforting to

American accountants. They may have encouraged a false sense of security. When American judges, and especially juries, came to determine the skill, care and caution which a reasonably competent auditor should use, the accounting profession was sometimes startled to read their conclusions.

Early American Cases

The earliest American case noted by Levy was *Smith* v. *London Assurance Corp.* in 1905. Here the judge said, "Public accountants now constitute a skilled professional class, and are subject generally to the same rules of liability for negligence in the practice of their profession as are members of other skilled professions."

There was nothing alarming in this dictum. In fact, some thoughtful CPAs believed that clarification of legal liability would lead to higher standards of accounting practice.

In 1908 the farsighted Joseph E. Sterrett touched on this subject in a speech before the American Economic Association, to which allusion has been made earlier. He said:

It must be borne in mind that a balance sheet of any large corporation is not a statement of facts that can be demonstrated with mathematical accuracy so much as it is an expression of an honest and intelligent opinion. In this expression of opinion the public accountant is now being recognized as an authority, and what is being widely done through the voluntary action of corporations that desire to deal fairly with their investors will doubtless become a legal requirement, and before many years the independent audit of all corporations offering their securities to the public will be firmly established.

With this, or possibly preceding it, will also come a civil liability on the part of the accountant for the faithful and diligent performance of his duties. As yet there are no decisions in this country upon the question of the liability of an auditor, but under the English law his liability both civil and criminal is pretty well established. . . .

Civil liability on the part of the accountant is, I believe, certain to come in this country, and while each member of the profession may well pray that the offense shall not come by him, it is nevertheless true that the effect of a clearly defined civil liability will be salutary. It will give confidence to the business public in the accountant's certificate as nothing else will do, and while the best accountants today recognize their moral responsibility quite as much as it will ever be necessary for them to recognize any legal responsibility, the knowledge that a civil and possibly a criminal liability attaches to them will deter the careless or the indifferent.

The key words here are *"clearly defined* civil liability." Unfortunately the evolution of common law in this area has not yet provided a clear definition.

Liability to Client

It was 25 years after Mr. Sterrett's speech that the audit of publicly held corporations became a legal requirement. But it was only nine years before "the offense came by" an old and prominent accounting firm, to quote Mr. Sterrett's words.

This was the case of *Craig* v. *Anyon,* finally decided in 1925. Barrow, Wade, Guthrie & Co., which the venerable James T. Anyon had managed in the United States since 1886, had audited the accounts of Bache & Co., a prominent firm of brokers, from 1913 to 1917. In the latter years it was learned that a Bache employee had stolen more than a million dollars from the firm. The auditors were charged with negligence. The jury found the defendants guilty and brought in a verdict for the total amount of the loss. The court then directed a general verdict for the plaintiffs of $2,000, the aggregate amount of fees paid to the auditors for their services. This judgment was affirmed on appeal.

There was an important element of contributory negligence on the part of the client in this case, which doubtless influenced the courts in limiting the damages.

Third-Party Liability

In the meantime, in 1919, a CPA firm had won a case in which an investor, alleging negligence, had sued to recover a loss he had suffered in purchasing stock in reliance on a financial statement certified by the accountants. The courts held that since there was no contractual relation between the plaintiff and defendants they owed no duty to the former; therefore, there was no cause of action for negligence.

Both these cases were reassuring to the profession: they seemed to reflect the views of the early English decisions in limiting the scope of accountants' legal liability. But several years later an action was brought which was to change the course of judicial opinion radically.

The Profession Reacts

Meanwhile, the subject of liability was receiving more attention than formerly. In May 1923, *The Journal of Accountancy* published an article by Bernard Rose, on "Responsibility of Auditors," which reflected the evolving nature of accounting practice as well as the growing concern with legal responsibility. The author said, in part:

> In former years the public accountant was engaged usually to balance the books of account or to assist the bookkeeping force in finding errors . . . Then . . . business began to engage accountants for organization and dissolution, auditing and cost analysis, systematizing and improvements in the general run of industry. Many accountants were called to conduct special investigations, especially those necessitated by misappropriation of funds and other assets . . . The federal and state income and capital-stock-tax laws have educated and induced businessmen to engage expert accountants to assist in the preparation and filing of returns and claims. . . .
>
> If accountancy is to remain on the plane with other professions, such as law and medicine, the accountant must be prepared to fulfill

his duties and obligations, not only to his clients, but also to the public and to his chosen profession. In his engagements to audit books and report thereon *he can no longer accept the oral statements of his client as to the assets and liabilities, but must secure such verifications as may be necessary from outside sources,* conducting his audit "not as a bloodhound, but as a watchdog." His conclusions must be of impartial fairness, stating conditions as he finds them and not as he is told of them without any confirming evidence. [Emphasis supplied. This was a remarkable statement six years after publication of the Federal Reserve bulletin.]

The author quoted Montgomery's *Auditing* as follows:

Acting in a professional capacity, an auditor must do more than ascertain the mere arithmetical accuracy of the account. If the accounts do not represent the true financial position of the undertaking under examination, and if the fact is apparent or can reasonably be deduced from the face of the accounts themselves, then the auditor is under a legal obligation to discover and disclose the true state of affairs.

Mr. Rose then summarized legal-liability cases in Great Britain where court decisions on auditor's liability were said to be "prolific." No American cases were cited.

Liability Insurance

The subject of insurance against losses suffered by accountants through claims based on alleged negligence began to receive lively attention. For many years, British firms had secured such insurance from Lloyds Underwriters in London, and the larger American firms had done likewise. But Lloyds were not interested in small policies, and since no American insurance company had written coverage of this kind, the smaller firms represented in the American Institute lacked any source of protection.

The Institute took steps to remedy this situation.

In 1925 the executive committee reported that after discussion with insurance agents, an American insurance company had submittted a form of accountants' indemnity policy which the company was willing to write. This was the first accountants' liability-insurance policy available in the United States. The executive committee decided not to approve this or any other particular form of policy officially, but rather to bring the policy to the attention of the members with a recommendation that those who cared to protect themselves by this kind of insurance should consider it.

Institute as Amicus Curiae

In 1926 an incident occurred which, while not directly related to the question of liability, had some indirect implications for future actions in that area.

For the first time the Institute intervened as friend of the court (amicus curiae) in a case involving a member. The case was tried in Massachusetts. The issue was the accountant's right to possession of his working papers. The defendant lost in the lower court. On appeal the Institute filed a brief in support of the accountant in the Massachusetts Supreme Court (*Ipswich Mills* v. *Dillon*). The Supreme Court overturned the decision of the lower court and held that the working papers of the accountant were his own property. This experience encouraged the Institute to intervene in later litigation involving issues of importance to the entire profession.

A New Concept

In 1929 a case was brought to court in New York which finally upset the widely held assumption that accountants could be held liable for negligence, however gross, only to those with whom they had a contractual relationship. This was the well-known *Ultramares* case.

The plaintiff was a creditor of the client, and had made substantial advances to the client, allegedly in reliance on a balance sheet certified by the accountants. It developed that false entries had been made in the books, which were undetected by the auditors, and as a result the balance sheet showed net worth greatly in excess of the actual position. The creditor sued the accountants to recover the loss it had suffered.

In the trial the complaint alleged both negligence and fraud. The judge dismissed the fraud count. The jury brought in a verdict for the plaintiff, but the judge set aside this verdict, basing his decision not on the facts, but on the law—i.e., that accountants were not liable for negligence to parties with whom they had no contractual relationship.

An intermediate appellate court unanimously affirmed dismissal of the cause of action for fraud, but, by a divided court of three to two, reversed the decision on negligence and reinstated the verdict.

The case then went to the Court of Appeals, the highest court in New York.

Thoroughly alarmed, the Institute, supported by the New York State Society of Certified Public Accountants, intervened as friend of the court. The amicus brief summed up the profession's position as follows:

> If the rule contended for by the plaintiff should finally be sustained, the more reputable and responsible firms of accountants will not be able to afford to take the financial risk of a jury finding that the action of some subordinate constituted negligence by reason of which the accountants would be liable to the world for an indefinite and unlimited period. Such a rule would very seriously affect all business transacted where statements, certified by accountants, have been customarily used, as in connection with the lending of money by banks and the purchase of securities from bankers.
>
> The audit for credit purposes and the certified balance sheet have their place, and the liability of an accountant to his employer, hitherto recognized, for the proper performance of such professional duties, is fair and proper. To increase this liability, as contended for

by the plaintiff in this case, would necessitate the accountant charging fees which would be prohibitive. If his liability for such service is to the world, and for an indefinite and unlimited amount, an accountant would be obliged to carry his examination to such an extent as would enable him to "know" that the statement was, in all its details, correct. Such an examination would be impractical, and would cause the present practice and service to be discontinued. The utmost that is expected of an accountant under such circumstances, is an "opinion," and it is a matter for the judgment of the accountant how far, under the circumstances surrounding each case, his examination must be carried in order to enable him to express an opinion.

In the case at bar there was no privity of contract and no direct relationship between the plaintiff and the accountants, while on the other hand the fraud of the employer of the accountants intervened between the plaintiff and the accountants, without which fraud the loss of the plaintiff would not have been suffered, and to which fraud the loss of the plaintiff can be attributed as proximately due. To hold accountants liable under such circumstances would work great hardship upon the profession.

The 62-page brief then supported these assertions with extensive argument based on the facts of the case and on the law.

Judge Cardozo, on behalf of the Court of Appeals, rendered the decision, which has become a landmark. To an extent he supported the Institute's position, in the following words:

> The defendants owed to their employer a duty imposed by law to make their certificate without fraud, and a duty growing out of contract to make it with the care and caution proper to their calling. Fraud includes the pretense of knowledge when knowledge there is none. To creditors and investors to whom the employer exhibited the certificate, the defendants owed a like duty to make it without fraud, since there was notice in the circumstances of its making that the employer did not intend to keep it to himself . . .
>
> A different question develops when we ask whether they owed a duty to those to make it without negligence. *If liability for negligence exists, a thoughtless slip or blunder, the failure to detect a theft or forgery beneath the cover of deceptive entries, may expose accountants to a liability in an indeterminate amount for an indeterminate time to an indeterminate class.* The hazards of a business conducted on these terms are so extreme as to enkindle doubt whether a flaw may

not exist in the implication of a duty that exposes to these consequences. [Emphasis supplied.]

However, Judge Cardozo proceeded to develop a concept that until then was novel in American jurisprudence, at least in its application to accountants. He held that negligence might of itself be evidence from which an inference of fraud could be drawn, even though there was no evidence of intent to deceive anyone. He said:

> Our holding does not emancipate accountants from the consequences of fraud. It does not relieve them if their audit has been so negligent as to justify a finding that they had no genuine belief in its adequacy, for this again is fraud. It does no more than say that, if less than this is proved, if there has been neither reckless misstatement nor insincere profession of an opinion, but only honest blunder, the ensuing liability for negligence is one that is bounded by the contract, and is to be enforced between the parties by whom the contract has been made. We doubt whether the average businessman receiving a certificate without paying for it, and receiving it merely as one among a multitude of possible investors, would look for anything more.

In the case before it, the court held that a jury might find that the defendants had made a statement as true to their own knowledge, when they had no knowledge on the subject—that they might have acted without information leading to a sincere or genuine belief when they certified to an opinion that the balance sheet faithfully reflected the condition of the business.

The Court of Appeals did not find the defendants guilty of fraud. It affirmed the trial judge's dismissal of the cause of action based on negligence alone, as a matter of law. However, on the reasoning quoted above, it reversed the judgment dismissing the cause of action based on fraud, and granted a new trial.

The new trial was never held. The case was settled out of court.

What the Cardozo decision did, in effect, was to erase

what accountants had previously considered to be a clean line between negligence, for which liability extended only to parties with whom a contractual relationship existed, and fraud, for which liability could extend to anyone who relied on certified financial statements.

Under this decision, it appeared unnecessary to prove intent to deceive in order to establish fraud. Negligence so gross as to support an inference that an accountant had no genuine belief in his own representation might justify a jury in a verdict of fraud.

The principles enunciated in the *Ultramares* case were soon applied in two other cases, in which controlling decisions were effective in 1937 and 1938, although the actions were commenced in 1928 and 1932, respectively.

It was evident that claims against accountants alleging "constructive fraud," a la Judge Cardozo, would become more frequent.

Defensive Actions

In 1932 the American insurance company which had agreed in 1925 to provide indemnity-insurance policies for accountants discontinued the coverage—not, it was said, because the experience had been unfavorable, but because of other factors. A special committee of the Institute, with the help of brokers, succeeded in developing coverage by another underwriter. Again, it was decided that the Institute should not sponsor any particular policy, but should simply inform members of its availability.

At the same time, no doubt as a result of the shock emanating from the *Ultramares* decision, the executive committee offered to consult with members against whom suits for damages might be filed. The committee pointed out the possibility of attempts, through litigation, "to force the accountant into the position of an insurer." It indicated that strike suits against accountants might be increasing, and advocated co-ordination of proper resistance against unjust claims, so that the strongest possible body of case law, determining the legal responsibilities of the profession, might be developed.

The Securities Act

Meanwhile, the securities legislation of 1933 and 1934 imposed statutory liabilities on accountants. Indeed, as described earlier, the 1933 Act provisions were far more harsh than those imposed by the courts.

This is how it was, as the accounting profession ended the first 50 years of existence as an organized group in the United States. Public accountants had suddenly been removed from what they had believed to be a position of reasonable security, so far as legal liability was concerned, and placed in what seemed a legal no-man's-land, against whose perils no adequate defenses were available.

CHAPTER 15

Developing Standards of Competence

THE American Association of Public Accountants had always shown a strong interest in education for professional accounting.

One of its earliest projects, as mentioned previously, was an unsuccessful effort to establish its own school. Thereafter, accounting was taught only in proprietary schools until the Wharton School at the University of Pennsylvania, and New York University, around the turn of the century, introduced accounting as a part of the curriculums of accredited institutions.

By 1916, when the Association was reorganized as the American Institute, the number of colleges and universities offering courses in accounting had increased to 20. However, the content of accounting courses varied widely, and the scarcity of suitable textbooks and competent teachers had retarded the development of high-level accounting education. Accounting instructors were not held in high regard by other faculties, and thus enjoyed limited prestige or influence in the academic community.

Relations With Academia

Yet there were men of great ability and dedication engaged in the teaching of accounting—Elwell, Hatfield, Kester, Paton, Scovill, and later Dohr and Greer, to name a few. They felt the need of an organization which would serve as a medium for the exchange of information and ideas, and as a means of facilitating joint action in advancing their common interests.

The new Institute, like its predecessor, required experience in public accounting as a basis for membership. Teachers who lacked practice experience, no matter how high the level of their technical competence, were ineligible for full membership, though they could become non-voting associates.

Partly for this reason, perhaps, just a few months after the formation of the American Institute in 1916, some 20 or 25 teachers of accounting formed the American Association of University Instructors in Accounting.

The Association grew slowly. In 1918 it approached the Institute with a view to developing co-operative relations. The first result was that members of the instructors' association were given access to the Institute's library.

In 1919, Fayette H. Elwell, then president of the Association, was invited to the Institute's annual meeting. He presented a "brief," suggesting that instructors in accounting be eligible to take the examinations of the Institute, and be admitted as full members, not merely as associates.

His proposal, if not rebuffed, was at least ignored, and this created resentment among many instructors which persisted for a long time.

Many practicing members of the Institute disapproved of its apparently unco-operative attitude toward the academicians. Finally, in 1924 the Institute's constitution was amended to provide that instructors who were CPAs and had sufficient teaching experience could become full members.

At the same time the Institute enlarged its committee on education, including three professors: John R. Wildman, David Himmelblau, and J. Hugh Jackson. In that year, too, the president of the Institute was invited for the first time to speak at the annual meeting of the Association. The foundation for co-operative relations between the practicing and academic branches of the profession had been established.

In 1926 the Association of University Instructors launched a quarterly publication, *The Accounting Review,* which soon secured a firm place in the professional literature. This was largely due to the efforts of William A. Paton, who almost single-handedly produced the early issues. Concerning itself mainly with accounting theory, research, accounting curriculums, and other academic matters, but also addressing itself to problems of accounting practice, the *Review* has had a significant impact on accounting thought.

The Association, and particularly the editor of *The Accounting Review,* from 1929 onward continually prodded the Institute to do more research leading to the development of accounting principles.

In 1935 the Association changed its name to the American Accounting Association, and opened its membership to practitioners and all other persons interested in promoting accounting research and education. This change was first proposed in 1921, heavily backed by Professor Paton, Howard Greer, Eric Kohler, J. O. McKinsey and others, but was defeated. It took 14 years to bring it about.

A new objective of the reorganized Association was to assist the accounting profession, through research, in developing principles which would place corporate financial reporting on a more rational basis.

Its efforts in this direction were to produce some tension between the Institute and the academic community. In fact, there is reason to believe that the Institute first looked askance on the Association's change of name and enlarged membership, suspecting that a rival organization was in the making. Even the launching of *The Accounting Review* years before had been opposed in some quarters, on the ground that it might compete with *The Journal of Accountancy*.

Particularly distasteful to many practitioners was the thought that college professors might issue pronouncements on accounting principles and methods, which were supposed to be the exclusive province of the practicing auditors. The Securities and Exchange Commission, however, encouraged the Association's efforts in this direction. The pressure from both the SEC and the American Accounting Association undoubtedly accelerated the Institute's efforts to narrow the areas of difference among acceptable accounting principles.

Educational Activities

The Institute's committee on education continued the periodic surveys of colleges and universities which taught accounting.

The committee also sought the co-operation of the university business schools in preparing students for the CPA examinations and for the Institute's examinations. Participation in this effort by the state societies was encouraged.

The committee addressed the state boards of accountancy, suggesting a uniform examination for the CPA certificate, and on the whole received encouraging replies. It also sent out a questionnaire related to preliminary education and experience requirements, in an effort to develop uniform standards among the states.

Preparation for Examinations

At the fall meeting of Council in 1917 it was suggested that the committee on education, in close co-operation with the Board of Examiners, which prepared the Institute's examinations, should formulate a curriculum to be followed by schools of accountancy. It was asserted that the schools which were attempting to prepare students for the CPA examinations were entitled to guidance as to the subject matter to be taught and the textbooks to be read. There was some question whether a curriculum prepared under Institute auspices would be kindly received by the academic community, since at that time no instructors of accounting were serving on either the committee or the board. However, the Council apparently felt that the teachers would welcome assistance.

Preparing a curriculum evidently was not as easy as it sounded. No progress was reported in the next two years.

Then, in 1919, as an initial step, the Council resolved that the committee on education be instructed to collaborate with the Board of Examiners in the preparation of a list of textbooks for study preparatory to the examinations.

The committee on education complied with this request. It noted that more than 20 states were then using the Institute's examinations, but that the Institute had not published any syllabus for the guidance of candidates.

The available literature had grown markedly. Reference was made to a "five-foot bookshelf" which had been recommended in 1912 for accountants and students of accountancy, including 28 titles.

To this list the 1919 committee added 13 titles. It also recommended the preparation of a syllabus of the examinations.

In 1921 the Board of Examiners produced the first "Circular of Information," for the guidance of applicants for membership in the Institute and candidates for the CPA certificate in states co-operating with the Institute in the conduct of examinations. The circular described the content of the examinations and the procedures followed in administering them.

It also included a bibliography of suggested texts for reading in preparation for the examination. This document proved to be of great assistance to candidates, and probably had some influence on the content of accounting courses in the universities.

Accounting Curriculums

In 1924, responding to the Council's suggestion seven years earlier, the committee on education submitted a tentative outline of a standard curriculum for university courses in accounting. This was offered in tentative form, it was said, in the hope that it would serve as a framework on which to build a comprehensive course in the future. The tentative program covered four printed pages in the 1924 *Yearbook*.

There is no evidence that the outline was received with enthusiasm in academic circles, although it may well have influenced individual teachers in designing their own courses.

In any event, a new Institute committee on education, under the chairmanship of John R. Wildman, set out on a new tack intended to reach the same goal—a curriculum in accounting to prepare students for professional practice.

Mr. Wildman's committee undertook an investigation of the activities which constituted the practice of accountancy. Its 1925 report said, "Once these activities have been defined, differentiated, classified, and weighted as to importance, it will be the purpose of the committee to determine the type of knowledge and technique of application necessary to meet the requirements of practice." Then it was proposed to offer educational institutions a graded course of study suitable for the preparation of students for public accounting.

This might be regarded as the first effort to describe the "common body of knowledge" of the accounting profession.

In 1926 Mr. Wildman presented, on behalf of the committee, a "Classification of Accountancy Services," which the Council referred to the annual meeting of members without recommendation. It proved to be a highly controversial document. There was disagreement among accountants in firms of all types and sizes over the suggested definitions of the appropriate scope of their activities.

The "Classification" described 14 types of accounting services, as follows: (1) General Audits; (2) Balance Sheet Audits; (3) Cash Audits; (4) General Examinations; (5) Limited Examinations; (6) Investigations; (7) Preparation of Statements From Books or Records Without Verification; (8) Tax Engagements; (9) General Accounting Systems; (10) Cost Systems; (11) Budgets; (12) Bookkeeping and Accounting Engagements; (13) Opinions; and (14) Miscellaneous.

The first five items, dealing with audits and examinations, were described at length and in detail, while the last seven were stated concisely, almost telegraphically, in a way which may have seemed to many practitioners to minimize their importance.

The document evoked differences of opinion on other grounds—the very titles used to describe the different types of services, the distinctions drawn among the several kinds of audits, examinations and investigations, the relegation of all advisory services to a mere phrase in the "miscellaneous" section, and so on. There may also have been some concern about the possibility of excerpts being quoted against members in cases involving accountants' legal liability.

The "Classification" was printed and distributed to the membership in 1927, with a request for opinions. Three appeals elicited responses from only about 10 per cent of the membership, and the views submitted were highly divergent. A special committee was appointed to study the comments and report back its findings. This committee took its time. It was not until September 1931 that the Council finally acted on the "Classification of Accountancy Services." After lengthy discussion, it was unanimously resolved that it would be unwise and impracticable for the Institute to adopt a classification of services at that time.

Nevertheless, the document served a useful purpose. It provoked animated discussion. It prompted accountants to devote some thought to the scope of their work; and it provided teachers with an insight into the nature of accounting practice.

Educational Policies

Some accounting teachers disapproved of the Institute's efforts to develop accounting curriculums, which they considered the exclusive prerogative of academicians. On the whole, however, relations with the academic community had improved considerably. Some accounting professors maintained a mistrustful, sometimes even a hostile, attitude toward the Institute. But a number of outstanding educators had been drawn into the Institute's official family.

Professor William A. Paton of the University of Michigan became chairman of the Institute's committee on education, which included also J. Hugh Jackson, formerly of Harvard and then of Stanford, and Roy B. Kester of Columbia. George E. Bennett of Syracuse and James E. McConahey, a practitioner who also taught at the University of Washington, were the other members. By virtue of his chairmanship, Professor Paton also became a member of the newly created special committee on development of accounting principles.

In its 1934 report, this committee on education offered five propositions for serious consideration:

1. That a comprehensive college or university training was becoming an indispensable part of the preparation required for the career of a professional accountant

2. That the educational background should include both a broad foundation and a period of two years of systematic study

in accounting and allied fields such as economics, finance, money and banking

3. That the Institute should not attempt to formulate a detailed curriculum, since this could better be done by educational organizations, nor should the Institute attempt to accredit or approve specific educational institutions, text materials or teachers

4. That only individuals of marked ability, adequate preliminary training and high promise be encouraged to enter the accounting field

5. That formal educational preparation be given greater emphasis in legislation specifying the qualifications of accountants to become CPAs

While no formal action was taken on these propositions at the time, they gradually became embodied in Institute policy.

A Contrary Approach

In 1935 the committee on education, then under the chairmanship of Professor Kester, made a survey of accounting courses offered in colleges and universities. On the basis of this factual study, the committee recommended that the Institute formulate an educational policy which would specify standards of education for the practice of public accounting; would encourage strengthening of the training then available in some collegiate schools of business; would encourage amendment of the statutes of the several states to raise educational requirements; and would encourage strengthening the examinations for entrance to the Institute in accordance with these suggestions.

A year later the committee reported that the educational standards set by the profession were too low. In no state was anything more required than graduation from a high school or secondary school, with one exception. New York had adopted a requirement, to be effective January 1, 1938, that each candidate be a graduate of a four-year collegiate course with a prescribed curriculum in accountancy, law, finance and economics, as well as basic liberal-arts courses.

The Council approved the four propositions in the 1935 report, and requested specific recommendations. The committee recommended that four years of collegiate training beyond high school should constitute a minimum education requirement for the successful practice of public accounting; that the four-year course of 120 semester hours should be evenly divided between cultural and professional subjects; and that the professional courses should include accounting, auditing, systems, financial reporting, business law, finance and economics.

The committee also recommended that an attempt should be made to develop standards covering courses and their content, faculty personnel, library and laboratory equipment and financial resources. These standards would be used as a basis for rating the various schools offering professional accounting training.

This recommendation was directly contrary to that of the preceding committee under the chairmanship of Professor Paton.

The 1936 committee also recommended that the Institute actively encourage amendment of CPA laws to set up higher educational requirements, and that ultimately five years of cultural-professional education should be required—three years of professional training based on two in the liberal arts.

The Council approved college training as preparation for the profession, and authorized the education committee to proceed in its endeavor to formulate suggested standards for university courses, despite the fact that previous efforts of this nature had failed. Nor did this latest project come to fruition.

Yet these efforts were by no means wasted. They evoked discussion and debate, which ultimately led to official policies. They encouraged the adoption of higher educational requirements for the CPA certificate in state after state. Accounting education was rapidly advancing.

Education of Practitioners

The educational background of accounting practitioners in those days was revealed in 1926 in a study by the Institute's special committee for placements, whose activities will be described shortly.

The study showed that of Institute members admitted from 1917 to 1926, 240 were not even high-school graduates; 278 were graduates of high school only; and 179 were college graduates, of whom 57 were from New York University, 12 from Harvard, ten from the University of Wisconsin, and fewer than ten from any other college. Of those educated outside the United States, 91 were not high-school graduates, 71 were high-school graduates, and 15 were college graduates. In summary, only 22 per cent of the members admitted during the ten-year period had a degree from a recognized college.

While in earlier days many able men did not attend college, and were successful nonetheless, by 1926 the need for attraction of recruits with better educational backgrounds was becoming apparent.

Beta Alpha Psi

In 1922, Beta Alpha Psi was founded as an honorary professional accounting fraternity. *The Journal of Accountancy* said, with obvious approval, "Membership in this fraternity is obtained by invitation only, and is based on a high scholastic standing in accounting courses pursued in the university, good moral character and an expressed interest in the accounting profession."

Chapters had been established at four universities: Illinois, Northwestern, Washington and Oregon, and at Oregon Agricultural College. The *Journal* compared the fraternity, as a distinguishing mark for accounting students, to Phi Beta Kappa in the field of literature and arts. Beta Alpha Psi was to have a strong influence in encouraging high standards of scholarship among accounting students.

The Uniform CPA Examination

The examination for professional accreditation and the educational preparation for the profession are inevitably interrelated. Textbook writers and curriculum designers may find it difficult to ignore the subject matter which their students will have to master in order to pass the profession's tests.

This is not necessarily good—if the professional examinations reflect only a narrow view of the profession's functions, or if they reflect only traditional practice without regard to the changes which may be evolving in response to a new environment. In these cases, to the extent that instruction is influenced by the examinations, students may be ill-prepared to adapt to the realities of practice.

Some claim that this happened in accounting. In the early years the CPA examinations focused heavily on auditing and financial reporting—much as did the Wildman committee's "Classification of Accounting Services," which undoubtedly reflected the practice of that day, at least in the larger firms. Many textbooks and college courses followed the same pattern. But as the scope of practice expanded, and new techniques were introduced, there was a time lag, both in the examinations and in curricula, in catching up with the changes.

On the one hand, it was difficult to include in the examinations, which are subject to state government control, subject matter which was not being taught generally in the colleges and universities. On the other hand, the academic institutions which took pride in the success of their accounting students in the examinations were inclined to keep teaching the subject matter covered in *past* examinations.

As the CPA examination gradually became uniform throughout the country, the difficulty of making radical changes in it increased. It was not until the "modern era" of the profession that a planned, deliberate effort was made to move both the examination and accounting instruction forward simultaneously to meet the needs of changing times.

Meanwhile, some prestigious business schools and some adventurous professors of accounting rejected the assumption that they were preparing students for the CPA examination, and taught accounting as they thought it should be taught.

In the period from 1916 to 1936 the emphasis was on attaining a uniform standard for the CPA certificate. The diversity in preliminary requirements and in the quality of examinations had been a major reason for creation of the Institute.

Immediately after its formation, its Board of Examiners held the first written examination for admission to the Institute. Thirty-four candidates sat.

More than a year before, John F. Forbes, as a member of Council, had suggested that if the new Institute was to prepare written examinations for admission to its membership, the same examinations might be offered to state boards in testing applicants for the CPA certificate—thus avoiding duplication of effort, and making it unnecessary to require two examinations for those who wished to become both CPAs and Institute members.

The idea had much appeal. In its 1917 report the Board of Examiners said:

> One of the most important matters considered . . . had been the necessity of establishing uniformity of standards for accounting examinations throughout the country. With the hope of bringing about

something approaching uniformity, a meeting was held in New York at the time of the Council meeting in April, at which representatives from the accountancy boards of several states were present. As a consequence of this meeting, and of suggestions received from various sources, the Board communicated with state boards of accountancy in every CPA state and offered to the state boards the use of the examination questions of the Institute, provided the examinations were held simultaneously. The Board also offered to mark the papers and return them to the state boards afterwards. Three states accepted the offer in the first instance, namely, New Hampshire, Oregon and Kansas, and other boards have since indicated their intention of following the same plan.

Thus began the Uniform CPA Examination, which 35 years later was to include all states and other jurisdictions of the United States.

The arrangement with the state boards was called the "Plan of Co-operation in the Conduct of Examinations." It was, of course, purely voluntary.

The only requirements were that the examinations be given on the same days everywhere, and that no changes be made in the examination as the Institute submitted it.

The questions and problems were submitted by firms and individuals—mostly drawn from actual practice cases—and then were selected, edited and arranged by CPAs employed by the Institute on a part-time basis.

In 1918, the Board of Examiners reported that 16 states had either co-operated with the Institute in the conduct of examinations or had indicated their intention to co-operate whenever candidates for examination appeared. There was reason to believe, it was stated, that other states would adopt the Institute's examinations in the near future. Nearly all the co-operating states had submitted the candidates' answers to the Institute's Board for grading. "One satisfactory result of the increasing utilization of the Institute's questions and markings," the Board reported, "is the building up of a considerable list of successful applicants who . . . will be eligible for admission, without further examination, if at any subsequent time they fulfill the constitutional requirements and apply."

The Institute, naturally, desired new members if they could meet the standards. It was soon apparent that CPAs who had already passed a written examination prepared by their own state boards would not be eager to take another examination to attain Institute membership. Thus the drive for a uniform examination, while obviously desirable from the viewpoint of the whole profession, also had advantages for the Institute itself.

The Board of Examiners reported in 1919 that the plan of co-operation with state boards had finally been worked out in the form of a definite written program. Twenty-two states had indicated their approval of the plan and their intention to adopt it.

From the start there was concern about the relatively small proportion of candidates who passed the examination. An editorial in *The Journal of Accountancy* for March 1921 stated that in a recent Institute examination, out of 820 candidates for CPA certificates in the co-operating states, only 110 passed —a little over 13 per cent.

On the other hand, applicants for admission to the Institute who took the examination before the Institute's Board had a much better record—almost 70 per cent passed. The difference was ascribed to the Institute's rigid preliminary practice requirements.

A reason for the failure of so many of the candidates before state boards was said to be the inferior proprietary accounting schools which had sprung up over the country. Through flamboyant advertising, it was alleged, such schools were attracting many young people who did not have the essential qualifications to become accountants: after taking an accounting course in one of these schools they might try the CPA examination, but would almost certainly fail.

Nevertheless, the argument continued perennially—were the examinations too hard, or the candidates inadequately prepared? There may never be a final answer.

In 1936, at the end of the profession's first 50 years, 30 states were participating in the plan of co-operation. The trend was strong, and it seemed only a question of time before complete uniformity would be attained.

The Association oj CPA Examiners

It became customary for the Institute's Board of Examiners to invite the co-operating state boards to a special meeting, held in conjunction with the annual meeting of the Institute, where free discussion was invited of any problems involved in the conduct of the examinations.

These meetings developed later into a revival of the Association of CPA Examiners, which had existed many years before, but which had lapsed into inactivity. Norman E. Webster of New York was a moving spirit in the revival.

Through this formal organization of the state boards, with its own elected officers, directors and committees, more activity was generated and the trend toward uniformity in requirements and procedure was gradually accelerated. In fact, as the years went on so much business came before the Association that it employed a part-time secretary. In 1967 the Association changed its name to National Association of State Boards of Accountancy, in order to indicate more clearly the constituency of its membership.

The Sells Medals

In 1923 a number of friends of Elijah Watt Sells, who had recently retired, contributed to a fund in his name, the income of which was to be given as a prize to the candidate sitting for Institute examinations who passed with the highest grade throughout the country. The Council approved this action unanimously and authorized the Institute to administer the fund.

Over the years the fund grew. Out of the income gold and silver medals have been purchased and given to the candidates with the highest and next highest grades at each examination. The winning of a Sells medal has come to be regarded as a great honor both to the candidate and his state and thus it has been an incentive to excellence.

The Bureau of Placements

The first organized effort to attract college graduates to the ranks of the accounting profession began in 1926. It was the brainchild of Warren W. Nissley, himself a Princeton graduate, and the first native American to become a general partner of Arthur Young & Company. Nissley was convinced that the demands of CPAs required personnel with better educational background than that possessed by many practitioners and staff assistants at that time.

Warren Nissley was a man of great physical and mental energy. Having made up his mind that the profession needed college graduates, he developed a plan to accomplish the purpose, presented it to the Institute's executive committee and secured its approval.

In brief the plan was this: a bureau for placements was created to act as a clearing house between co-operating accounting firms and college students who were interested in obtaining employment in the profession. Student interest was aroused by circulation of a pamphlet, "Accounting Is a Career for Educated Men," drafted by the Institute's assistant secretary, a young man recently graduated from Yale, and edited by the committee of which Nissley was chairman.

The pamphlet was followed by personal visits to college campuses. Interested students were told what the profession had to offer them. Those who desired to apply were asked to fill out a questionnaire and submit to a personal interview by an Institute representative. The candidates selected by the bureau on the basis of scholastic achievements and extra-curricular activities were referred to co-operating firms on an impartial rotation basis.

The firms agreed to guarantee continuous employment for three years—to protect these selected applicants against lay-offs in the dull season. The firms also agreed to pay these men a starting salary of $125 a month—a princely sum in those days—with stated increases each year. Furthermore, the firms paid to the bureau a fee of $50 for every applicant employed through its efforts.

In the first year, 1926, thousands of copies of the recruiting pamphlet were circulated; 143 accounting firms in 44 cities expressed interest in obtaining recruits through the Bureau; and 19 men from 14 different colleges were actually employed.

In each succeeding year the numbers increased. Through 1930, 1,220 graduates had applied, from more than 200 colleges, and 223 had secured positions in more than 50 firms. In 1930, however, due to "exceptionally quiet business conditions"—the beginning of the Great Depression—the bureau was unable to find positions for all the approved applicants, though even in that year 50 men were placed.

Thereafter, the effort was abandoned. Hardly anyone was employing new assistants in the thirties. Many firms were compelled to reduce their staffs.

The bureau, nevertheless, started a trend. A number of the men it placed became partners of the firms which hired them. It had been demonstrated that college graduates, in general, were more promising material than high-school graduates with bookkeeping experience, who had been an important source of recruits prior to 1926.

After the depression and World War II, progressive accounting firms began to do their own recruiting on college campuses, which became by far the most important source of new blood for the accounting profession.

If the bureau for placements did not single-handedly start this trend, it certainly dramatized and accelerated it.

Summary

In the first 50 years accounting education spread slowly at first, and then rapidly, among the colleges and universities in all parts of the country. The academic branch of the profession was greatly strengthened. A strong trend toward a Uniform CPA Examination was started, which, together with debates about curriculums, began to shape a common core of subject matter in the accounting courses taught in the schools.

The organized profession committed itself to college education as a basis for admission to the profession, and New York started the movement to make such education a requirement for the CPA certificate.

A beginning was made in establishment of honors and awards to encourage a high level of scholarship in accounting. The first organized effort to attract college graduates to the profession was launched, and it succeeded.

Another long step had been taken toward attainment of true professional status.

CHAPTER 16

Regulation Under State Law

From 1896, when the first CPA law was enacted in New York, to 1916, when the new Institute was formed, 39 states had adopted CPA legislation. But the standards varied widely from state to state.

While a major objective of the Institute was to establish a uniform national standard for accreditation as a professional accountant—through membership in the Institute itself—the men who set the Institute's policies were largely the same men who had governed the predecessor American Association, which was dedicated to extension and strengthening of CPA laws. Almost all of these men were certified public accountants themselves. It was impossible for them to repudiate or abandon the CPA movement.

Rather, they seemed to reconcile themselves to the CPA laws as a form of local accreditation, with each state setting its own standards, while shaping the Institute into a national accreditation agency with a uniform standard.

Although this ambivalence now seems rather curious, it is not difficult to understand in the light of the environment of 1916. As industry spread across state lines, the practice of accounting inevitably followed. In order to secure the confidence of bankers who underwrote issues of securities and lent large sums of money, not to mention the increasing interest of federal agencies, it seemed imperative to create some identification of professional competence and responsibility on a nationwide basis. At the time it was next to impossible for users of financial statements to evaluate the qualifications of CPAs of one state as compared with those of another, or the qualifications of public accountants in the nine states which had no CPA laws.

The suggestion that the Federal Reserve Board set up a register of "approved" accountants was sufficient indication that the profession had to do something.

Accordingly, while the Institute sought to be the national "qualifying body" of the profession, it also proclaimed itself to be the defender of the CPA certificate. While it invited non-certified public accountants as well as CPAs to apply for Institute membership, its committee on state legislation continued to assist state societies in the preparation of sound CPA laws, and in the defeat of undesirable bills.

One of the first acts of the Institute's Council after the reorganization was approval in 1917 of a model CPA law.

But conditions changed rapidly and unpredictably. In the five years immediately following the reorganization the nine remaining states enacted CPA laws—many of them substantially in accord with the Institute's model bill. By 1921 CPA laws existed in all states.

Furthermore, the Institute's plan of co-operation in the conduct of examinations provided the state boards with a ready solution to the problem of preparing and grading examinations. The Institute's examinations were being used in 36 states by 1921. Many of the remaining 12 were the states with older CPA laws, which continued to prepare their own examinations, but for the most part their standards were equivalent to those of the Institute.

As a kind of by-product of the reorganization, and almost without conscious planning, a uniform national standard of professional competence had been largely established in a short five years.

Passage of a CPA law in the District of Columbia was a long, hard struggle, partly because it had to be enacted by a Congress never deeply concerned with District affairs. Finally, however, in 1923 this law, too, came into being. It followed the lines of the Institute's model CPA bill, and Institute spokesmen appeared at hearings to advocate it. At the time it was considered highly important that the District of Columbia, seat of the federal government, should have a CPA law similar to the laws of the several states.

The National Association of Certified Public Accountants

One reason was that in 1920 a "diploma mill," taking the name, National Association of Certified Public Accountants, had been organized in Washington, D.C., where no CPA law at that time existed. The association in effect sold certificates designating the holders as "CPA-NA." The resulting flood of bogus certificates naturally alarmed all legitimate CPAs.

This was, in fact, one of the reasons for widespread resentment against the Institute, the traumatic results of which will be described in a later chapter. It was supposed that the Institute, having set its own standards and examinations for membership—thus giving credence to an appearance of competing with the CPA certificate—was indifferent to the fate of the CPA movement.

Actually, however, the Institute, through its legal counsel, the reliable Judge Covington, sought and finally obtained an injunction against the National Association of CPAs, prohibiting it from issuing so-called CPA certificates. This put the association out of business. But with characteristic caution, amounting almost to secrecy, the Institute had gone about this task without publicity, and received no credit until the final result was known. By that time, many CPAs who had earlier resented the Institute's apparent lack of concern failed to realize what it had done.

Shortly after enactment of the District of Columbia CPA law, the territories of Alaska, Hawaii and the Philippine Islands enacted similar laws. Puerto Rico completed the roster in 1927.

Restrictive Legislation

For some time the idea had been spreading that the practice of public accounting should be restricted to CPAs. Until 1917 all existing CPA laws were of the so-called "permissive" type, permitting anyone to practice as a public accountant, but reserving use of the title "certified public accountant" or the initials "CPA" to those who had satisfied the legal requirements.

The constitutionality of this type of law had been tested and upheld in Minnesota, New York and Louisiana.

In 1923, for example, the Supreme Court of Louisiana, in the *deVerges* case said, "Anyone is at liberty to practice as an accountant, notwithstanding this law, so long as he does not represent himself to be a certified public accountant, as defined thereby, or use the abbreviation 'CPA' or similar letters or device to indicate that he is a certified public accountant. It is true that neither morals, health nor safety of anyone is jeopardized by the practicing of this profession, however incompetent a person may be, but the power of the state in matters of this sort is not confined to professions involving such consequences. It may also act whenever the general welfare requires to protect the public in the skilled trades and professions against ignorance, incompetence and fraud. We think, therefore, that the legislature, in the public interest and for the general welfare, unquestionably had and has the power to regulate the highly skilled and technical profession of public accounting in the measure which it did."

In 1917, however, Oklahoma enacted a law restricting the practice of accounting to certified public accountants of that state. It made no provision for continuation of practice by non-certified public accountants already on the scene, and it defined the scope of accounting very broadly.

This law was held unconstitutional in 1924.

The Oklahoma Supreme Court held that it deprived non-certified accountants of their right to earn a living through continuing to offer their services to the public, thereby abridging the right of private property; also that it infringed the right of private contract (between a client and any accountant he selected); and that it tended to create a monopoly for the benefit of certified public accountants—all without relation to the public welfare.

This decision strongly influenced future regulatory accountancy legislation. It was clear that provision must be made for non-certified accountants who were in practice when such a law was passed to continue thereafter; and that the scope of accounting services to be restricted to licensed persons must be defined narrowly enough to sustain the contention that the public welfare would be adversely affected if such services were performed by unqualified persons.

In 1924 a regulatory law was enacted in Maryland which confined the practice of public accounting to certified public accountants and a limited class licensed as "public accountants," consisting of persons in practice but not certified at the time of the passage of the act. This version of regulatory legislation came to be known as the "two-class law."

In the same year a similar bill was introduced in the New York State Legislature.

The Institute's approach to this kind of legislation was cautious and tentative. It was recognized that there were constitutional questions involved in efforts to limit the practice of accounting to licensed persons. Accordingly, the Institute at first neither opposed nor approved the two-class laws. It stood by and watched the experiments.

The New York bill, known as the McGinnies Bill, passed both houses of the legislature but was vetoed by Governor Alfred E. Smith. His message stated that "the present law gives us ample protection by setting up a professional class of accountants, but leaves the field open for other people, probably equally competent, but not admitted to the profession." His memorandum in general expressed concern about limiting the practice of public accounting to persons who qualified under CPA standards, which he felt would deprive many young people of an opportunity to render useful accounting services.

In spite of this defeat, two-class laws were enacted in Louisiana in 1924, and in North Carolina, Tennessee and Michigan in 1925.

In view of these developments, the Institute's committee on state legislation sent a questionnaire to the state societies, seeking their views on regulatory legislation. The majority favored restriction of the practice of public accountancy to CPAs "and other qualified public accountants."

A special committee on restrictive legislation was appointed to study the new phenomenon. This committee reported that while the majority of the states apparently favored this type of law, the difficulty of defining the practice of accountancy to be restricted appeared to be a serious obstacle in formulating such legislation.

The committee strongly urged that there should be no restriction without reciprocity—i.e., recognition of the right of CPAs of other states to practice within a state where restrictive legislation existed.

But on the whole, the committee expressed the opinion that restrictive legislation should receive the Institute's endorsement.

The Council, however, did not respond to that recommendation. In fact, when the committee on state legislation revised the model CPA bill and presented it in 1926, the Council deferred action pending settlement of the question of restrictive legislation, and subsequently resolved that the model bill should not include any clause restricting the practice of accounting. The revised version was therefore published in the "permissive" form in 1926.

Thereafter there was a lull.

In 1931, however, the executive committee reported that it had been suggested again that the Institute take a definite stand on the question of restrictive legislation.

Bills of this nature had been introduced in many states. The opinion of Institute counsel had been sought on the constitutionality of this type of law. He indicated doubt as to the constitutionality of restrictive provisions of the sort which had appeared in many bills. The report concluded, "Up to this time the executive committee has been unable to discover a method of restricting the practice of accountancy to certain persons which seems practicable and desirable from the viewpoint of the profession as a whole."

In 1932 the Supreme Court of Tennessee held unconstitutional the restrictive accounting law in that state. In *Campbell v. McIntyre* the court held that the definition of public accounting contained in that law, "including the service of as many as two employers under private contract, is convincing that the restriction is designed for the protection of accountants certified and licensed, and not for the protection of the public in general, and we are persuaded that the statute confers upon this class a right of private contract which is unreasonably withheld from others."

The court did say that there were some specific types of accountancy and auditing work which might be affected with the public interest, and therefore might be a proper subject of regulation.

In 1934, the Institute's committee on state legislation submitted a lengthy report analyzing the restrictive accountancy laws which had been enacted in some states and proposed in others.

The committee came to the conclusion that restrictive legislation was undesirable on several grounds, noting that the supreme courts of some states had held such laws to be unconstitutional; that many of such laws were so drawn as to impede the interstate practice of accounting; and that the enactment of such laws necessarily extended state recognition to unaccredited accountants who were in practice at the time of enactment, thus diluting the prestige of the certified public accountant certificate.

The committee recommended, therefore, that the Council resolve that restrictive accountancy laws of the so-called two-class type were inimical to the interests of the CPAs and of the business public.

The Council adopted that resolution, thus placing the Institute in a position contrary to that of many state societies. Later the Institute's Council withdrew the resolution, taking a neutral position on the subject, and ultimately it endorsed a modified version of regulatory legislation.

Interstate Practice

The Institute was much concerned with legislative impediments to freedom in interstate practice. Most of the larger firms—local, regional and national—were represented in the Institute, and they were the ones most likely to have clients requiring service in more than one state. Furthermore, the trend toward mergers of corporations and the rapid development of nationwide operations by large companies made it necessary that accounting firms be able to move across state borders.

A questionnaire was sent to the members of the Institute seeking their opinions on this question, with the result that "there is evidently an overwhelming preponderance of opinion in the Institute favorable to reasonable facility in crossing state lines in the practice of accountancy."

Smaller local firms, however, many of whose partners were then not Institute members, had no clients with interests outside their own states, and no dealings with metropolitan bankers. Interstate practice troubled them not at all. Local pride encouraged them to support strict requirements for recognition of CPAs of other states, to assure no dilution of the quality of their own certificates. Furthermore, the competition of firms headquartered in the metropolitan centers, which were establishing branch offices in state after state, was a source of growing concern to some local firms.

Whether by oversight or intent, the restrictive laws enacted or proposed in some states did not contain adequate provision for establishment of offices by out-of-state firms, or in some cases even for reasonable freedom to conduct audits within such states.

Reciprocity

Reciprocity, or recognition of "foreign" CPA certificates among the states, had also been a problem for a long time.

It was not until 1923 that New York indicated its willingness to recognize CPA certificates of other states whose standards were comparable to those of New York. In retaliation other states made it hard for New York CPAs who wanted to practice as CPAs within their boundaries.

The difficulties of establishing reciprocity among the states seemed insoluble. One state would not recognize the certificates of another unless the other reciprocated. Any variation in standards between the two would make reciprocity impossible.

The increasing mobility of members of the profession resulted in many individual hardships, when a CPA of one state would move to another, only to find that he could not practice as a CPA there because of the absence of reciprocal arrangements.

New York's breakthrough, in according "recognition" regardless of whether reciprocal relationships had been established with the other state concerned, set a useful precedent. In New York each applicant from another state could have his application considered on its individual merits. If he satisfied the standards prevailing in New York he could receive "endorsement," and be entitled to practice as a CPA in New York.

Turbulence

Partly, perhaps, because of the depression there were many attacks on CPA laws during the thirties. In 1933 alone attempts were made in 22 states to amend or repeal accounting acts. Many of the proposed amendments were outright waiver bills, providing for the issuance of CPA certificates without examination. Two such bills were actually enacted into law in Arizona and Montana. The CPA law of Alaska was repealed without substitute. Freak legislation appeared in Minnesota, Missouri and Ohio, providing respectively for an autonomous society of accountants, for "certified practical accountant" certificates, and for "certificates of qualification" for accountants.

The Institute gave what help it could to the state societies in resisting such adverse legislation. During 1933 the committee on state legislation wrote 475 official letters and received 350 communications. Its report said, "It is an obvious conclusion that eternal vigilance seems necessary if the certified public accountant is to protect what he has won. The attack is being launched on many fronts, and the Institute's committee can be, and is eager to be, of service in co-ordinating the defense."

All through these years the committee on state legislation kept careful track of accountancy bills introduced in the various states. It subscribed to a legislative reference service, which gave early notice of the introduction of any bills related to accounting. Often the Institute learned of the introduction of legislation affecting the accounting profession before the state society concerned had heard of it. In some cases the Institute sent representatives to legislative hearings in defense against bills which would lower standards.

In spite of all the turbulence, however, the CPA movement was incomparably stronger in 1936 than it had been in 1916. While there was much arguing, struggling and fighting ahead, and while the outlook was discouraging at times, it can fairly be said that at the end of 50 years the accounting profession had firmly established the CPA certificate as the hallmark of the professional accountant in the United States.

CHAPTER 17

Relations With the Outer World

A GREAT thirst for public recognition pervaded the young accounting profession throughout its first 50 years— and later. This thirst was never fully slaked, but even a few drops of favorable publicity from time to time were gratefully received.

The old American Association and the new Institute were under constant pressure to get the profession's name in the paper. Yet for many years the profession was not doing much of interest to the general public that could legitimately be described as news.

The more sophisticated members, many of them among the profession's leaders, knew that prestige and respect were gained through public service, and that publicity which recognized the profession's contributions to the public welfare, and its concern for the public interest, would flow naturally after the fact.

Relations With Bankers

Bankers were natural targets for the profession's public relations efforts. If they could be convinced that independently audited financial statements were useful to credit grantors, immediate benefits might flow. Bankers were in a position to encourage borrowers to engage independent auditors. Furthermore, bankers were respected and influential citizens, and their support could do much to enhance the prestige of the emerging profession.

To the delight of the accountants, the American Bankers Association recommended to its members in 1908 that paper purchased from notebrokers should be accompanied by financial statements audited by certified public accountants. So far as was known, this was an unsolicited testimonial.

The American Association was stimulated to follow up on this auspicious event. A survey was made of 850 bankers in all parts of the country, asking their attitudes toward certification of borrowers' statements by public accountants. The response was favorable, and the replies provided material for a booklet on audits and commercial credit, which was widely distributed.

Subsequently several local clearing-house associations went on record as approving independent audits in conjunction with loan applications.

The Journal of Accountancy for July 1914 contained an article by Joel Hunter, head of his own firm in Atlanta, and a member of Council, entitled "The Public Accountant and the Credit Man." The author had corresponded with the officers of each credit men's association in the United States, as listed by the National Association of Credit Men. About 175 letters were sent out. Sixty-two replies were received, 52 of which made specific suggestions.

The consensus was in favor of certified balance sheets. Twenty-four respondents were satisfied with that, but 21 added the thought that the accountant could best serve the credit man by devising appropriate accounting systems. Among the specific suggestions were the following: the accountant should be a business adviser; he should ascertain collectibility of notes and accounts receivable and disclose contingent liabilities; he should disclose the cost of doing business; financial statements should be in uniform style; inventories should be scrutinized; a false-statement law should be enacted in each state; the statements of large creditors should be verified.

Mr. Hunter wrote, "I think that it is as the business adviser that the accountant finds his highest mark of usefulness. . . . When a business fails auditors are generally called in. . . . How much better would it be to forestall or perhaps reduce the total loss and call in the advisory or consulting accountant before the failure occurs."

But not all the news was good. In 1914 an item in *The Journal of Commerce* said: "A movement has been started by leading New York banking houses to eliminate the employment of the less reputable certified public accountants. In recent years, and particularly since the passage of the Corporation Tax Law, there have sprung up a great many accounting and auditing firms which employ questionable methods and charge exorbitant prices for their services. Statements put out by mercantile concerns desiring credit are frequently accompanied by accountants' certificates, and banks which buy commercial paper look with disfavor upon certificates issued by accountants unknown to them."

The editor of the *Journal* denied the charges: "As a matter of fact the number of disreputable firms is small, and the fees, particularly in the large centers, are in a measure standardized. But with the broad statement of our contemporary there is no possible quarrel. Every accountant of standing and repute will welcome anything which will tend to raise the standards and to eliminate the unfit. . . . **The public should have sufficient knowledge of the fit and the unfit to be able to make its own selection. If it fails to do so, the result must be on the public's head."**

However, bankers and credit men generally continued to support the concept of independent audits.

In 1915 the American Association's committee on general relations published a brochure entitled "Acceptability of Commercial Paper," which was sent to state societies for distribution to banks. The result was not too encouraging. Only six state societies participated in the effort.

This brochure pointed out that the Federal Reserve Board, in accepting commercial paper as a basis for issuance of currency, demanded financial statements as evidence of the soundness of the original maker. The brochure advocated independent audit of such financial statements, citing the American Bankers Association resolutions in favor of audits for credit purposes.

A second bulletin, "Some Evils of Competition," covered the disadvantages of competitive bidding for accounting work.

The National Association of Credit Men adopted a committee report in 1915 recommending, among other things, "that rating books prepared and issued by mercantile agencies should indicate by symbol whether the rating assigned is based on an audited statement."

In 1916 the Association's committee on general relations issued a third bulletin, entitled "Protection of Investments." Referring to the vast accumulations of capital seeking avenues for safe investment, and to new rules of stock exchanges and state blue-sky laws, the bulletin said that American practice had failed to utilize fully one of the most important safeguards.

The American investor, it continued, "permits the election of directorates, ostensibly in his name, actually self-perpetuating. In too many cases he leaves to these directors not only the conduct of the business but the preparation of reports which are the only means he has of ascertaining the financial condition of his property and the efficiency of its operation. It is better that independent auditors should be chosen by the directors than that the services of such auditors should not be secured, but the best plan is that the shareholder shall elect the auditors. . . . It is vital that every owner of securities have direct access to the unabridged report of the auditor, because in some instances the auditor's report is suppressed or emasculated before it reaches the proprietors. The English Companies Act is generally regarded as the most adequate legislation governing corporate activities . . . there must be annual statements approved by independent auditors, and . . . the auditors shall be elected at the annual meeting of shareholders. The law provides that there cannot be a change of auditors without an opportunity for the retiring auditors to be heard by the shareholders."

After the organization of the Institute as successor to the Association, an unsuccessful effort was made to persuade the commercial credit agencies, Dun and Bradstreet, to specify in their reports whether or not financial statements had been certified by public accountants.

In 1922 formal co-operative relations were established between the Institute and the bank credit men's organization, the Robert Morris Associates, "in the hope of bringing about better understanding between the two professions and with the firm intention of removing evils which exist."

Since then, the bankers have often been called the best friends and severest critics of the accounting profession.

In announcing the formation of the co-operating committees, the *Journal* for May 1922 clearly stated the dilemma which persisted through the following decades:

> The banker . . . expects the accountant to render services in excess of the accountant's engagement and he expects him frequently to display an insistence upon details which the banker himself does not require of his customer. . . . the banker himself is not blameless in the matter. We firmly believe that if the banker and accountant would unite in the demand for access to all matters which have a bearing upon the financial condition of the client, the banker will find that the accountant can render an indispensable service.
>
> It has been openly stated by bankers that they hesitate to insist upon properly certified statements for fear of losing business. If this is true,

as we believe it is in many cases, the banker is not exactly in a position to criticize adversely the accountant who is unable to bring pressure to bear upon the client sufficient to induce a complete exposition of conditions.

A banker speaking at a regional meeting of the Institute in 1924 conceded that until recently bank loans had been made on the basis of confidence in the applicant, based on personal acquaintance, character, or favorable past experience.

The widespread dispersion of business throughout the country and the growth of large corporations, however, made it impossible for any banker to know all those who wished to borrow. The personal element diminished in financial transactions. Bankers needed financial data on which they could rely, and came to recognize that an independent audit by a certified public accountant was a substantial safeguard, in spite of their complaints that some audited statements did not tell them all they needed to know, and that some audits were substandard.

Frequent meetings between the committees of the Robert Morris Associates and the Institute did much to clear the air.

Reference has already been made to their joint recommendations regarding "pro forma" or "giving-effect" financial statements.

In addition, the Robert Morris committee would submit questionable financial statements and auditors' certificates, without names, for the consideration of the Institute's committee, and the points involved would be discussed orally at the meetings. Then for the edification of its own members, the Robert Morris committee would publish in the organization's bulletin items indicating types of reporting that the Institute committee considered substandard.

This educational work was much appreciated. The Committee on Co-operation with Public Accountants became one of the most important agencies of the Robert Morris Associates.

In 1932 co-operative relations were established with the Industrial Securities Committee of the Investment Bankers Association, but no continuing program was developed comparable to that maintained with the Robert Morris Associates. Investment bankers as a group have never shown as keen an interest in accounting and auditing as the credit officers of commercial banks.

The Federal Budget

An example of the effort to exercise some influence in public affairs, even without any direct relation to accounting practice, was the Institute's interest in proposed legislation providing a budget system for the national government. Harvey S. Chase had written extensively on the need for a federal budget, and *The Journal of Accountancy* supported his views. Chase had been appointed as a member of President Taft's Commission on Efficiency and Economy, and vigorously advocated the proposed legislation.

The Budget and Accounting Act of 1921 was praised in the August 1921 *Journal*. The editorial said, "the vigorous manner in which the present administration has taken hold of the organization of the budget system promises well for effective results. . . ."

At the 1923 annual meeting there was a discussion on the national budget system, led by Harvey Chase. General H. M. Lord, Director of the Budget, was also present and addressed the meeting.

This Act, which established the Bureau of the Budget, the office of the Comptroller General and the General Accounting Office, was also to provide in later years additional opportunities for service by the accounting profession. The presence of a national auditor reporting to the Congress not only greatly strengthened federal financial controls, but provided a channel through which the accounting profession could make recommendations for strengthening the system. As the activities of the federal government broadened in scope, the

Institute had frequent occasions to co-operate with the Comptroller General in various ways.

Publicity

The craving for visibility which afflicted most of the members was not satisfied by these limited activities.

When the Institute finally adopted a rule of professional conduct prohibiting advertising by firms or individual practitioners, a resolution was adopted calling for some kind of institutional effort to publicize the profession.

In response, a special committee on professional advancement presented in 1922 a plan for a campaign of publicity, to be financed by a fund of $100,000 raised by voluntary subscriptions. Prior to the 1922 annual meeting about $12,000 had already been subscribed. An additional $6,500 was raised by the members present at the meeting.

The committee noted that while the members' interest in educational advertising by the Institute was high, the response to the appeal for subscriptions had not been commensurate with the interest expressed. The possibility of abandoning the project was discussed at the annual meeting, but it was finally resolved to refer the entire matter to the Council for consideration.

At the next annual meeting there was a general discussion of publicity for the profession, led by Homer S. Pace, CPA, the founder and head of Pace Institute, a highly successful school which eventually became Pace College.

Mr. Pace told the members that for years there had been much talk and various proposals on the subject of publicity for the profession; that efforts had recently been made to raise money for this purpose, but that no precise program had been formulated.

The members' interest in the subject had been heightened,

he said, by the adoption of Rule 11 of the Rules of Professional Conduct forbidding advertising by individual members or associates. Mr. Pace proposed the formation of a bureau of public affairs in the Institute, and the employment of the necessary staff to do its work.

This bureau, as he envisaged it, would make studies of problems of interest to the business and financial community, publish and distribute the results, and send out news releases summarizing the findings. Thus the name of the American Institute of Accountants would be identified with subject matter of direct interest to the public. In addition, the bureau would arrange speeches by members before business groups, and would obtain publicity for the various activities of the Institute, including its annual meeting.

This was a sound idea, Mr. Pace was persuasive, and the members enthusiastically and unanimously recommended to the Council that the plan be adopted. All that was needed was money.

The Council promptly authorized appointment of a special committee on public affairs. Homer S. Pace was chairman. The committee was charged with carrying out, so far as possible, the plan presented at the annual meeting. An appropriation of $5,000 was made for the use of the committee.

Meanwhile, the amounts contributed in response to the previous solicitations for a campaign of national publicity were returned to the subscribers, but new appeals for financial support of the bureau of public affairs were soon necessary.

In 1924 the new special committee on public affairs reported on its activities. It had published two bulletins. The first of these encouraged the use of arbitration in the settlement of business disputes. The Arbitration Society of America had co-operated in its preparation. Eight thousand copies had been printed and widely distributed. Accountants were being engaged as arbitrators more frequently than before. The bulletin had also been noticed in the press.

The second bulletin, on "The Crime Tendency," attracted even more widespread interest. Fifty thousand copies had already been distributed, and another 50,000 were being printed. The bulletin dealt with measures designed to combat crime related to financial affairs, such as embezzlement. The text had been reproduced in many trade and technical periodicals. The bulletin had also obtained wide newspaper publicity.

The bureau had also made a beginning in providing speakers from the profession for outside organizations, and in the preparation of articles by members for newspapers and periodicals. Newspaper publicity for various activities of the Institute was also being secured.

Contributions to a special fund were obtained to finance these activities.

The committee had requested a budget of $30,000, of which staff salaries constituted $14,000, printing and postage $16,000.

The staff of the bureau consisted of Arthur R. Tucker, assistant secretary for public affairs, a secretary and a typist. Mr. Tucker was a former newspaper man, imaginative and energetic. He had been discovered by Mr. Pace, it seems, and employed at his recommendation.

While housed in the Institute's headquarters, and making use of its services, Mr. Tucker naturally assumed that he was responsible to the committee on public affairs, and principally to its chairman. The secretary of the Institute, A. P. Richardson, however, naturally assumed that he was in charge of the entire full-time staff, as he always had been. The intrusion of Tucker into Richardson's offices, while working independently of the rest of the staff and reporting, in effect, to Pace, was a source of irritation.

The irritation grew to tension between Richardson and both Pace and Tucker.

Furthermore, in the minds of the more conservative members of the executive committee and the Council, publicity—even institutional publicity—was a questionable activity. Aggressive efforts to attract public attention were regarded by some as undignified. The rising costs of the program were also viewed with concern.

However, the majority of the members seemed so pleased

with the results achieved by the bureau of public affairs that its budgetary requests were honored and the work went on.

In its second year, 1925, the bureau published a bulletin on "Credit Frauds," of which about 100,000 copies were distributed to accountants, credit men, bankers, businessmen, trade associations, chambers of commerce, attorneys and other organizations. The bulletin was widely praised by the National Association of Credit Men and others.

The bureau also had in preparation a bulletin on "Federal Tax Simplification."

In addition, hundreds of newspaper articles had been distributed, assistance had been rendered in preparing programs for regional meetings, and articles and speeches by members had been encouraged.

At the 1925 annual meeting the work of the special committee was highly praised, and members were urged to contribute to the special fund required to support the work. A budget of $40,000 for the bureau was suggested for the ensuing year.

By 1926, in the three years of its existence, the bureau of public affairs had published six bulletins, more than 300,000 copies of which had been distributed. It had also obtained a large quantity of newspaper and magazine publicity. It had encouraged hundreds of members to participate in public affairs; it had arranged many speeches; it had brought about publication of many articles.

The record was impressive. But the sources of funds were drying up.

At the end of the 1926 fiscal year, Mr. Pace resigned as chairman of the committee on public affairs, and Mr. Tucker resigned as assistant secretary.

The report of the executive committee noted that the program of the bureau of public affairs had been undertaken as an experiment; that it had accomplished a great deal, but efforts to finance the program by membership subscription had not been successful. The Institute's regular income was insufficient to support an activity of this magnitude.

The work of the committee and the bureau was therefore discontinued.

However, there was no diminution of the members' concern for adequate communication with the public. The Institute, therefore, established a small public-relations department in its headquarters staff. The department consisted, at first, of one man, a former journalist, whose principal job was to get out press releases on Institute activities of interest to the financial community, and to stimulate magazine articles on subjects related to the profession's affairs.

After 1929, in the climate created by the stock-market crash, there was a keener public interest in accounting and auditing than in previous years, and the press was more receptive to news of this type. Modest success attended these more modest efforts to obtain publicity.

National Bureau of Economic Research

The person-to-person type of public relations continued as opportunity arose.

In 1929 the National Bureau of Economic Research sought the Institute's co-operation in a study of corporate profits. A special committee was created to work with the Bureau.

Members of the Institute were supplied by this committee with data sheets, on which they were requested to supply certain information for each of their corporate clients for the years 1927, '28 and '29. This information was obtained for some 700 corporations, and turned over to the Bureau for study. Due precautions were taken to prevent identification of either the accounting firms or their clients.

Professor William A. Paton was retained by the Bureau to analyze the data.

The ultimate product was a book, *Corporate Profits as Shown by Audit Reports,* published by the National Bureau of Economic Research in April 1935, with a preface by George O. May, and due credit to the Institute.

This book indicated the average rate of earnings on total net assets, and the average profit rate on stockholders' equity for the entire sample for the three-year period. It also showed the variations in earning rates as between different years and different kinds of enterprises. The study included an analysis of sources of capital; the ownership ratio of trading corporations as compared with manufacturing corporations; dividend policies and corporate savings, and other operating and financial characteristics of the companies represented in the sample.

What Price Public Relations?

The Institute learned a good deal from its various experiments in the esoteric field of public relations. Sustained, broad-scale publicity campaigns cost more than it could then afford. Public service, as in the war, or community service in peacetime, and co-operation with other organizations in areas of mutual interest—such as the bankers and the National Bureau—developed lasting respect in small but influential groups. These activities also often resulted in free publicity when the results of the co-operative efforts were of general interest. Maintenance of a small, full-time public-relations staff was not unduly expensive, and it provided a continuous flow of information about the profession's activities into channels which would reach those who might be interested.

From the 1930's onward that staff function was maintained.

CHAPTER 18

Incidental Intelligence

Since its organization the Institute had its hands full enough, in its efforts to establish technical standards, to develop and enforce a code of ethics, to adjust to expanding legal liability, to deal with the income tax and the Securities Acts, to encourage better accounting education, to press toward a uniform CPA examination, to support sound CPA laws, and to improve the profession's public relations.

But in addition to all this the Institute was becoming involved in the most severe internal struggle in its entire history.

Dissatisfaction with Institute policies resulted in the formation of a rival organization. This in turn led to a schism within the profession which widened steadily for 15 years. The climax was an open fight, which happily was followed by reunion and reconciliation.

There are lessons to be learned from this experience, and for that reason the story will be told in some detail. But first, to complete the record, a few additional facts about the Institute's activities must be recited, and the creation of two other important accounting organizations must be described.

Headquarters Offices

The creation of the library also led directly to the accession of headquarters offices for the Institute. Until 1917, the secretariat had been lodged in "desk space" in the offices of one of the larger firms at 55 Liberty Street. George May's plan for housing the library envisaged that the same quarters would be occupied by the secretariat and the editorial staff.

The income from the Endowment Fund of $150,000 was sufficient to pay not only the salaries and direct expenses of the library itself, but a substantial share of the rent of enlarged offices which could be occupied also by the Institute's regular staff.

Consequently, in 1918, offices were rented at One Liberty Street, New York, and the Institute had a home of its own.

But these offices were swiftly outgrown. In 1920 it was decided to purchase a small building at 135 Cedar Street to accommodate both the growing library and the growing staff. The purchase was financed with little difficulty by the sale to members of $90,000 of 7 per cent 20-year bonds issued by a real-estate corporation formed to hold the property. The bonds were called by lot and redeemed at the rate of $5,000 a year.

For the next 18 years, 135 Cedar Street was the Institute's address.

The Publications Program

Indirectly and accidentally, the library was also partly responsible for significant enlargement of the Institute's publishing activities.

In 1918 the only Institute publications were the *Yearbooks, The Journal of Accountancy* and a monthly *Bulletin* designed to keep the members informed of the month-to-month activities.

To this list were added the special library bulletins. In addition, it was decided that the Endowment Fund would finance publication of *The Accountants' Index*. Also published under the auspices of the Fund in subsequent years were *The Duties of the Junior Accountant*, by W. B. Reynolds and F. W. Thornton; *Introduction to Actuarial Science*, by H. A. Finney; *Audit Working Papers*, by J. Hugh Jackson, and *The Balance Sheet*, by Charles B. Couchman. The Institute's examination questions were also published in book form.

A. P. Richardson, the Institute's secretary and editor of the *Journal*, was a man of letters. Being a trained journalist, writer and editor, he liked the publishing business. The modest success which had attended these ventures into the book publishing field encouraged him to broaden the scope of the effort. In addition, he was tiring of the administrative duties of the secretary's office, and particularly the political infighting, yet to be described, which was going on within the Institute. He had been the target of criticism, much of it unjust, by those who disagreed with policies adopted by the executive committee and the Council.

In 1930, with approval of the executive committee, Mr. Richardson made arrangements with The Century Company to act as publishers of books produced or procured by the Institute.

It was then announced that he had given up the office of secretary, would continue as editor of the *Journal* and other publications, and would devote himself to the areas of accounting education, research, and professional literature.

Four new books were added to the Institute's list of publications in 1931, under the new arrangements with The Century Company: *Fraud, Its Control Through Accounts,* by George E. Bennett; *CPA Laws of the United States,* a compilation arranged by the Institute; *Accounting Terminology,* a tentative report of the Institute's committee on terminology; and *Ethics of a Profession,* by A. P. Richardson himself.

However, the arrangements with The Century Company proved unsatisfactory, and were terminated by friendly agreement in 1932. The Institute created its own subsidiary publishing company, the American Institute Publishing Company, Inc., which took over the entire program.

The list of books published was increased in 1932 by the following: *Law for Laymen,* by Harold Dudley Greeley; *Basic Standard Costs,* by Eric Camman; *Duties of the Senior Accountant,* by F. W. Thornton; a third supplement to the *Accountants' Index;* a new volume of examination questions, and a book of unofficial answers to examination questions. The sales of these and earlier books continued to produce a modest profit.

In 1934 and 1935, six new titles were added: *Financial Examinations,* by F. W. Thornton; *Accounting Evolution to 1900,* by A. C. Littleton; *The Accounts of an Oil Company,* by H. G. Humphreys; *Land Accounts,* by Walter Mucklow; *Cemetery Accounts,* by the same author; and *Legal Responsibilities and Rights of Public Accountants,* by Wiley Daniel Rich.

These contributions to professional literature were significant at the time. Many of them provided information available nowhere else. The foundations of a continuing publishing program by the Institute had been solidly laid.

The Journal of Accountancy had its ups and downs in this period. While the Institute always kept editorial control, The Ronald Press Co. acted as publisher under a contractual arrangement executed in 1914 and renewed periodically by mutual agreement.

A current extension of this contract expired in 1922. It was decided then that the Institute would take over full responsibility for the publication of the *Journal,* including promotion of subscriptions, advertising and fulfillment. This resulted in an increase in staff, for which office space was made available at 135 Cedar Street.

In 1916 the circulation of the *Journal* was 4,940. Two years later it reached a peak of 10,046, and in 1919 advanced to 11,501. By 1922 it was about 14,000, and strenuous efforts to increase advertising volume had produced revenue of $7,000 in that year.

Thereafter a decline set in: by 1926 circulation had dropped to the 11,000 level again, and in 1931, the second year of the depression, the *Journal* showed a small deficit—the first deficit in many years.

The committee on publications said in its report: "The great revolution in customs which has been brought about by the automobile, radio and moving pictures has interfered with reading of all kinds, but especially the reading of magazines, and it seems doubtful if there will ever be a return to the heyday of 20 or 30 years ago."

However, the decline was arrested in 1934, and steady increases occurred in the following years.

The Benevolent Fund

In 1934 the Institute established the American Institute Benevolent Fund, Inc., for the assistance of needy members and their families. The depression had wrought severe financial hardship on some members who were old or ill, and it seemed fitting that their more fortunate colleagues should come to their relief through their national professional organization.

This Fund has been supported by annual voluntary contributions of members and by bequest. Over the years the Fund has given financial assistance to scores of members, or surviving members of the families of deceased members, who were in financial difficulties owing to illness or other misfortunes.

International Relations

The American accountants always attached a good deal of importance to the maintenance of close relations with their colleagues abroad, particularly those of the British Empire, later the Commonwealth. The profession and its traditions had originated in Great Britain, the chartered accountants had attained world-wide respect, and it was pleasant to have their friendly interest in the American profession manifested by official visits to this country.

The International Congress in St. Louis in 1904 had given a great lift to the American accountants. It became customary subsequently for the presidents of the Canadian and United States organizations to exchange visits at the respective annual meetings. Not infrequently official representatives of the English Institute would also appear at meetings in America.

However, there had been no formal international congress since 1904, until the Netherlands Institute of Accountants organized the Second International Congress of Accountants, held in Amsterdam in 1926.

This 1926 Congress apparently was not taken too seriously by the American Institute. It was referred to in the minutes as "an international meeting of accountants." Only a few Americans attended. Three official representatives of the American Institute of Accountants were listed in the book of proceedings—although Professor Robert H. Montgomery was listed as representing Columbia University! Other American accounting organizations were also represented by small delegations.

However, the Dutch Congress inspired Robert Montgomery to propose that the Third International Congress be held in the United States in 1929.

This proposal was approved at the Institute's 1927 annual meeting. Preliminary arrangements were referred to the incoming executive committee with power. This committee resolved that a special committee of not less than 21 be appointed to make the arrangements, and that other societies in the United States should be invited to "assist the Institute" in this task.

In 1928, however, differences of opinion appeared. It had

first been assumed that the Institute would sponsor the Congress. But in April 1928 the Council reconsidered the proposal to hold such a meeting under the control of the Institute. Because of its wish to avoid "misunderstanding among other organizations" the proposal was dropped. Said the Council report: "At the same meeting of Council a resolution was passed authorizing the executive committee, if it saw fit, to appoint a representative to confer with anyone who might be interested in holding an international congress."

The Institute had appointed a special committee on international congress, consisting of 22 members of the Institute with F. H. Hurdman as chairman. On December 30, 1927, a meeting had been held in Washington, to which representatives of other organizations were invited, to discuss plans for the international meeting. At this meeting suggestions were made which were at variance with the intentions of the Council. Said the executive committee, "Question therefore arose as to whether an international congress would be desirable or not in view of the attitude of other organizations which had been invited to co-operate."

It appears that the other organizations were not enthusiastic about accepting a subordinate position in an international congress sponsored by the Institute. Rather than yield its leadership the Institute's Council decided to drop the matter.

Robert Montgomery, however, was not prepared to abandon the project. He formed a committee composed of representatives of all the organizations, including one representative of the Institute. Montgomery was elected president of the Congress, and went ahead with the plans.

The Congress was held in New York in 1929, largely boycotted by the Institute's official family, though the Institute was listed as one of the sponsors.

This incident and others marked a growing estrangement of Colonel Montgomery from the inner circles of the Institute. His views were liberal on most questions. He had come to favor policies which were unpopular with most of the members of Council. As a consequence, Montgomery's name does not appear in any important posts in Institute affairs for the next five years.

In spite of the Institute's passive role, the 1929 Congress in New York was a grand affair. Representatives of 16 countries were present. Honorary presidents were Joseph E. Sterrett, president of the First International Congress in 1904, and E. van Dien, president of the Second International Congress in Amsterdam in 1926. The total attendance, largely from the United States, was about 1,600, making this the largest meeting of accountants ever held in America up to that time.

At the Institute's 1929 annual meeting in Washington, D.C., which immediately followed the International Congress, many of the overseas delegates to the Congress were entertained.

The Fourth International Congress was held in London, England in 1933. It was sponsored by the several accountants' societies of Great Britain under the leadership of the largest, the Institute of Chartered Accountants in England and Wales. Lord Plender, president of the English Institute, was also president of the Congress. Forty-nine societies of accountants from 20 countries were represented. The attendance was well over a thousand.

The American Institute of Accountants displayed great interest in this Congress due, no doubt, to the strong bond between the accounting professions in the English-speaking countries. There were 28 official delegates from the United States and four "visitors." This was the largest representation from any one country outside Great Britain itself.

These three international congresses, occurring in the space of seven years, greatly strengthened personal acquaintances and organizational relationships among the accounting societies of the world. Many warm friendships were formed, which were maintained by correspondence and occasional personal meetings, as members on professional business or on holiday visited other countries. Gradually, a sense of community developed which was to grow stronger over the years.

The result was fruitful co-operation in the advancement of the profession internationally.

National Association of Cost Accountants

At a Council meeting in 1919, a communication from C. B. Williams suggested the creation of a cost-accounting section of the Institute, comprising accountants who specialized in cost work. The matter was referred to the annual meeting of members and was the subject of general discussion. Among those in support of this idea was J. Lee Nicholson, a respected member of the Institute. However, the opinion prevailed that a separate organization would be preferable to a cost-accounting section of the Institute, and the proposal was rejected, on the ground that the primary purpose of the Institute was to serve practicing public accountants.

To be sure, the practicing public accountants were proud of the advances that had been made in cost accounting in the United States, and many of them provided clients with services in this area. However, the structure of the Institute did not provide for the formation of branches or sections in specialized areas. In any event, the Institute was facing enough problems at that time, and probably would not have undertaken another major organizational change for any reason.

Accordingly, those interested in the proposal, among whom Mr. Nicholson was a leader, organized the National Association of Cost Accountants. It was an almost immediate success, due largely to the genius of its secretary, Dr. Stuart C. McLeod. He was not an accountant, but a professor—a teaching fellow in Harvard's department of government, and a professor in the department of public affairs at New York University.

Far from being an absent-minded professor, however, McLeod proved adept at organization and public relations. He was mainly responsible for the organizational structure of NACA, based on centralized control, but decentralization of activity among chapters, which were organized in cities or regions rather than on a state-wide basis.

Stuart McLeod was not only highly intelligent; he was a genial, humorous, convivial soul, who enjoyed immense personal popularity. He traveled the country incessantly, and the membership of NACA grew rapidly.

Dr. McLeod developed a competitive system among the chapters, through which prizes were awarded annually for various achievements, one of which was the production of technical papers, presented at chapter meetings, of high enough quality to be accepted for publication in the *NACA Bulletin*. As a consequence a rich store of literature on industrial accounting was developed over the years.

It was largely due to McLeod's influence that the NACA never undertook any legislative programs, or attempted to set technical standards, which might have brought it into competition with the Institute. He insisted to the day of his death in 1944 that NACA was purely an educational organization, giving thousands of young men an opportunity to learn from others, and in the process, developing a valuable body of technical literature. As a consequence, the NACA and the Institute lived happily side by side over the years.

Controllers Institute of America

Soon after Homer Pace and Arthur R. Tucker resigned their positions in the Institute in 1926, the energetic Mr. Pace launched a new accounting magazine, *The American Accountant*. Arthur Tucker was the managing editor.

The market for accounting magazines was thin, however, and *The American Accountant* found it difficult to obtain sufficient circulation or advertising volume to make it a profitable venture.

In his experience with the Institute and with the new magazine Mr. Tucker had conceived the idea that the controllers of the larger corporations in the country needed an organization through which they could advance their interests.

The National Association of Cost Accountants, being exclusively an educational organization, admitted members without regard to technical competence. Tucker's conception was an organization which would admit only controllers and other senior financial officers of corporations of sufficient size to justify the assumption of a high level of competence, and an interest both in managerial accounting and financial reporting.

The idea was attractive to a number of controllers. The Controller's Institute of America was founded in 1931, and Tucker was engaged as its managing director.

During its first five years, the Controllers Institute was preoccupied largely with building membership, organizing local chapters, and launching its magazine, *The Controller.*

Thereafter, however, the scope of its activities broadened, and especially in the field of accounting principles it developed close working relations with the American Institute. Many years later the Controllers Institute changed its name to Financial Executives Institute.

CHAPTER 19

The Great Schism

W HEN in 1916 the membership by mail ballot approved the constitution and bylaws necessary to change the American Association of Public Accountants into the Institute, perhaps few members realized how radical the change was.

The old Association had become virtually a federation of state societies, whose delegates had ultimate control of the organization. The new Institute was so far as possible modeled on the Institute of Chartered Accountants in England and Wales—a national professional society, setting its own standards for admission, enforcing its own code of ethics, self-governing, independent of legislative influence, and dedicated to high standards.

In the confused, untidy circumstances of 1916—when this emerging profession was struggling with a host of problems, but seemed unable to do much but talk about them—the new Institute's simple, direct approach to a solution must have had strong appeal. The Gordian knot had been cut—or so it seemed.

In truth the knot had not been cut; it had been ignored. And it was going to have to be untied.

In the abstract, the conception of the new Institute was sound enough. If the profession as a whole had adopted this concept in the beginning, there might have been no trouble. But when the first CPA law was passed in New York in 1896 the die was cast. Professional accreditation under state law was chosen as an alternative to accreditation by a private professional society—a "qualifying body."

This choice was, after all, the American way of doing things. Doctors, lawyers and other professions were licensed by duly constituted legal authorities in their own states. In Great Britain and some other countries the accreditation process was conducted by authorized professional societies.

The new Institute immediately found itself in an ambivalent position. To an outside observer it seemed quite plain that this new organization was setting out to compete with the CPA certificate—to make Institute membership a form of accreditation superior to that of the CPA designation.

Yet the vast majority of Institute members were CPAs, and proud of it. Furthermore, under the banner of the Association, only a few months before, they had been dedicated to the promotion of CPA legislation, and to strengthening of CPA standards.

Also, the majority of the members belonged to state societies. Some members of the new Institute's Council had been presidents of their state societies. Others had been delegates of state societies to the board of trustees of the Association. Yet suddenly, under the new Institute structure, the state societies, which had been an integral part of the Association, found themselves without any official ties to the national organization.

A case of schizophrenia was developing. Institute spokesmen sometimes seemed to be talking out of both sides of their mouths. Suspicions of people's motives were aroused. Had a dark plot been hatched by sinister, nameless monarchists to destroy the American way of life and turn the American accounting profession over to King George V? Or, perhaps worse, to turn it over to the New York gang, or to the national firms?

There was no plot. The men who conceived the Institute, and then led it, were men of intelligence, integrity and candor. They saw a young but rapidly growing profession, faced with brilliant opportunities but beset by critical problems, all but immobilized in an organizational structure which thwarted decision and action.

Joseph E. Sterrett, of unimpeachable rectitude, who had lived a life of service to his profession, and whose career reflected honor upon it, was prominent in the movement for the change. He and many others saw that the accounting profession could not move forward without attracting public confidence, and that to attract confidence it was necessary to maintain standards—technical and ethical standards, and standards of competence to be met by those who received professional accreditation.

These men also saw that increasing intervention of the federal government in the economy, and the increasing interest of bankers and investors in what the profession was doing, would require prompt and decisive action on many matters.

The achievements recited in the preceding chapters demonstrate beyond doubt that the new Institute, in the period from 1916 to 1936, accomplished incomparably more in establishing standards, in reacting to changes in the environment, and in enhancing the profession's stature than it had been possible to accomplish in the 30 years preceding.

Nevertheless, the new Institute faced serious political problems, and they were not always well handled. Perhaps because their eyes were fixed upon the stars, the leaders forgot that the most important factor in an organization is people.

The political problems were compounded by the difficulties of transportation. There were no jet airplanes: there were no commercial airlines at all until 1926, and even in the early 1930's it took some 20 hours to fly from New York to San Francisco. By rail the same journey consumed three days and four nights.

It was therefore not easy to talk to people face to face in the various parts of this vast country. Institute officers could spend two or three weeks on a barnstorming trip, but meet the CPAs in only comparatively few cities.

Consequently, rumor had virtually free play, and local gossip could distort facts beyond recognition.

The political problems were finally resolved, not without trial and error, conflict and compromise over the 20-year period. How it happened is a fascinating story of social adjustment. And there are lessons in this story for present times.

What came out was an organization better either than the old Association or the new Institute as originally conceived— an organization which has surmounted the ever-more-complex problems of the modern era.

The New Start

The American Association ended its last year in 1916 with 1,105 members and 64 associates. At the end of its first year, in 1917, the Institute had 1,100 members and 120 associates. There were at that time about 3,300 CPAs in the entire country.

In its zeal for high standards the Institute had set stringent admission requirements: five consecutive years of practice as a partner or sole proprietor, immediately preceding the date of application; and passage of an examination—written or oral. In addition there was an initiation fee of $50.

It was easier to become an associate. The requirements were only to present evidence of "satisfactory" education, training and experience in public accounting and to pass an examination. But associates could not vote, and few self-respecting, mature CPAs wanted to be in an inferior classification. Nor did many CPAs who had already passed an examination want to take another one—to say nothing of the $50 initiation fee.

Long lines of applicants did not form at the Institute's doors. The membership grew very slowly, and this became cause for concern. As John Forbes said later, the feeling grew around the country that the Institute's objective was "to keep the bahstads out."

One of the first things the new organization did was change its name. "The Institute of Accountants in the United States of America" was euphonious. It rolled pleasantly on the tongue, and it had a dignity comparable to "The Institute of Chartered Accountants in England and Wales." But it was too big a mouthful for impatient Americans. On January 23, 1917, legal steps were taken to change the name to the American Institute of Accountants.

There was hardly time to do much else before the country was plunged into the First World War, and the Institute became engrossed with the war activities which have already been described.

There was time, however, for discussion of organizational problems.

Institute vs. CPA

At the very first Council meeting following the organization of the Institute, held in April 1917, concern was expressed about the Institute's policy toward the CPA certificate.

Reference was made to an editorial in the *Journal* which seemed to disparage the CPA. A Council member said, "Now we are all probably prepared to admit . . . that a good deal of CPA legislation is unsatisfactory, that many of the laws are bad and that many of them are badly administered. While admitting all that . . . the bulk of the membership of the Institute is composed of certified public accountants, and it seems to me that . . . we should pursue the policy which was pursued under the old administration, namely, that of a fatherly interest in the welfare of the certified accountant."

These remarks signaled the beginning of disquietude which gradually spread through the country—a feeling that the Institute was cutting itself loose from the CPA certificate and from the state societies, and setting itself up as the superior qualifying body for the profession.

Many CPAs were offended by the Institute's invitation to non-certified public accountants to join it. Furthermore, oral examinations were permitted under certain circumstances, and this made it possible, theoretically at least, that a non-certified accountant could become an Institute member by oral examination, whereas candidates for the CPA certificate had to sit for written examinations.

The Board of Examiners explained that the principal reason for holding oral examinations was to enable men who had long practiced accounting, and who might have lost touch with much of the theory found in textbooks, to demonstrate their eligibility for membership. The questions in the oral examinations were taken largely from the written papers. Complete stenographic reports of the entire oral examinations were made. The orals were held before at least two members of the Board, and the transcript was submitted to a quorum of the Board, in each case.

Unpleasant comments about Institute policies impelled the editor of the *Journal* to respond somewhat defensively:

> The American Institute of Accountants is seeking to avoid any charge of being a closed corporation . . . it would be pure folly to attempt to restrict membership anywhere short of the boundary line of reputation and ability. The Institute wants on its roll every accountant who is honestly engaged in public accounting. . . . Inquiries which have been received . . . indicate that the great majority of practicing accountants will probably apply for membership in the Institute. . . . strangely enough, failure to satisfy some of the boards

of accountancy is not necessarily an indication of lack of ability. We have it on excellent authority that men whose accounting ability is of the highest order have failed.

These predictions were almost completely erroneous. Each year the proportion of members of the Institute who were certified public accountants increased. Few non-certified accountants applied. This was natural, since a man who was willing to sit for the examination would prefer to obtain the CPA certificate and then become eligible for admission to the Institute, if not on the basis of the examination he had already passed, then by oral examination.

Institute vs. State Societies

At the Council meeting in the fall of 1917, a member suggested the development of closer relations between the Institute and the state societies. He suggested provision for local chapters of the Institute, which the local societies could become. He urged that relations between the state societies and the national organization be cemented: "We need it badly in Massachusetts, for whom I plead."

The response was that this matter had been considered, and that it was too early to attempt to organize chapters of the Institute. The president, W. Sanders Davies, said, "We have only just broken away from the society membership; we have only just had one year of individual membership . . . and it seems to me we ought to wait a little longer before we take the matter up. . . . We have been doing all we could to make the local societies strong, and it seems to me that until a year or two years from now we ought not to have chapters."

George May said that the question was a delicate one, and that Institute chapters might be construed as adverse to the state society idea. He suggested allowing a sufficient period to develop a feeling of mutual confidence between the Institute and the state societies. The matter was dropped for the time being.

Federal Recognition?

However, at the same annual meeting some suspicions were aroused by adoption of the following resolution:

> Resolved, That the American Institute of Accountants favors the enactment by the United States Congress of an act providing for the incorporation of companies engaged in interstate commerce, and of trade, professional and educational associations whose activities are national in their scope.

In the debate the resolution was supported on the ground that businesses incorporated under the laws of one state were subject to discriminatory treatment as foreign corporations in other states, which made it difficult for organizations of national scope to operate efficiently. It was pointed out also that several states had enacted income-tax laws, and that others were likely to do so.

A proponent of the resolution said that while the sovereignty of the state had been close to the hearts of the people, "we are, however, at that period in our history when state lines are disappearing and evidence of that is this organization of our own. The necessity of our country having a centralized power . . . is manifesting itself in business and in world politics and in many other directions. . . ."A federal incorporation law, it was said, would supersede state legislation, "which is now an annoyance." This suggested application of the proposed law to the accounting profession.

While ostensibly directed to the problems of business, the inclusion of "professional associations" in the resolution hinted that the real objective of the Institute might be a national charter enabling it to issue accounting credentials—like the

English Institute—and to free the profession from the "annoyance" of the state CPA laws.

Slow Growth

A year later, there was a net loss in membership of five. This was ascribed to the war. The secretary reported, "In view of the extraordinary conditions prevailing it is probably unreasonable to expect the membership of the Institute to increase to any great extent until peace shall have been restored."

However, to encourage membership, the constitution was amended to provide that applicants who had been in the employ of practicing public accountants for five years next preceding the date of their application would be eligible as full members. Previously only partners and proprietors in practice had been eligible as members.

It was evident that dissatisfaction was growing. In his final report as president, Mr. Davies referred to differences of opinion which had arisen within the membership, but urged all to accept the principles laid down by the majority:

> For surely uniformity in practice and strict conformity to the rules of ethics will find favor with the public at large and enhance the reputation of the individual member as well as that of the Institute as a whole. So I would beg of you to remember that we are the pioneers of the profession, and that the standards set by us today will either make or mar its future.

Truer words were never said. The technical and ethical standards being developed then did much to make the future of the profession. But the political problem remained.

In 1919 the war was over, but peace did not bring a sudden growth in Institute membership. There was a net gain of only 25 since the preceding year.

"It is evident," the secretary reported, "that the membership of the Institute is not increasing as rapidly as might reasonably be expected. The enormous demands for accountants' service are bringing more and more men into the profession, and it appears logical to expect that the membership of the Institute would increase at least proportionately. Evidently there must be some reason why accountants do not avail themselves of the privileges of membership."

The reasons should not have been difficult to discern. CPAs were the principal source of members, but many CPAs thought the Institute was trying to downgrade their certificates.

Chapters?

The problem of increasing membership might be solved, some believed, by the formation of local branches of the Institute.

Accordingly, a special committee studied the question of affiliated or subsidiary organizations of the Institute. This committee, headed by the prestigious Robert H. Montgomery, recommended the formation of chapters of the Institute in states or districts, provided that no chapter be formed without approval of the state society in any state where such a society existed.

This report was referred by the Council to the general meeting in 1919, where it was approved.

The dilemma was obvious. The Institute wanted local branches subject to national control. It knew that most state societies would not accept a subordinate position. Yet it could not afford to offend the state societies by establishing competing local organizations against their will.

Growing Dissatisfaction

At the same annual meeting a signal was given which might have been noted by an attentive ear.

It was proposed that members be allowed to describe themselves by the initials "MAIA" and associates as "AAIA," but the motion on being put to a vote was lost.

Resistance against competition with the CPA certificate was growing, even among members most sympathetic with the Institute's professional goals, who were those most likely to be in attendance at the annual meeting.

Despite this warning, however, another step was taken which seemed a needless and almost deliberate irritation.

In 1920 the executive committee recommended that the letters "CPA," and every other designation be omitted from the certificates of membership, and from any other publication of the Institute, such as the *Yearbook*. The Council unanimously adopted the recommendation—it was not referred to the annual meeting, doubtless being considered a minor administrative matter.

In the next issue of the *Yearbook* the asterisks before the names of members who held CPA certificates—the vast majority—were omitted.

The executive committee said it was making this recommendation, "in the belief that membership in the Institute is the first consideration, and not the question of whether a member is a certified public accountant or a chartered accountant or neither."

This was a further indication of the inconsistent attitude of the Institute toward the CPA certificate. While on the one hand making sincere and constructive efforts to strengthen CPA laws, and to establish a uniform CPA examination of high quality, it seemed clear that the Institute intended to make membership in its own ranks a hallmark superior to the state-granted designation.

Each additional evidence of this intention increased the resentment of many CPAs in all parts of the country, who were proud of their title, who believed in states' rights, and who didn't need much encouragement to be suspicious of a national organization whose headquarters were in New York, and many of whose prominent members were of British origin.

In 1920, there were only 1,185 members and 178 associates. In four years the net gain had been a mere 194, while the numbers of CPAs throughout the country had increased from 3,186 in 1916 to 4,997 in 1920.

Something was wrong. There was obvious anxiety about the Institute's becoming remote from the rank and file of the profession. A plan for holding regional meetings was adopted, "as a means to stimulate interest in the Institute." The question of forming local chapters of the Institute was also revived and referred to a committee for further investigation.

Also, membership requirements were again relaxed slightly. In 1920 it was provided that accountants who had been in practice for not less than ten years, one year of which immediately preceded the date of application, would be eligible after examination. Previously, membership had been open only to those who had been in practice for five continuous years immediately preceding the date of application.

A Rival Organization

At the meetings of Council and members in September 1921, there may have been premonitions that something important was going to happen—that the possibility of forming a rival organization was under consideration.

A special committee on subsidiary organizations reported to the Council. John F. Forbes was chairman. It will be recalled that he was one of only two Council members who in 1916 voted against the change from Association to Institute, mainly on the ground that it severed relations with the state societies. His committee's report recommended that chapters of the Institute be formed in each state, and that subchapters subordinate to the state chapters be permitted in cities where ten or more members resided.

So far so good. But then came the bomb. It was further recommended that state chapters consist of the existing state societies, and that all members of existing state societies which became chapters of the Institute, if such members possessed CPA certificates, be admitted to membership in the Institute without further examination.

The report also recommended that in states where no CPA societies existed, or if after 18 months existing state societies did not apply for admission as chapters, independent chapters might be formed. This recommendation was accompanied by the following warning: "It should be kept in mind that this committee clearly discerns the danger in the multiplicity of state societies and in competing state societies."

These recommendations must have been painful to those who had labored to make the new Institute a viable organization. In large measure the Forbes report added up to a reversal of course, a return to a structure similar to that of the old Association—except for the possibility, implicit rather than explicit, that if the state societies became chapters of the Institute they would be subject to central control, as were the NACA chapters, rather than autonomous members of a national federation.

In any event, Mr. Forbes was a man of substance and influence. He was not to be brushed off. His report was discussed seriously by the Council, and finally was referred to the annual meeting of members in 1921, where it was the subject of extended debate.

Mr. Forbes pointed out that the membership of the Institute had increased by less than 300 members and associates in the first five years of its existence. He added that few members living on the Pacific Coast, for example, could come to the Institute meetings. He said that most California CPAs did not understand the benefits of Institute membership, and were not interested in joining it. He contended that if the local societies, in which the members were actively interested, were permitted to become a part of the national body, the profession would be stronger.

The proposal was opposed on the ground that changes in

the Institute's constitution and bylaws would be required, since the admission of state society members to the Institute en masse would violate the existing constitutional requirements for individual application and examination.

A member from New York said that the New York State Society would not wish to become a chapter of the Institute, nor would it wish to have an independent Institute chapter established in that state.

Durand W. Springer of Michigan, who was to become the first president of the rival organization to be created in a few months, made his position clear. He said:

> I believe that those who have studied the history of national organizations have long since come to a realization of the fact that when we changed from the old type of federation to the institute, we cut the props from under us. No national organization has succeeded in acquiring a large membership except as it has done it through state organizations. . . .
>
> It seems to me that the report of the committee is a step looking forward for the purpose of rectifying the error that was made, in the judgment of a good many of the members, when the Institute was formed and we were pulled away from the state societies.

W. P. Hilton, head of his own firm in Norfolk, Virginia, responded that "the admission of all certified public accountants who are not now members of the Institute without further examination—if that should be undertaken, we not only knock down all the structure of our constitution and our Institute and our Board of Examiners, but we depreciate the certificates granted those men who had stood the examination."

Finally a motion was adopted "that the spirit of the committee's report be approved, that the committee be continued and to act in conjunction with the Council, and if that involves amendment to the bylaws, with the committee on constitution and bylaws, to the end that during the coming year a concrete, workable program can be presented to this meeting next year."

Federal Chartered Accountants?

However, at the Council meeting held in conjunction with the same 1921 annual meeting, a proposal was presented in direct conflict, philosophically, with the thinking of the Forbes committee. It was proposed to seek a federal charter incorporating the "Institute of American Chartered Accountants."

A Council member objected that there would be confusion over the existence of two titles side by side. References were also made to anti-British feelings among the membership, which would arouse resentment at the use of the title "chartered accountant." It was also suggested that it would be sufficient merely to obtain a federal charter for the existing American Institute of Accountants.

Proponents of the proposal stated that it was contemplated, if the new corporation should be formed, that the American Institute of Accountants would transfer its membership and assets to the new Institute of Chartered Accountants.

It was suggested that the matter be referred to the general membership for discussion. This was opposed on the grounds that it would result in delay, which might jeopardize the enactment of legislation providing for federal incorporation. If the new corporation were formed, it was said, the membership would have an opportunity to vote on whether they wished to transfer the present Institute to the new organization.

In spite of obvious uncertainty, and some confusion in the minds of many members of the Council, a motion was adopted authorizing introduction of the necessary legislation in Congress.

When news of this action reached the dissident elements it was the last straw. The word spread about the country like wildfire that the Institute was going to form an Institute of Chartered Accountants under federal law. It seemed that the gauntlet had been thrown down before the state societies and the CPAs in general. To some CPAs countermeasures appeared to be an urgent necessity.

But this particular bomb turned out to be a dud. The proposed Institute of Chartered Accountants got nowhere.

The Institute did sponsor a bill in Congress designed for this purpose. However, in conference with interested members of Congress it appeared that "certain legal questions arose," on the basis of which counsel for the Institute suggested that no further effort be made to press for the legislation. The proposal was never revived.

Large Firms and Small Firms

Another motive for creation of a rival organization was revealed by Durand Springer in a debate over the proposed rule against advertising. He said:

> It seems to me that the discussion . . . is based upon a fallacy that accounting is a profession. I do not believe that it is, as things are now constituted. There is such a large proportion of the accounting work that is done by the large interlocking concerns, that the element of personality is entirely lost, and the element of personality must be present in every professional proposition. [The stenographer at this point inserted, "Applause."]
>
> Until the time comes when groups of accountants will, by means of firms or corporations, take care of their own communities, as do the lawyers and the doctors and the dentists and those who are legitimately known and understood to be professional men, we might just as well quit talking about accounting being a profession and admit that it is a business concern of the very highest type, and as a business organization of the highest type, we should determine the methods by which we put it before the public.
>
> When the State of Michigan wrote into its laws the fact that its degrees were given to individuals, as individuals, and that firms and corporations would be prohibited from utilizing the title "certified public accountant," we were met by the objection on the part of some of these organizations that have institutions in various cities, with the statement that they could hardly recognize our justification for putting that into the law. . . .
>
> Now I . . . would not for a moment wish to impute that it is the concerns with offices in a large number of cities that are the greatest violators so far as bad advertising is concerned . . . but I do believe

that we are overlooking the fundamental trouble . . . by considering that we are a profession when, as a matter of fact, accounting throughout the length and breadth of the country is a business of the very highest type.

Tension between the small local firms and the large multi-office firms was growing. Partners of the largest firms were active and influential in the Institute, though many local-firm partners were also deeply involved in its affairs. The organizers of the rival organization were, however, with few exceptions, partners of local firms, the most influential of whom were outside the large metropolitan centers.

The American Society

The American Society of Certified Public Accountants was incorporated in the District of Columbia on the fifth day of December 1921. The organizational meeting was held in Chicago a week later. It is significant that of the 15 officers and directors during the first year of its existence, 12 were also members of the American Institute.

The reasons for the Society's formation could have been foreseen. What they boiled down to was disaffection with the Institute's attitude toward the state societies and the CPA certificate, culminating in the proposal to incorporate an Institute of American Chartered Accountants under federal law.

Another stimulus was the activity of the "diploma mill" (the so-called National Association of Certified Public Accountants which offered CPA certificates to its members).

The single objective stated in the Society's first constitution and bylaws was protection of the CPA certificate.

Later it added "assistance of government authorities in regulating the public practice of accountancy; the improvement of standards of the profession; and the encouragement of an affiliated relation between the American Society and the state societies."

Possession of a CPA certificate was the only requirement for admission. There was only one class of members. Dues were $15, as contrasted with $25 for members of the Institute. Provision was made for affiliation of state societies with the Society.

The Society did not attempt to enforce a code of ethics, but encouraged state societies to handle their own disciplinary problems.

Its directors were nominated and elected by successive mail ballots of the membership, on a regional basis, and the directors elected the officers, who rotated annually.

The Society strongly advocated legislation which would restrict the practice of public accounting ultimately to CPAs— a type of law on which the Institute first took no position, later an adverse position, and finally a favorable position.

The Society published a monthly magazine entitled *The Certified Public Accountant*.

In 1932, in further support of the state societies, membership in the American Society was restricted to CPAs who were also members of state societies.

The Society encouraged all professional activities at the state level, and assisted the state societies in every way possible.

The Society's headquarters were in Washington, and it also worked hard on federal legislation and government agency matters affecting the profession.

The Society did not develop technical standards, or services of the sort which occupied a large part of the Institute's attention, but it competed effectively in the areas where the Institute was weakest. The two organizations were often at odds on policy questions.

The guiding genius of the American Society was Durand W. Springer. Born in 1866, a minister's son, he obtained a master's degree at the University of Michigan, where he later served for a time as auditor. He became a CPA in Michigan in 1906, not long after the CPA law was enacted. He was the first president of the Michigan Association of Certified Public Accountants, and was secretary of the Michigan State Board of Accountancy for 25 years—1913 to 1938.

Mr. Springer was interested in education and organization work, as well as accounting. He served as a high-school principal, and from 1912 to 1917 was secretary of the National Education Association. Later he became secretary of the Association of Governing Boards of State Universities and Allied Institutions.

Five years after serving as president of the American Society, Durand Springer became its full-time secretary in 1926 and continued in that position throughout the Society's life. He had been a member of the American Association and the Institute since 1905, and never relinquished this membership.

Mr. Springer was a man of energy and force. He had a breezy Midwestern manner, put people at their ease, and made friends easily. His varied experience had given him a keen sense of human relations. He was expert in the politics of organizations.

While he may have practiced accounting on his own account at periods, the record does not indicate that he had engaged extensively in professional practice.

He was a man of strong opinions and had no distaste for controversy. He traveled tens of thousands of miles and made hundreds of speeches in building up the American Society, though at the date of its formation he was already 55 years old, and was 60 when he became secretary.

Intraprofessional Competition

In January 1922, one month after organization of the American Society, the editor of the *Journal*, who it must be remembered was also secretary of the Institute, presented an impassioned defense of the Institute's position with respect to the CPA certificate:

> Certain persons, either ill-informed or evilly disposed, have been journeying up and down the face of the land asserting with a great deal of vehemence that the American Institute of Accountants has done nothing and is doing nothing to sustain the prestige which attaches to the title "certified public accountants" as used in the United States.

Since the American Society had just been organized, the implication seemed clear that the Society's emissaries were engaging in "obviously malevolent attacks of this kind," as the editorial put it.

"But for the Institute," declared the editorial, "the CPA degree would today be a thing of 48 varieties, many of which would be utterly unworthy. . . . It must appear to the impartial observer that the Institute has gone to considerable lengths to foster and protect the CPA designation."

Officially, the Institute at first tried to ignore the American Society. In 1922 the Council reported that the National Association of Certified Public Accountants—the diploma mill which peddled spurious CPA certificates—had been put out of business. In making this announcement the Council's report observed, in passing, "other organizations of accountants have been brought to the attention of the executive committee during the year, but their activities have not seemed to call for serious consideration."

It was not to be long, however, before the activities of the American Society would require the most serious consideration.

To strengthen membership support and attract new members the Institute formed regional groups in the Midwest, New England and the Southeast. In 1922, regional meetings were held in Des Moines, Pittsburgh, Hartford, Indianapolis, Cleveland and Boston.

The president of the Institute, or its secretary, or both together, visited and conferred with groups of members in 35 cities in that year.

This face-to-face, two-way communication was useful to all concerned.

For one thing, after the officers had listened to members in the "grass roots," the requirements for admission to the Institute were modified by providing that certified public accountants who had passed examinations satisfactory to the Board of Examiners, other than the Institute examinations, could be admitted to the Institute without further examination; provided, of course, that they met the experience requirements.

At the Council meeting in the spring of 1922, Edward E. Gore introduced the resolution to make this change. He said that many reputable CPAs, who had had long years of practice, dreaded the thought of taking even the oral examinations then required for admission to the Institute. He continued:

> There is also abroad in the land a feeling that the Institute is so functioning as to militate against the interests of the CPA, and that feeling has been carried on to such an extent and has been so traded upon that there has been organized, as you all know, a society called the American Society of Certified Public Accountants, which I am informed comprises five or six hundred men in its membership at this time. . . . I think the Institute should get itself into a form to do all that possibly can be done to encourage those who are really fitted to become associates and members to do so.

J. S. M. Goodloe of New York, formerly of Ohio, expressed the opinion that there was strong feeling on the part of many qualified CPAs who did not feel it should be necessary to submit to a second examination in applying for membership in the Institute.

"I have felt for a long time," he said, "that the requirements for membership, according to the present constitution and bylaws, were entirely too prescriptive, that it was more a matter of whom we kept out than of who would be taken in."

He pointed out that there were 245 members of the New York State Society who were also members of the Institute; 274 members of the state society who were not members of the Institute, and 181 Institute members in New York who were not members of the New York State Society.

John B. Niven, chairman of the Board of Examiners, supported Mr. Gore's resolution and promised that the Board of Examiners would be glad to work under it.

After further discussion, the motion was unanimously adopted. This made membership readily available to CPAs who had passed examinations in most states not using the Institute's examinations.

Mr. Gore then suggested that the matter of organization of Institute chapters be deferred, in the hope that the modification in the requirements for admission might draw into the Institute enough CPAs "to practically convert the state societies into material suitable for chapters."

However, John F. Forbes, as chairman of the committee on subsidiary organizations, reminded the Council that the last annual meeting had resolved "that the spirit of his committee's report be approved." He said that the organization of chapters would require a change of bylaws, and if the matter were held over until the time of the next annual meeting, another year would have been lost.

It was suggested that immediate provision might be made permitting members of the Institute to form local chapters of the Institute. Mr. Forbes replied that a multiplicity of organizations in the same state might lead to quarrels. He felt that the state societies ought to be afforded the opportunity of coming in as chapters: "All through the West you hear about the society of cost accountants (NACA) but you never hear anything about the American Institute, and that is because they have local chapters."

It was stated that it would be impossible to take all the members of the state societies into a chapter of the Institute when some of the individuals were not members of the Institute.

Mr. Sterrett expressed the opinion that while the western societies might be willing to come in as chapters of the Institute, many of the eastern state societies would not. He also contended that chapters formed along state lines would not be successful. Rather, he suggested the formation of chapters in cities in which the members resided. In view of the modification of the membership requirements just approved, he suggested the matter be referred back for further study and discussion at the coming September meeting. This motion was adopted.

The final result was the following amendment to the constitution, recommended both by the special committee on subsidiary organizations, and a special committee of the Council:

> Upon application to the Council of the Institute and subject to its approval there may be organized in any state, by members resident or having a place of business therein, a subsidiary body to be known as a chapter of the American Institute of Accountants, under such rules and regulations as the Council of the Institute may prescribe.

Under the new bylaw, chapters of the Institute were formed in 1923 in Pittsburgh, Illinois, Minnesota and Texas. A California chapter was also approved.

Admit Only CPAs?

Another important proposal was made at Council meeting in the fall of 1923. The committee on constitution and bylaws recommended an amendment providing that no one thereafter could be admitted to the Institute who was not a certified public accountant.

This was a sound and timely suggestion. In 38 states the

Institute's examinations were being used as examinations for the CPA certificate. Furthermore, the Board of Examiners had just been authorized to accept satisfactory examinations other than those of the Institute, which opened the door to hundreds of CPAs in New York, Pennsylvania, and other states not using the Institute's examinations. The membership was already composed mainly of CPAs. All states had enacted CPA laws.

Restriction of Institute members to CPAs in the future would have deprived the American Society of one of its selling points, as the injunction against the National Association of Certified Public Accountants had deprived it of another.

Nevertheless, the proposal to admit only CPAs in the future was opposed. It was suggested, for one thing, that if any such restriction was adopted provision should also be made for admission of chartered accountants of other countries. No doubt some members of Council disliked the idea of appearing to be stampeded into a change of policy under the pressure of the American Society's competition.

In any event, the proposed amendment was put to a vote and failed to obtain approval. The Council recommended that the amendment not be adopted.

Yet Edward E. Gore, who had become president, renewed the proposal immediately.

In his report to the annual meeting he expressed concern about an impression abroad that the Institute "if it is not actually hostile to the CPA degree, is at least indifferent as to its possession by Institute members. . . .

"To make plain that the impression referred to is utterly without foundation, and because no further need exists for the extension of the privilege of membership to those who are not certified public accountants, it is recommended that the bylaws be so amended that after the expiration of a brief period applications for membership in the Institute will be entertained only if they emanate from those who hold the degree of certified public accountant . . . or of reputable accountant societies of Canada or Great Britain. This measure

. . . would thus secure the friendly feeling of a considerable body of accountants who have been misled by the false representation made."

This report must have been written prior to the meeting at which the Council had acted adversely on the proposed amendment to substantially the same effect; or possibly Mr. Gore deliberately ignored the Council's action and took his appeal to the membership directly. Nevertheless, the amendment was defeated on the floor of the annual meeting.

Among those who opposed it was Durand W. Springer, a leader of the American Society, who took part in the discussion on the floor of the annual meeting. He suggested that the issue was extremely complicated, and that it would be untimely to adopt the proposed amendment restricting membership in the Institute to CPAs without further study.

Growing Concern

At the final meeting of Council, immediately following the 1923 annual meeting, a member urged that steps be taken to bring back into the Institute the membership of the recently formed American Society of Certified Public Accountants.

A motion was made that a committee be appointed to explore this matter. It was opposed by numerous members of the Council on various grounds: for one thing, admission of members of the American Society as a group would include many individuals who could not qualify under the Institute's standards.

However, there were also evidences of personal rancor. It was said that the attitude of the Institute toward the CPA certificate had been misrepresented in an effort to develop support for the American Society. It was recalled that the Institute had obtained the injunction against the National Association of Certified Public Accountants; yet that association's activities had been one of the alleged reasons for the formation of the American Society, in the supposition that the Institute was doing nothing about it. It also pointed out that the Institute had spent money and taken action to improve state CPA laws and to defeat efforts to weaken them.

The proponent of absorbing the Society said it had been rumored that the American Society might offer the states a CPA examination in competition with that of the Institute, which could destroy the approach to uniformity.

Nonetheless, his motion was defeated.

Following the 1923 annual meeting, A. P. Richardson asked the Council for a leave of absence. He was exhausted, and in poor health. The double duty as secretary and editor was demanding, and the internal conflicts added an emotional strain.

Mr. Richardson was a scholarly type, widely read, sensitive, who really preferred his literary labors to dealing with his varied constituency as secretary. But he had worked hard at building the Institute, had traveled widely making speeches and meeting members, and he naturally had a strong sense of identity with the organization. When the Institute was criticized he took it personally, and the reactions absorbed nervous energy.

In addition to a leave of absence, he requested permission to employ an assistant secretary, when a suitable person could be found, to relieve the secretary-editor of part of the workload.

The Council unanimously granted both requests, with an expression of concern for the secretary's health.

A year later more of the Institute's leaders were showing concern about the progress and activities of the American Society. While the Society had been in existence for only three years, the disadvantages of having two national professional organizations were becoming apparent. Pressures to modify some of the Institute's policies were developing.

At the spring Council meeting in 1924, John B. Niven, chairman of the Board of Examiners (who, incidentally, was about to become the president of the Institute), proposed a minor but significant change in policy. In introducing the change, he said:

> I would remind you that in 1916 the American Association went out of existence and the Institute came into existence, and the general idea underlying that change was that the members of the profession and of the Institute should be put in better position to control their own affairs. Whether that was a wise move or not has been the subject of a good deal of question. . . .

He recalled that in order to make the method of entry into the Institute "a little more simple," the rules had already been changed so as to admit applicants who had passed the CPA examinations of states which had not used the Institute's examinations. However, not as many new members had been obtained by reason of that change as expected. Mr. Niven explained that, in a sense, this put applicants who had taken Institute examinations and whose papers had been graded by the Institute at something of a disadvantage, since the non-Institute states might not grade as severely as the Institute's examiners.

He then stated that legal questions had arisen about the right of some boards to send their papers out of the state for grading by the Institute, and proposed that the Institute offer its examinations on an optional basis, for a lower fee, to states that preferred to do their own grading without reference to the Institute. This would be done with the understanding that if an individual in one of these states should apply for admission to the Institute later, the Board would have a right to review his papers.

"We who are reading the handwriting on the wall," Mr. Niven continued, "think it may throw open the doors quite considerably to entry into the Institute. It won't quite get back to the point of the old American Association idea where every CPA who came along was entitled to membership, but it goes a good way in that direction."

At this point, Colonel Montgomery rose to express some doubts that had arisen in his own mind about the best course of action. He pointed out that under a regulatory bill, which had passed both houses of the New York legislature, only CPAs would be entitled to practice. But apparently many public accountants then in practice could become CPAs without examination. This, he suggested, might result in more than 2,000 CPAs in New York, while the Institute had only some 400 members in that state.

"The question is," said the Colonel, "do we want to encourage them to come into the Institute. . . . If we talk frankly about the American Society, which purports to be a national body of CPAs, that society of course will welcome those new CPAs into its membership. If the American Society should become a vastly stronger society numerically than ours, it will then bring about more confusion in the mind of the public as to the two national bodies. . . . A few years ago, before I became president of the New York State Society, I was as keen as anyone in the Institute for the highest possible standards. . . . I was very reluctant, in the beginning, to reduce the standards." But he said that he had become inclined to be interested in a society that contained most of the CPAs of the country. "Is it possible to look in the near future toward a liberalization, or shall we stand pat?"

Arthur W. Teele said that if the Board of Examiners accepted applicants whose papers had not been graded by the Institute's examiners, it would change the standards of the Institute. He suggested moving slowly, and deferring action on the new plan.

Colonel Montgomery agreed that the Institute probably should go for one thing or the other—a policy of taking in all CPAs, or else maintaining a very high standard. While a start had been made on liberalization, he suggested that a special committee study the whole problem with a view to plans for the future.

This suggestion prevailed, and a motion was adopted that a special committee study the whole matter.

The Board of Tax Appeals Incident

In 1924 the American Society gained another talking point at the expense of the Institute. The Board of Tax Appeals had issued its rules admitting only lawyers and CPAs to practice before it. The Institute, which included some 200 non-certified members, requested an additional provision for admission of "members of any professional society of accountants, admission to which is dependent upon the passing of professional examinations of a standard at least equivalent to that of any state."

The American Society opposed this provision, holding that only CPAs and lawyers should be admitted. Charles D. Hamel, chairman of the Board of Tax Appeals, informed the Institute that the Board "had not found it desirable to modify its rules" as suggested.

The incident, however, got under President Gore's skin. In his report at the 1924 annual meeting he said:

"With about 1,700 members of our organization who are certified public accountants," said Mr. Gore, "can anyone imagine that the Institute would do anything to injure their interests?" With respect to the Institute's proposal that about 200 members who were not CPAs also be admitted to practice before the Board, he said, "The Institute could not do less and retain the respect even of those who are certified." It would be easy, he said, for the executive committee and officers to ignore the 200, "but it is inconceivable that the Institute should do anything of that kind. The Institute has being accused of betraying the certified public accountants; it has been accused of trying to change the rules so that the tax expert could practice. I want to refute these statements."

Conciliatory Gestures

As a partial antidote to the anti-CPA charges, the Institute in 1924 quietly reversed another policy. It resumed the practice of indicating by asterisks against their names in the *Yearbook* those members and associates who were CPAs. Since these were 86 per cent of the total, the new *Yearbook* made an impressive visual exhibit of the actual state of affairs.

In the same year the olive branch was held out to the academic community by reversal of another earlier action.

An amendment to the bylaws was adopted providing that accountants engaged in accountancy instruction were eligible for full membership if they had taught accounting for a period of not less than five years next preceding the date of application, in schools recognized by the Board of Examiners, and were certified public accountants.

In 1924 additional chapters of the Institute had been organized, making a total of 15 chapters in all: California, Illinois, Kansas City, Maryland, Massachusetts, Michigan, Minnesota, Northern Ohio, Oregon, Philadelphia, Pittsburgh, Rhode Island, St. Louis, Southern Ohio, and Texas.

As the process of liberalization and improvement of membership relations gradually continued, informal conversations were undertaken between representatives of the Institute and the American Society. These talks resulted in a communication from the American Society expressing willingness to submit to its membership any plan for a policy of co-operation which might be formulated by a joint committee and would be satisfactory to the governing bodies of both organizations.

Thereafter, a special committee of the Institute, headed by John B. Niven, met with representatives of the American Society to continue the discussions. The executive committee reported, "The substance of the opinions of the two committees seems to be that there should be no thought of departing from the standards set up by the Institute, but that there might be some points of contact upon which committees of the two organizations could co-operate or confer."

In 1925 the special committee on co-operation with other organizations published a memorandum for the information of the membership. It stated in part, "There has been an unfortunate prevalence of misconception in regard to the aims and accomplishments of the Institute." The memorandum reviewed the reasons for formation of the Institute in 1916. It continued with the statement that the Institute was the premier national organization, but if other organizations having no special professional requirements for admission embraced accountants who had not yet reached the standard demanded by the Institute, the Institute would co-operate with such organizations.

It was further stated that the existing requirements for admission as associates of the Institute were quite liberal. Any practicing accountant who had two years professional experience, if he were a certified public accountant of a state having acceptable standards and had passed a satisfactory examination, could be admitted to the Institute without further examination.

The memorandum then reviewed the activities of the Institute in obtaining an injunction against the National Association of Certified Public Accountants.

The formation of the American Society was described. The Institute's activities in strengthening and supporting CPA laws were stated to be "the means of saving the certified public accountant's certificate from disrepute and disregard." It was said that most of the CPA laws in the country were founded on the model bill approved by the Institute.

The memorandum continued, "The campaign of misrepresentation conducted during the past year relative to the action of the Institute's officers in regard to the rules of the Board of Tax Appeals was definitely laid to rest by the action of the Institute at its meeting of September 1924, at which there was unanimous approval of what had been done."

The plan of co-operation in the conduct of examinations in which most of the states were participating was described.

The memorandum concluded: "There is a great appeal in the suggestion that there should be one all-inclusive body, and the committee has given much thought to the suggestion that there should be a consolidation of all national accounting organizations. Alluring as this suggestion may be, the committee regrets that it has been compelled to reach the conclusion that such fusion is not practicable and in many ways would not be desirable. The Institute is primarily an organization of selective membership. It cannot admit everyone who may happen to make application based upon qualifications not equivalent to its standards."

The conclusion was that there must be no lowering of standards for admission to the Institute. Enforcement of the code of ethics must be universal. Yet the Institute must not relinquish its interest in the strengthening of the certified public accountant certificate.

Meanwhile, however, the work of removing targets for criticism continued.

In 1925 the bylaws were amended to provide that applicants should have had at least one year of the required public accounting experience in the United States of America. This appears to have been a concession to critics of "foreign" influences in the Institute, though by that time there could have been very few accountants from abroad who would apply for admission to the Institute without having practiced in the U.S. for a year. The amendment was largely symbolic, but an indication that the Institute was learning the importance of symbolism.

Also in 1925 the Board of Examiners raised the age requirement for oral examinations from 30 to 40 years. Indeed, it raised the question whether oral examinations should be discontinued, but the Council preferred to defer that decision.

At the same time an amendment was proposed again to provide that no applicants should be admitted to the Institute who did not hold a CPA certificate issued by the state in which the applicant resided or practiced.

Surprisingly, Edward Gore this time spoke against the amendment.

"During the last four years," he said, "I have advocated the enactment of an amendment substantially the same as that which has been read. I have, however, come to a change of mind and I have been very much encouraged in that change of mind by the action of the legislature in my own state during the past half year. I have seen a state legislature used to carry out the purposes of politicians, men who know nothing about the accounting profession, and I have witnessed the possibility that lies before us in the treatment of the CPA laws of the various states whenever they may become the football of the politicians. The result convinces me that the place of the American Institute is one of independence. It must stand as the guardian of the standards of public accountancy in the United States. . . . I think no more serious error could be made than to enact the amendment that has been proposed."

The proposed amendment was defeated with only two votes in its favor.

Mr. Gore then offered a resolution that the Institute reaffirm its belief in the necessity of a strong national organization, immune from the caprices of legislators; and that the Institute should do all that lay within its power to protect the interests of those engaged in the legitimate practice of the profession, particularly endeavoring to aid in the preservation and improvement of state laws which provided for the registration of CPAs.

This resolution was unanimously adopted.

Thus, the Institute declared its support for the CPA certificate, but refused to make the certificate a requirement for membership in its own ranks. While, in retrospect, this seems a puzzling attitude, there can be no doubt of the sincerity of those who, like Mr. Gore, felt it logical to take both positions at once.

There were political attacks on CPA laws. There were many people in the country who had received CPA certificates without examination or without experience in public accounting. There was a need for a strong national organization setting a high professional standard.

At the same time there was a need for an organization which could unite CPAs of the country; the American Society of Certified Public Accountants was threatening to fill that role.

In his presidential address to the annual meeting in 1925, Mr. Niven made the following remarks: "I cannot help expressing the personal conviction which I have always held, that we ought to avoid any possibility of clashing with state societies. In all our chapter activities, we should co-operate to the largest extent with state societies and in every way possible avoid duplication of effort."

It may be inferred that there was evidence of clashing or duplication between Institute chapters and state societies.

"This leads," Mr. Niven continued, "to a reference to our relations with the American Society of Certified Public Accountants, with whose representatives a committee of the Institute met during the year, to discuss matters of mutual interest. The question even of amalgamation was discussed, but while this was not considered feasible, the principle of co-operation was, I am glad to say, cordially accepted by both committees, which I hope may bear much fruit."

Competition in Examinations

In 1928 the American Society aligned itself against the Institute on another issue. It suggested that the plan of co-operation in the conduct of examinations be modified by offering a number of questions and problems from which a state board of accountancy might select at its discretion.

The Society's communication stated that uniformity in examinations was unlikely, and that no other profession had achieved it. The letter stressed that state boards had the legal responsibility to set their own examinations. It said that if the Institute would modify its plan, the American Society would not take any action. If not, the Society would offer state boards questions and problems from which they could select at their discretion.

The Institute rejected this offer and the Society proceeded

with its plan, in which a number of states not already using the Institute's examinations participated.

A New Secretary

As recounted earlier, the executive committee in 1930 approved an expanded publishing program, under arrangements which had been discussed with The Century Company.

In reporting on this matter the Council said: "It seemed to the committee inevitable that this new venture would greatly increase the activities of the Institute in the field of publication, and in view of the fact that the secretary had expressed a wish to be relieved of the technical duties of the secretaryship in order to devote greater attention to questions of education, research and professional literature, it was resolved that A. P. Richardson be appointed editor and that his place as secretary be filled by John L. Carey, who had been assistant secretary since June 1925. At the same time it was resolved that Mr. Richardson be requested to hold himself in readiness to give information or advice to any officer of the Institute in order that the Institute should not be deprived of his experience and knowledge." These actions were approved and the elections confirmed by the Council at its meeting on April 14, 1930.

The new secretary was 26 years old. He had been graduated from Yale in 1925, with a major in English, a Phi Beta Kappa key, and some minor evidences of indifferent athletic ability. Four days after graduation he went to work for the Institute, with vast enthusiasm and equally vast ignorance of what it was all about. But in five years as assistant secretary, under A. P. Richardson's effective tutelage, he had learned a lot. With some trepidation, but with an outward expression of calm confidence, he donned the mantle of the secretary, which Mr. Richardson was glad to doff.

Following his interim appointment in January 1930 the new secretary and the president, Frederick H. Hurdman, traveled widely, appearing at meetings of state societies or their chapters in Tulsa, Dallas, San Antonio, Houston, New Orleans, Birmingham, Atlanta, Chicago and St. Paul.

The annual meeting in 1930 was held at Colorado Springs, and subsequent to that meeting the new president, Charles B. Couchman, and the secretary visited state society groups in Salt Lake City, Portland, Seattle, San Francisco and Los Angeles.

The objective was to bring the Institute into closer personal touch with the largest possible number of CPAs, both members of the Institute and prospective members. The fact that the American Society was gaining membership steadily had not gone unnoticed.

To make it easier for applicants to obtain admission to the Institute, the bylaws were again amended in 1930 to provide that the continuity of public accounting practice might be considered unbroken by a temporary interruption consisting of activity which in the opinion of the Board was equivalent to public accounting. The process of liberalization was continuing.

When the full force of the depression hit the Institute in 1931, the membership declined for the first time in years. By early fall of that year it was 2,182, as compared with 2,196 the year before. There were more than 13,000 CPAs in the country.

A Turning Point

In 1932 John F. Forbes was elected president of the Institute, after many long years of laboring in the vineyard. He was one of the outstanding leaders of the profession in California, and there had been some resentment among his colleagues there that he had been passed over for the presidency in earlier years.

But as noted frequently in these pages, he was an independent and not always a conventional thinker. He was one of the two Council members who had voted against the reorganization of the old American Association in the form of the new Institute. He had been chairman of the committee which had recommended taking in state societies as chapters of the Institute. He was not, therefore, regarded as entirely "safe" by the conservative elements in the Institute.

However, Mr. Forbes was a loyal Institute member. He had keen political insight. He knew that the gains made by the American Society were largely the result of ineffective communications on the part of the Institute with the rank and file of the profession, and actions and attitudes on the part of the Institute which were unnecessarily irritating to many CPAs.

Furthermore, Mr. Forbes enjoyed a contest. He made up his mind that the Institute would give the American Society a run for its money.

Charles B. Couchman, the retiring president, was also of a liberal and progressive frame of mind. He applauded Forbes' objectives.

Frederick H. Hurdman, who had preceded Couchman in the presidency, and had indoctrinated the new secretary, was wholly sympathetic with the views of Forbes and Couchman. Hurdman became convinced that there was no need for two national organizations, and that one way or another one of them must be eliminated—either by merger or through competition.

These three men—Messrs. Forbes, Couchman and Hurdman—made a powerful combination—intelligent, experienced, and skillful in dealing with people. With Forbes' election as president, a turning point had been reached.

He was a highly pragmatic man and a skillful tactician, with a clear understanding of the uses of power. At this time he retired as a partner of Haskins & Sells, and opened an office as a consultant in San Francisco. This enabled him to spend more time on Institute affairs than otherwise would have been possible. Later he formed the West Coast regional firm of John F. Forbes & Co. He had accepted defeats as a member of Council. Once in office, however, he had no hesitation in using the influence of the presidency to move the Institute in what he considered the right direction.

His immediate goal was to build the Institute to a position of strength from which it could negotiate a merger with the American Society, if necessary, without weakening the Institute's basic structure or altering its major objectives.

His formula was relatively simple: to make it as easy as possible to join the Institute; to travel as widely as possible for face-to-face meetings with the state societies and Institute members; to publicize as widely as possible, through speeches and other available media, the effective work that the Institute was doing in maintaining professional standards, working with the federal government, the stock exchanges and other important groups, and serving its members through publications, the library, and the bureau of information. He hoped to increase the membership, and secure the goodwill of the state societies by removing relatively unimportant irritants without impairing the quality of the Institute as an organization.

During his first term in office, for example, he gained approval for a refund of initiation fees hitherto required of applicants for membership—$50 for members and $25 for associates. Later these fees were eliminated completely.

At the 1933 annual meeting an amendment to the bylaws was adopted making it easier for a member who had resigned or had been dropped for non-payment of dues to rejoin the Institute.

In his first presidential address Mr. Forbes said:

> While under our form of organization the formation of chapters in the Institute is permitted, we have never encouraged permanent local organizations subordinate to the Institute for the reason that we have felt that all local organizations should be a part of or subordinate to the state societies. We feel that the state societies

should control the situation within the state, and that the Institute should concern itself principally with other matters of nationwide or world-wide interest. We have felt, too, that the creation of strong, local Institute units might in some way retard the development of the state societies, and for this and other reasons have not encouraged their extension.

Mr. Forbes was using the editorial "we." He had not asked the Council for an expression of policy on this question, and there is no doubt that many of its members would have disagreed with this statement. But he went ahead and made it, and got away with it. There is no doubt that it was well received by the state societies.

President Forbes also created a special committee on development of the Institute, consisting of about 50 members resident in all parts of the country. Their duties were to spread the Institute's gospel and to encourage applications for membership. As a result, in spite of the depression, there were 319 applications in the year 1932-33—the largest number in any single year in the Institute's history.

However, 1933 was the low point of the depression, and again there was a net loss in membership, which declined by 14 to a total of 2,169. The losses through death, resignation, and most of all non-payment of dues, were the heaviest the Institute had known in a single year. But by the end of the fiscal year 1933-34, despite continued heavy losses, there was a net gain of 143, bringing the total to 2,312, largely as a result of the policies and energetic efforts of the president.

CHAPTER 20

The Profession Is Reunited

By 1933 neither the Council of the Institute nor the directors of the American Society were eager for a merger. The Society was flourishing, and the Institute was making substantial progress. The leaders of both groups had worked hard in building up their organizations, they had developed strong loyalties, and they sincerely believed that their philosophical differences were irreconcilable.

But the rank and file, for the most part, had a different view. They saw little fundamental difference between the two national organizations. Both were to all intents and purposes organizations of certified public accountants. The number of non-CPAs remaining in the Institute was insignificant, and was declining steadily. Both organizations proclaimed support of the CPA certificate and sought the support of the state societies. The Institute's abortive efforts to obtain national accreditation had been abandoned, and its chapters were lapsing into inactivity. The Society was doing the better job in serving the state societies, in promoting regulatory legislation, and in maintaining relations with Congress and government agencies in Washington—the site of its headquarters office. The Institute was doing the better job in developing technical and ethical standards, in providing technical publications, in developing a uniform CPA examination, in serving members through its library and bureau of information, and in maintaining relations with bankers and the New York Stock Exchange.

Many hundreds of CPAs belonged to both organizations, and many hundreds belonged to neither. The state societies felt obliged to deal with both, but would have preferred national leadership from one source.

With increasing frequency CPAs were asking why the two organizations should not get together, stop squabbling, and pool their resources for the benefit of the profession.

The time was ripe for someone to mobilize the rank and file, and to apply pressure on the policymakers of the two national organizations.

The New York State Society assumed this role. It was the largest state society. Its membership had grown to a number only a little less than that of either the Institute or the American Society. The redoubtable Colonel Montgomery had been president of the New York State Society some years before, and probably had more influence among its members than any one man. He had become convinced that a merger of the two national organizations was essential. His partner, Walter A. Staub, was president of the New York State Society in 1933.

Pressure from Outside

In that capacity Mr. Staub wrote a letter to the president of the Institute, John Forbes, suggesting consolidation of the

Institute with the American Society, and stating that a circular letter on the subject was also being sent to the presidents of all state societies.

This letter was considered at the Council meeting in April 1933. A motion was offered that the chairman appoint a committee to co-operate with a like committee of the American Society to consider the question. There was visible resentment at the intervention of the New York State Society in this delicate area. The motion was defeated, 19 to two.

Mr. Staub then requested an opportunity to address the Council at its next meeting, October 16, 1933, and President Forbes readily consented.

At that meeting, Mr. Forbes introduced Mr. Staub to an audience which with a few exceptions was clearly hostile.

Mr. Staub was well prepared. He spoke calmly and persuasively. He said that when the Securities Act of 1933 was under consideration both national organizations had committees attempting to present their separate views on the proposed legislation. The appearance of Colonel Carter, as president of the New York State Society, before the Senate committee, Mr. Staub suggested, might have been due to the fact that there were two national organizations instead of one. Personally, Mr. Staub would have preferred that the profession speak with one voice through one national organization.

After the Securities Act became law, he continued, the committees of the two national organizations made contact with the Federal Trade Commission with a view to participating in the framing of regulations. The chairman of the Commission was reported to have asked why the two organizations did not get together.

Mr. Staub said that the competitive relations between the Institute and the American Society tended to delay policy decisions on a national scale. He also referred to the difficulty of establishing close co-operative relations with the state societies when there were two national organizations. The state societies, he said, "have to pursue a sort of middle-of-the-road policy and show favoritism to neither, and the consequence

355

is that the co-operation is really of a lukewarm character."

As background information, Mr. Staub presented an analysis of memberships: Of 1,800 members of the New York State Society, 150 were members of both the Institute and the American Society; 245 were members of the Institute but not the Society, and 250 were members of the Society but not the Institute. There were 1,151 who were not members of either. In addition, there were 50 New York members of both the Institute and the American Society who were not in the New York State Society. There were 217 in the Institute who were not in either the American Society or the New York State Society, and there were 135 in the American Society who were not in either the Institute or the New York State Society.

The original intention to make Institute membership the major national symbol of professional qualification, Mr. Staub said, was no longer realistic. The designation "certified public accountant" had acquired widespread recognition in the 17 years since the Institute had been organized, and the standard of examinations nationally had greatly improved, largely due to the Institute's efforts.

In conclusion, Mr. Staub did not ask the Council to express any opinion on the desirability of unification, but simply to authorize appointment of a committee to study the subject.

After these remarks, Mr. Staub withdrew from the meeting and the regular business of the Council was transacted.

Then the chairman asked whether, if the Council wished to discuss Mr. Staub's remarks, he should be invited to return to the room during such discussion. It was moved that Mr. Staub be invited to participate in the discussion. The motion was seconded and put to a vote. Sixteen members voted in the affirmative and ten in the negative. Mr. Staub was invited to return, and did so.

A motion was made to appoint a committee in accordance with Mr. Staub's suggestion, although the mover stated that he personally opposed a merger with the American Society. The motion was seconded.

During the ensuing discussion, Council member after Council member spoke of the impossibility of effecting a merger. It would result in the admission of many members of the American Society who were not practicing accountants. It would lower the standards that the Institute had labored so long to elevate. The philosophies of the two organizations were incompatible. Each filled a separate need. The entire matter had been explored by committees of the two groups some years before, and in all goodwill it had been agreed that there was no basis for unification.

It was moved that the motion to appoint a committee be tabled. The motion to table was carried, 19 to seven.

Ira B. McGladrey of Iowa then requested the floor. He was a rugged individualist, born in a log cabin in upper Michigan, who after long years of hard work had built up the highly successful regional firm of McGladrey, Hansen & Dunn. He said that while the majority of the Council was clearly opposed to consideration of a merger, most CPAs were strongly in favor of it. If the Institute took the position that it wouldn't even discuss the matter, he said, meanwhile apparently "slapping the face" of the greatest state society in the United States, "you are certainly making my task in my own state a great deal harder in my work for the American Institute of Accountants."

After further remarks in support of these points Mr. McGladrey moved that a committee be appointed with power to examine the entire question—not only possible amalgamation of the two societies, but the possibility of co-operative action in certain matters. In the absence of a second, Clem W. Collins of Colorado, who expressed agreement with Mr. McGladrey's views, moved that the matter be referred to the executive committee with a request to consider the possibility both of amalgamation and of co-operation with the American Society.

After lengthy discussion, this motion was tabled by a vote of 21 to five.

Charles B. Couchman then sought the floor and described

some of his experiences when as president of the Institute he had visited some 22 state societies, in company with the secretary. Mr. Couchman declared that the Institute was generally unpopular, that there was widespread misunderstanding of its objectives and activities, and that it was the object of all manner of baseless accusations.

He expressed the view that a failure of the Institute to appoint any committee even to consider the possibility of an amalgamation with the American Society would only increase hostility toward the Institute.

Several other motions were offered, withdrawn or amended. Finally, Frederick H. Hurdman stated that in view of the remarks of other speakers he would move that the president be authorized to appoint a special committee to consider the matter of amalgamation or co-operation with other bodies of accountants, and report back to the executive committee. This motion was seconded and carried—possibly because the opposition was exhausted.

President Forbes soon appointed a special committee on co-operation with other organizations, with Fred Hurdman as chairman. The other members were Walter Staub, George Armistead of Texas, Robert O. Berger of Illinois, and James J. Hastings of New Jersey.

Moving Away from the Defensive

A year later, at the October 1934 meeting of Council, Colonel Montgomery appeared in person. He strongly urged amalgamation of the two national organizations. Mr. Hurdman, as chairman of the special committee on co-operation with other organizations, reported that he had been in communication with the American Society, and had requested certain information from the Society, but up to this time had been unable to arrange a meeting. Meanwhile his committee had accumulated facts and figures bearing on the proposal before it.

It was the sense of the Council that the Institute was doing everything that it could reasonably do to undertake serious consideration of the matter.

These efforts, however, did not result in relaxation on the part of President Forbes in his drive to attract members, and to strengthen relations with the state societies. The president, the secretary and other representatives of the Institute traveled thousands of miles to speak at meetings of state societies and chapters. Numerous publications were produced for distribution to the entire membership and to other CPAs.

The Institute assisted state societies in obtaining speakers for their meetings, offered help in the establishment of local libraries and employment exchanges, and requested each society to appoint a special committee to co-operate with the Institute, through which channels of communication might be maintained. A periodic letter to officers of state societies was published, transmitting information of national interest.

As an additional step to conciliate those who might feel that the Institute was not wholeheartedly supporting the CPA certificate, the bylaws were amended by adding to the first article, stating the Institute's objectives, the following clause: "To assist in the maintenance of high standards for the certified public accountant certificate in the several states."

A result of all these efforts was the greatest increase in membership in a single year since 1923.

An Internal Split

Under the surface, the proposed merger had become an issue which divided the Institute into two political parties.

A logical candidate to succeed Mr. Forbes as president would have been one of the members of the executive committee who had labored long and faithfully on behalf of the

Institute. But he was known to be irreconcilably opposed to a merger with the American Society. As a consequence, after sharp disagreements in the nominating committee, George Armistead of Texas was selected as the nominee, in the belief that he was a middle-of-the-roader on this sensitive question.

Mr. Armistead headed a flourishing local firm in Houston, was highly regarded by his colleagues in that state, had been active in the Institute, and was a man of unquestioned integrity. He also was a skillful orator. He was duly elected president at the 1934 meeting.

Subsequently it appeared that Mr. Armistead, too, was irreconcilably opposed to a merger with the Society. This resulted in heightened tensions through the year, culminating in the only contest for the office of presidency of the Institute in the history of the organization.

This happened at the following annual meeting in Boston in 1935, but in the meantime the merger issue reached a point of decision.

Taking the Initiative

Following the 1934 meeting, Mr. Hurdman and his associates had a brilliant inspiration. They decided to take the initiative. They would develop a plan of merger which would meet the most frequent objections to the Institute's policies, but would retain the one feature considered of vital importance—direct control over its own members. They would offer the plan publicly to the American Society, but anticipating a counter offer and long-drawn-out bargaining, they would try to have the Institute's bylaws amended in accordance with the plan, regardless of the Society's reaction. Then the Institute would be in a position to say that it had done all it could to meet the demands of the profession generally. It would have demonstrated its good faith. It would be up to the Society to persuade the profession that the

Institute's position was unreasonable, rather than vice versa.

This strategy worked, but not without a final battle within the Institute itself.

Prior to the Council meeting in April 1935, the Hurdman committee presented its plan to the executive committee. The essential features were as follows:

1. The Institute would continue as the active national organization.

2. All members of the Society in good standing would be admitted to the Institute without examination or initiation fee.

3. The bylaws of the Institute would be amended to provide that no further applicants would be admitted to membership or associateship except certified public accountants.

4. The experience requirement for admission as associates would be reduced to two years.

5. An Advisory Council of State Society Presidents would be formed by the Institute to advise and consult with the Council.

6. The Society would transfer all its properties to the Institute.

The corresponding committee of the American Society, but not its Board of Directors, had agreed that this plan was acceptable. The Society's Board of Directors later added the following additional conditions:

1. That the Institute's name be changed to American Institute of Certified Public Accountants;

2. That in the future the only requirement for admission to membership in the Institute be the possession of a CPA certificate;

3. That the governing body of the new organization be nominated and elected by and from geographical districts by mail ballot of the members in such districts.

The Institute's committee took the position that the change of name, the basis of admission to membership, and the method of electing the governing body should be left for decision of the members of the combined organization following the merger.

The majority of the Institute's executive committee refused to approve the Hurdman committee proposals. In fact, the executive committee carefully refrained from sending copies of the Hurdman committee's report to Council members in advance of the 1935 spring meeting—apparently fearing that if Council members studied the report in advance they might arrive at the meeting in a mood to approve it.

Instead the executive committee reported at the Council meeting that it had considered the proposed merger plan, without explaining it in detail, and recommended in effect that the plan be not adopted, but that American Society members be invited to apply for membership in the Institute.

Members of the Council then requested copies of the Hurdman committee's report. Copies were distributed while the meeting was in session.

There ensued an extended and sometimes acrimonious debate.

Mr. Hurdman said: ". . . that is the way I construed the suggestion of the executive committee, that the plan be abandoned and that we invite the American Society members to apply for membership." He warned the Council that if this effort to unite the two national bodies was unsuccessful, he believed that immediate steps would be taken to form a federation of state societies, with a total membership of some 6,000, as compared to the Institute's membership of about 2,000. After an impassioned defense of his committee's report, Mr. Hurdman concluded, "I think that the Institute is at the crossroads, and this Council has got to decide whether or not it intends to remain a smug, concise, small organization, representing high ideals and a certain group of the accounting profession, or whether it wants to go on and be truly representative of the entire profession. That is the question we have got to decide today."

Various parliamentary maneuvers were attempted. A motion to discharge the special committee was defeated. A motion to approve its report and submit it to the membership was also defeated. In the course of the debate, Mr. Hurdman made it clear that the plan of merger would not be implemented unless there were assurances that the American Society would be dissolved after its membership had been taken into the Institute en bloc.

Finally, it was moved that the Council approve the work done by the special committee, not in detail, but in its approach toward a workable basis for consolidation of the two bodies; that the plan be referred back to a joint meeting of the executive committee and the special committee on co-operation with other organizations, with the sincere hope that all difficulties between the two committees could be ironed out; and that they report back again to the Council. The motion was seconded.

This motion was the subject of further discussion, in the course of which Mr. Hurdman said, "I think we have made wonderful progress, if I do say it myself, in getting this thing worked out on a basis which I thought would be acceptable to this Council. I know, as a matter of fact, that the Society committee think they have sold themselves out entirely to this Institute committee. Apparently this group doesn't think so."

In the end the motion was carried.

On April 18 the executive committee and the special committee on co-operation with other organizations held a joint meeting and reached agreement on the following fundamental points:

1. Since legally the Institute could not turn over its assets [which were substantial, while those of the Society were minimal] to a new organization, it was necessary that the Institute continue in its present form with provision for admission of members of the American Society.

2. All members of the Society in good standing would be admitted to the Institute without examination or other test of eligibility, provided the American Society agreed to dissolve its organization upon completion of a mutually acceptable plan.

3. The executive committee of the Institute would recommend amendment of the bylaws providing that future applicants for membership in the Institute should be required to possess a CPA certificate.

4. The executive committee would recommend creation of an Advisory Council of State Society Presidents.

5. Amendment of the bylaws would be proposed to reduce the experience requirement for admission as associates from three to two years.

Subsequently the American Society's board of directors reviewed the plan, and agreed on the following points:

1. That a single national organization was desirable.

2. That future membership should be confined to CPAs.

3. That such recognition of state societies should be provided as would forestall the organization of a second national group.

This did not commit the Society to the details of the Institute's plan, nor foreclose it from insisting on additional conditions.

The New York State Society then called a meeting of presidents or other representatives of state societies in Atlantic City, August 22, 1935. At this meeting, the president and the secretary of the American Institute were present, as well as Mr. Hurdman, as chairman of the special committee on cooperation with other organizations.

The state society presidents approved the Institute's suggested plan in principle, with the following additions: that the name of the resulting organization should be "The American Institute of Certified Public Accountants"; that its Council members be elected by districts and by the members resident in the district; and that the Institute maintain an office in Washington, D.C.

These were, of course, conditions urged by the American Society, which Hurdman knew it would be difficult for the Institute's Council to accept.

The Showdown

By the time the Institute's Council reassembled on October 14, 1935 at Boston, things had come to a head. After sharp infighting, resulting in a split within the nominating committee, two candidates for president had been proposed. The pro-merger forces nominated Robert H. Montgomery, and the anti-merger forces nominated Will-A. Clader of Pennsylvania. Mr. Clader was head of his own firm, a member of Council and the executive committee, chairman of the committee on state legislation, and a dedicated supporter of all that the Institute stood for. He was a tireless worker and a courageous fighter. To him the proposed merger was anathema.

The elections were to take place at the annual meeting of members October 15, and when the Council assembled on the previous day there was tension in the air.

The special committee on co-operation with other organizations recommended that the Institute immediately amend its bylaws to give effect to three principal points of the proposed plan of amalgamation, regardless of the fact that the American Society had not yet approved the plan. These three points were:

1. That after January 1, 1936, all applicants for admission to the Institute be required to possess a CPA certificate.

2. That provision be made for the creation of an Advisory Council of State Society Presidents, in order to permit closer co-operation between the Institute and the state societies.

3. That the experience requirement for admission as an associate be reduced from three to two years.

In its report to Council the executive committee expressed "grave doubt as to the legality" of immediate amendment of the bylaws in the manner suggested: "It believes that necessary notice must be given to the members of the Institute of any proposed amendments to the bylaws."

The question was raised whether advice of legal counsel had been obtained, and the answer was negative.

A motion that opinion of counsel be secured as to the legality of acting on bylaw amendments without prior notice to the membership, was put to a voice vote and declared by the chair to have been carried. The ruling of the chair was challenged, and a vote by count was called for. Eighteen members of Council were counted in favor and 12 against.

Legal counsel was consulted by telephone. He responded that under the existing bylaws it was his considered opinion that amendments could be introduced on the floor of the annual meeting without prior notice to the membership. In any event, adoption of amendments depended on a vote of the entire membership by a mail ballot subsequent to the annual meeting.

In view of this report, the executive committee suggested that the Council recess while the committee reconsidered its position.

The handwriting was on the wall. The opposition faded. When the Council reconvened, the executive committee reported that it unanimously concurred with the principles embodied in the recommendations of the special committee on co-operation with other organizations. Believing that the plan recommended by the two special committees of the Institute and the Society provided a satisfactory basis for a merger of the two national organizations, the executive committee recommended that the plan be submitted to the annual meeting for approval or disapproval, in order that the sentiment of the membership might be known. Further, since certain features of the plan would enable the Institute better to serve the profession to the satisfaction of all certified public accountants, the executive committee recommended immediate amendment of the Institute's bylaws to put into effect the three changes mentioned above.

Detailed amendments to bylaws to give effect to these proposals were then presented.

The Council approved these recommendations and referred them to the annual meeting.

In his presidential address, at the opening of the annual

meeting the next day, the retiring president, George Armistead, made a stirring speech against the merger. He implored the members "not to yield to panic or join a stampede." His appeal fell mainly on deaf ears.

Proxy voting was permitted in those days. Colonel Montgomery was elected president by a vote of 1,210 against 438 for Mr. Clader. There were only somewhat over 2,000 members eligible to vote, and 1,648 did so.

The merger plan, as submitted by the Council, was discussed and approved by the members. It was also unanimously resolved that the bylaws be changed immediately to give effect to the three major points involved in the plan, regardless of what action the American Society might take.

These amendments were soon afterward submitted for vote of the entire membership by mail ballot.

The annual meeting was adjourned to reconvene January 6, 1936, in Washington, D.C., to permit final action on the merger plan if the American Society agreed to its consummation.

The "liberals" had achieved a complete victory. The Institute had set itself on a new course. It had demonstrated a sincere desire for the merger. By taking steps to amend its own bylaws to meet three of the major pre-conditions, it had placed the Society on the defensive.

The Conclusion

The adjourned annual meeting of the Institute reconvened in Washington in January. State society presidents had been especially invited to participate, and to form the new Advisory Council.

No word had been received from the American Society as to its position on the merger plan.

Mr. Hurdman reported that the bylaw amendments approved at Boston had been adopted by the membership by mail ballot and had become effective. This left only two major points raised by the American Society as a condition of merger which had not yet been met by the Institute: (1) that the Council be elected in a manner which would insure adequate regional representation; and (2) that the name of the Institute be changed to include the words "certified public accountant."

Mr. Hurdman announced that an informal vote of the members of the Institute had opposed the change of name, 667 to 383. Regarding the method of election of Council, he proposed an additional amendment to the bylaws to provide that the Institute's nominating committee be required to seek suggestions from members in the states concerned as to members to be nominated for Council. Nominees would be selected by the committee from among the names submitted.

Durand W. Springer, the secretary of the American Society, was present at the meeting as a member of the Institute. He announced that the merger plan would be submitted to the members of the Society in the near future. He then made a last gallant effort to include in the plan one feature which would perpetuate a major part of the Society's philosophy.

Mr. Springer offered a substitute for the proposed amendment to the bylaws. His substitute provided that the Council be nominated and elected by mail ballot of the members in regional districts—the method then followed by the American Society.

But it was too late. The Institute's plan had gained too much momentum. The merger was within sight, and the members were impatient to finish it. Mr. Springer's substitute amendment was promptly defeated. The amendment proposed by Mr. Hurdman was approved, and subsequently was adopted by mail ballot of the entire membership.

Thus the Institute had adopted unilaterally all the changes in its organization that had been agreed upon by the two committees up to then, except for the admission of members of the American Society to the Institute. In addition, it had met at least halfway the Society's desire for a change in the method of electing Council.

So far the members of the American Society had approved nothing.

Mr. Hurdman stated that the executive committee of the American Society had not yet communicated with him or with any officer of the Institute, and that his committee had finished its work. He requested that the committee be discharged, and that all future communications on the matter of the merger be handled by the Institute's executive committee. With enthusiastic expressions of appreciation for its labors, Mr. Hurdman's committee was discharged.

The next step was up to the Society.

Mr. Springer stated that the executive committee of the American Society had been in session on the day before, and would reconvene immediately after this meeting to consider the matter further. He also expressed personal support for the merger, and the belief that the Society had accomplished its objectives.

Subsequently all members of the American Society were informed of the current state of affairs, and were asked for their views as to whether the consolidation should be effected, even though not all the points regarded as essential by the Society had been adopted by the Institute. The response was favorable.

In the spring of 1936 the executive committees of the two organizations agreed on the merger plan, with the condition that upon its consummation the total membership of the merged organization would be given an opportunity to vote on the two unresolved issues—the name of the organization and the method of electing its governing body.

The final steps were taken at the 1936 annual meetings of the two organizations; one meeting in Dallas, Texas, and the other in Fort Worth, at approximately the same time. The Advisory Council of State Society Presidents began to function in Dallas. The members of the Institute approved the final changes in the bylaws, to admit the Society members, by a mail ballot. Entitled to vote were 2,835: in favor, 1,571; against, 70.

The memberships of the two organizations were approximately equal: 2,135 in the Society, and 2,239 in the Institute, plus some 400 associates. However, a large number of members belonged to both. The net increase in membership through the merger was 1,544. Only about 60 Society members failed to join the Institute. Following the merger, with 785 new accessions, the total membership in 1937 was 4,890. There were then some 16,500 CPAs in the nation.

The two moot questions were submitted for vote by mail ballot of the combined membership, and both failed to receive the required two-thirds affirmative vote.

Some years later, however, the name of the Institute was changed to "American Institute of Certified Public Accountants," and the state societies were given an influential voice in the nomination of Council members.

From the time of the merger, no new members were admitted who did not possess CPA certificates. Ultimately all the states and other political subdivisions adopted the Institute's Uniform CPA Examination, so it became unnecessary for any examination to be given for admission to the Institute —all new CPAs had already passed it. Yet the Institute did retain control over other admission requirements—education, experience and moral character—and also retained disciplinary control over its individual members.

The Advisory Council of State Society Presidents was later replaced by a provision that all state society presidents, or other representatives designated by state societies, be ex officio members of the Council. This move greatly strengthened the relations between the national and state organizations.

The compromises were sound. The structure developed in 1936, with occasional modifications, has worked satisfactorily throughout the following years. It gives every sign of working satisfactorily into the indefinite future.

Both Durand W. Springer, former secretary of the Society, and A. P. Richardson, former secretary and then editor of the Institute, expressed a wish to retire. Both were voted life-long pensions by the Council of the Institute. Mr. Richardson had served the Institute and its predecessor, the American Association, for 25 years, and had a large part in building it to its current strength and status. Mr. Springer had been largely responsible for the growth and success of the Society over the 15 years of its existence.

End of the First Fifty Years

Thus ended a turbulent period in the history of the accounting profession in the United States.

In 50 years it had come from nowhere to carve out a secure place in the American economic system.

It had established technical standards which provided a foundation for future progress. It had developed and enforced a respectable code of ethics. It had adapted to new tax and securities legislation, contributed to a war effort, and made itself known to the business public.

It had experimented with several forms of organization and methods of accrediting its members. By trial and error it had worked out an organizational pattern peculiarly suited to its own special needs. It was well on the way to a uniform examination for the CPA certificate.

The profession had learned many lessons. It had matured. It was united, stronger than it had ever been, and ready to move forward.

There were great opportunities ahead, and troubled waters as well, which will be described in Volume II of this work.

Appendix A

Officers of the
American Institute of Accountants and Predecessor Organizations to 1936

AMERICAN ASSOCIATION OF PUBLIC ACCOUNTANTS

Officers

1887-1888

President	JAMES YALDEN
Vice-president	JOHN HEINS
Secretary	JAMES T. ANYON
Treasurer	WILLIAM H. VEYSEY

1888-1889

President	JOHN HEINS
Secretary	JAMES T. ANYON
Treasurer	WILLIAM H. VEYSEY

1889-1890

President	JOHN HEINS
Vice-president	E. H. SEWELL
Secretary-treasurer	WILLIAM H. VEYSEY

President	John Heins
Vice-president	E. H. Sewell
Secretary-treasurer	M. C. Mirick

1891-1892

President	James Yalden
Vice-president	Henry R. M. Cook
Secretary	Frank Broaker
Treasurer	R. M. Chapman

1892-1893

President	Henry R. M. Cook
Vice-president	Richard F. Stevens
Secretary	Thomas Bagot
Treasurer	R. M. Chapman

1893-1894

President	Richard F. Stevens
Vice-president	Frank Broaker
Secretary	John W. Whitehead
Treasurer	R. M. Chapman

1894-1895

President	Richard F. Stevens
Vice-president	Frank Broaker
Secretary	T. Cullen Roberts
Treasurer	R. M. Chapman

1895-1896

President	Richard F. Stevens
Vice-president	Frank Broaker
Secretary	T. Cullen Roberts
Treasurer	Francis Gottsberger

1896-1897

President	Frank Broaker
Vice-president	W. Sanders Davies
Secretary	T. Cullen Roberts
Treasurer	Leonard H. Conant

1897-1898

President	W. SANDERS DAVIES
Vice-president	DAVID ROLLO
Secretary	T. CULLEN ROBERTS
Treasurer	LEONARD H. CONANT

1898-1899

President	DAVID ROLLO
Vice-president	LEONARD H. CONANT
Secretary	T. CULLEN ROBERTS
Treasurer	FERDINAND W. LAFRENTZ

1899-1900

President	LEONARD H. CONANT
Vice-president	FERDINAND W. LAFRENTZ
Secretary	T. CULLEN ROBERTS
Treasurer	FREDERICK C. MANVEL

1900-1901

President	LEONARD H. CONANT
Vice-president	FERDINAND W. LAFRENTZ
Secretary	T. CULLEN ROBERTS
Treasurer	JAMES GRANT

1901-1902

President	FERDINAND W. LAFRENTZ
Vice-president	JOHN R. LOOMIS
Secretary	T. CULLEN ROBERTS
Treasurer	ANDREW A. CLARKE

1902-1903

President	FERDINAND W. LAFRENTZ
Vice-president	JOHN R. LOOMIS
Secretary	T. CULLEN ROBERTS
Treasurer	ANDREW A. CLARKE

1903-1904

President	JOHN R. LOOMIS
Vice-president	ANDREW A. CLARKE
Secretary	T. CULLEN ROBERTS
Treasurer	FRANKLIN ALLEN

1904-1905

President	JOHN R. LOOMIS
Vice-president	ANDREW A. CLARKE
Secretary	T. CULLEN ROBERTS
Treasurer	FRANKLIN ALLEN

1905-1906

President	JOHN R. LOOMIS
Vice-presidents	Presidents of the several state societies
Secretary	A. LOWES DICKINSON
Treasurer	GUY H. KENNEDY

1906-1907

President	ELIJAH WATT SELLS
Vice-presidents	Presidents of the several state societies
Secretary	T. CULLEN ROBERTS
Treasurer	GUY H. KENNEDY

1907-1908

President	ELIJAH WATT SELLS
Vice-presidents	Presidents of the several state societies
Secretary	T. CULLEN ROBERTS
Treasurer	H. T. WESTERMANN

1908-1909

President	J. E. STERRETT
Vice-presidents	Presidents of the several state societies
Secretary	T. CULLEN ROBERTS
Treasurer	H. T. WESTERMANN

1909-1910

President	J. E. STERRETT
Vice-presidents	Presidents of the several state societies
Secretary	T. CULLEN ROBERTS
Treasurer	H. A. KELLER

1910-1911

President	EDWARD L. SUFFERN
Vice-presidents	Presidents of the several state societies
Secretary	T. CULLEN ROBERTS
Treasurer	H. A. KELLER

1911-1912

President	EDWARD L. SUFFERN
Vice-presidents	Presidents of the several state societies
Secretary	A. P. RICHARDSON
Treasurer	JAMES WHITAKER FERNLEY

1912-1913

President	ROBERT H. MONTGOMERY
Vice-presidents	Presidents of the several state societies
Secretary	A. P. RICHARDSON
Treasurer	JAMES WHITAKER FERNLEY

1913-1914

President	ROBERT H. MONTGOMERY
Vice-presidents	Presidents of the several state societies
Secretary	A. P. RICHARDSON
Treasurer	CARL H. NAU

1914-1915

President	J. PORTER JOPLIN
Vice-presidents	Presidents of the several state societies
Secretary	A. P. RICHARDSON
Treasurer	CARL H. NAU

1915-1916

President	J. PORTER JOPLIN
Vice-presidents	Presidents of the several state societies
Secretary	A. P. RICHARDSON
Treasurer	CARL H. NAU

Federation of Societies of Public Accountants in USA

Officers

1903-1904

President	Farquhar J. MacRae
Secretary	George Wilkinson
Treasurer	Robert H. Montgomery

1904-1905

President	A. Lowes Dickinson
Secretary	George Wilkinson
Treasurer	Robert H. Montgomery

1905-1906

President	A. Lowes Dickinson
Secretary	Robert H. Montgomery
Treasurer	J. S. M. Goodloe

The Institute of Accountants in the United States of America

Officers

1916-1917

President	W. Sanders Davies
Vice-presidents	Harvey S. Chase
	Carl H. Nau
Treasurer	Adam A. Ross
Secretary	A. P. Richardson

American Institute of Accountants

Officers

1917-1918

President	W. Sanders Davies
Vice-presidents	George O. May
	Waldron H. Rand
Treasurer	Adam A. Ross
Secretary	A. P. Richardson

1918-1919

President	WALDRON H. RAND
Vice-presidents	CHARLES S. LUDLAM
	E. G. SHORROCK
Treasurer	ADAM A. ROSS
Secretary	A. P. RICHARDSON

1919-1920

President	WALDRON H. RAND
Vice-presidents	ARTHUR W. TEELE
	H. IVOR THOMAS
Treasurer	J. E. STERRETT
Secretary	A. P. RICHARDSON

1920-1921

President	CARL H. NAU
Vice-presidents	W. P. HILTON
	T. EDWARD ROSS
Treasurer	J. E. STERRETT
Secretary	A. P. RICHARDSON

1921-1922

President	CARL H. NAU
Vice-presidents	JOHN B. NIVEN
	ARTHUR W. TEELE
Treasurer	J. E. STERRETT
Secretary	A. P. RICHARDSON

1922-1923

President	EDWARD E. GORE
Vice-presidents	JOHN R. LOOMIS
	NORMAN L. McLAREN
Treasurer	ARTHUR W. TEELE
Secretary	A. P. RICHARDSON

1923-1924

President	EDWARD E. GORE
Vice-presidents	FRANK LOWSON
	NORMAN E. WEBSTER
Treasurer	ARTHUR W. TEELE
Secretary	A. P. RICHARDSON

1924-1925

President	JOHN B. NIVEN
Vice-presidents	ERNEST RECKITT
	WILLIAM H. WEST
Treasurer	ARTHUR W. TEELE
Secretary	A. P. RICHARDSON

1925-1926

President	WILLIAM H. WEST
Vice-presidents	JOHN F. FORBES
	FREDERICK A. ROSS
Treasurer	ARTHUR W. TEELE
Secretary	A. P. RICHARDSON

1926-1927

President	WILLIAM H. WEST
Vice-presidents	FREDERICK H. HURDMAN
	JOHN R. RUCKSTELL
Treasurer	ARTHUR W. TEELE
Secretary	A. P. RICHARDSON

1927-1928

President	JOHN R. RUCKSTELL
Vice-presidents	JAMES S. MATTESON
	ROBERT H. MONTGOMERY
Treasurer	ARTHUR W. TEELE
Secretary	A. P. RICHARDSON

1928-1929

President	FREDERICK H. HURDMAN
Vice-presidents	ALBERT T. BACON
	LEWIS G. FISHER
Treasurer	ANDREW STEWART
Secretary	A. P. RICHARDSON

1929-1930

President	FREDERICK H. HURDMAN
Vice-presidents	STANLEY G. H. FITCH
Editor	OVERTON S. MELDRUM
Treasurer	ANDREW STEWART
Secretary	A. P. RICHARDSON

1930-1931

President	CHARLES B. COUCHMAN
Vice-presidents	ARTHUR H. CARTER
	JAMES M. McCONAHEY
Treasurer	ALLAN DAVIES
Editor	A. P. RICHARDSON
Secretary	JOHN L. CAREY

1931-1932

President	CHARLES B. COUCHMAN
Vice-presidents	GEORGE ARMISTEAD
	WILL-A. CLADER
Treasurer	ALLAN DAVIES
Editor	A. P. RICHARDSON
Secretary	JOHN L. CAREY

1932-1933

President	JOHN F. FORBES
Vice-presidents	FREDERICK B. ANDREWS
	WALTER MUCKLOW
Treasurer	ALLAN DAVIES
Editor	A. P. RICHARDSON
Secretary	JOHN L. CAREY

1933-1934

President	JOHN F. FORBES
Vice-presidents	P. W. R. GLOVER
	ELMER L. HATTER
Treasurer	ALLAN DAVIES
Editor	A. P. RICHARDSON
Secretary	JOHN L. CAREY

1934-1935

President	GEORGE ARMISTEAD
Vice-presidents	JOHN D. CHERRINGTON
	H. W. HENNEGIN
Treasurer	ARTHUR W. TEELE
Editor	A. P. RICHARDSON
Secretary	JOHN L. CAREY

1935-1936

President	ROBERT H. MONTGOMERY
Vice-presidents	WILLIAM B. FRANKE
	NORMAN L. McLAREN
Treasurer	ARTHUR W. TEELE
Editor	A. P. RICHARDSON
Secretary	JOHN L. CAREY

AMERICAN SOCIETY OF CERTIFIED PUBLIC ACCOUNTANTS

Officers

1922

President	DURAND W. SPRINGER
Vice-presidents	HOMER A. DUNN
	LESLIE S. EVERTS
Treasurer	GEORGE P. ELLIS
Secretary	WILBUR L. HARRISON
(Acting)	

1923

President	FRANK WILBUR MAIN
Vice-presidents	WILLIAM DOLGE
	HOMER A. DUNN
	RENE J. LeGARDEUR
	DURAND W. SPRINGER
Treasurer	CARL PENNER
Secretary	WILBUR L. HARRISON

1923-1924

President	ALEXANDER S. BANKS
Vice-presidents	FRANK WILBUR MAIN
	EDWIN L. PRIDE
	E. G. SHORROCK
	WALTER A. COY
	A. C. UPLEGER
Treasurer	SHEPARD E. BARRY
Secretary	WILBUR L. HARRISON

1924-1925

President	EDWIN L. PRIDE
Vice-presidents	ALEXANDER S. BANKS
	HENRY J. MILLER
	PHILIP B. PRICE
	E. J. POWELL
	E. G. SHORROCK
Treasurer	GEORGE W. ROSSETTER
Secretary	WILBUR L. HARRISON

1925-1926

President	HARRY E. LUNSFORD
Vice-presidents	CHARLES HECHT
	EDWIN L. PRIDE
	A. LEE RAWLINGS
	HENRY B. SCOTT
	H. IVOR THOMAS
Treasurer	JAMES A. COUNCILOR
Secretary	WILBUR L. HARRISON

1926-1927

President	JAMES A. COUNCILOR
Vice-presidents	PAUL W. PINKERTON
	JAMES F. HUGHES
Treasurer	T. COLEMAN ANDREWS
Secretary	DURAND W. SPRINGER

1927-1928

President	PAUL W. PINKERTON
Vice-presidents (1st)	ARTHUR C. UPLEGER
(2nd)	CHARLES F. COATES
Treasurer	FRANK A. WILLISON
Secretary	DURAND W. SPRINGER

1928-1929

President	ARTHUR C. UPLEGER
Vice-presidents (1st)	JAMES F. HUGHES
(2nd)	THEODORE J. WITTING
Treasurer	THOMAS H. EVANS
Secretary	DURAND W. SPRINGER

1929-1930

President	JAMES F. HUGHES
Vice-presidents (1st)	HERMAN C. J. PEISCH
(2nd)	R. W. E. COLE
Treasurer	EARL S. CLARK
Secretary	DURAND W. SPRINGER

1930-1931

President	HERMAN C. J. PEISCH
Vice-presidents (1st)	HENRY J. MILLER
(2nd)	JAMES F. WELCH
Treasurer	GARDNER W. KIMBALL
Secretary	DURAND W. SPRINGER

1931-1932

President	HENRY J. MILLER
Vice-presidents (1st)	RALPH W. E. COLE
(2nd)	PATRICK F. CROWLEY
Treasurer	HORATIO A. RONEY
Secretary	DURAND W. SPRINGER

1932-1933

President	RALPH W. E. COLE
Vice-presidents (1st)	GEORGE P. ELLIS
(2nd)	CHESLEY S. GOLDSTON
Treasurer	WILLIAM D. MORRISON
Secretary	DURAND W. SPRINGER

1933-1934

President	GEORGE P. ELLIS
Vice-presidents (1st)	WILLIAM C. HEATON
(2nd)	PAUL R. STROUT
Treasurer	CARL E. DIETZE
Secretary	DURAND W. SPRINGER

1934-1935

President	WILLIAM C. HEATON
Vice-presidents (1st)	WILLIAM D. MORRISON
(2nd)	ORION N. HUTCHINSON
Treasurer	WALTER D. WALL
Secretary	DURAND W. SPRINGER

1935-1936

President	WILLIAM D. MORRISON
Vice-presidents (1st)	HARRY M. JAY
(2nd)	CARL E. DIETZE
Treasurer	J. ARTHUR MARVIN
Secretary	DURAND W. SPRINGER

1936

President	HARRY M. JAY
Secretary	DURAND W. SPRINGER

Appendix B

Source Materials

Much of what appears in this book is based on unpublished sources—minutes and transcripts of meetings, memorandums and correspondence in the files of the American Institute of Certified Public Accountants, in addition to the personal observations and recollections of the author, who was on the scene from 1925 onward.

The *Yearbooks* of the American Association of Public Accountants and the American Institute of Accountants, *The Journal of Accountancy,* the Bulletin of the American Institute of Accountants, the *Certified Public Accountant,* records of Congressional hearings, the proceedings of the several International Congresses of Accountants, and speeches and articles too numerous to mention have also been sources of useful and interesting information.

Reliance has also been placed on the following publications:

Arthur Andersen & Co., *The First Fifty Years, 1913-1963,* privately published, Illinois, 1963.

Andrew Barr and Elmer C. Koch, "Accounting and the SEC," *The George Washington Law Review,* Vol. 28, No. 1, October 1959.

Ralph Lester Boyd, *A Study of CPA Legislation in the United States—1896-1940,* University of Illinois, 1941.

Commerce Clearing House, *Practice and Procedure Before the United States Board of Tax Appeals,* 1925.

C. W. DeMond, *Price, Waterhouse & Co. in America,* privately published, New York, 1951.

James Don Edwards, *History of Public Accounting in the United States,* Bureau of Business and Economic Research, Graduate School of Business Administration, Michigan State University, East Lansing, Michigan, 1960.

Ernst & Ernst, *A History of the Firm,* privately published, Cleveland, Ohio, 1960.

Paul Grady, Editor, *Memoirs and Accounting Thought of George O. May,* The Ronald Press Co., New York, 1962.

Thomas G. Higgins, CPA, *An Autobiography,* privately published, New York, 1965.

Sir Harold Howitt, *The History of The Institute of Chartered Accountants in England and Wales 1880-1965 and of Its Founder Accountancy Bodies 1870-1880,* William Heinemann Ltd., London, England, 1966.

A. C. Littleton, *Accounting Evolution to 1900,* American Institute Publishing Co., New York, 1933.

Robert H. Montgomery, *Fifty Years of Accountancy,* privately printed by The Ronald Press Company, 1939.

Samuel Eliot Morison, *The Oxford History of the American People,* Oxford University Press, New York, 1965.

Norman E. Webster, *The American Association of Public Accountants, Its First Twenty Years,* American Institute of Accountants, New York, 1954.

Stephen A. Zeff, *The American Accounting Association, Its First Fifty Years,* privately published, 1966.